"Andy and Joe have written a book that instructs, charms, and entices. *The Fearless Chef* is a book to cook through; start at page one and don't even think about stopping until you have cooked every single recipe and fed all your friends. That's certainly what we intend to do."

—Todd English, James Beard Award winner, and
Sally Sampson, coauthors, *The Olives Table*

"Andy Husbands and Joe Yonan have created that golden mix where the recipes are at once exciting and not at all daunting."

—Didi Emmons, James Beard Award–winning author,
Vegetarian Planet and *Entertaining for a Veggie Planet*

"You can call Andy a tattooed freak or an irreverent punk-rock chef. You can call him a bleeding heart liberal or as happy as a pig in mud at a barbecue contest. But when Andy's cookin', don't call me too late for dinner!"

—Tom Douglas, James Beard Award winner and author,
Tom Douglas' Seattle Kitchen and *Tom's Big Dinners*

"Andy Husbands has tenaciously defined the cuisine of one of Boston's most eclectic neighborhoods, the South End. Now, his book with Joe Yonan captures many of the qualities that make a chef successful—mystique, unconventionality, passion, and drive—and reveals how these qualities, even for a home cook, can easily be harnessed to produce boldly inventive, flavorful food."

—Ken Oringer, James Beard Award–winning
chef/owner, Clio, Boston

"Andy Husbands is well known in Boston, and increasingly beyond, for his distinctively adventurous American cuisine—and this wonderfully fun and flavor-filled cookbook promises to hasten the rise of this shining star! Drawing on influences from around the globe—from India to Japan to Mexico—Husbands exemplifies the best of the new generation of New American chefs."

—Andrew Dornenburg and Karen Page, James Beard Award–winning authors, *Becoming a Chef* and *The New American Chef*

"Andy Husbands and Joe Yonan write the way Andy cooks: with passion, the highest quality ingredients, and the commitment to serving others that is the hallmark of his restaurants and of his leadership in the community. Andy is as generous in sharing the secrets of his culinary success as he is in sharing his many strengths to help others. This is a must-have book!"

—Bill Shore, founder and executive director, Share Our Strength, and author, *The Cathedral Within*

"Andy and Joe bring a different voice and a great deal of fun to the kitchen in these creative, easy, and tasty recipes.This would be a great addition to any cookbook collection."

—Traci Des Jardins, James Beard Award–winning chef and co-owner, Jardiniere, San Francisco

The Fearless Chef

Innovative Recipes from the Edge of American Cuisine

Andy Husbands and Joe Yonan

Foreword by Chris Schlesinger

Adams Media
Avon, Massachusetts

Published by
Adams Media, an F+W Publications Company
57 Littlefield Street, Avon, MA 02322. U.S.A.
www.adamsmedia.com

ISBN: 1-59337-092-X

Printed in the United States of America.

J I H G F E D C B A

Library of Congress Cataloging-in-Publication Data
Husbands, Andy.
The fearless chef / Andy Husbands and Joe Yonan.
p. cm.
ISBN 1-59337-092-X
1. Cookery. I. Yonan, Joe. II. Title.

TX714.H863 2004
641.5--dc22
2004002028

Cover photo credits: Photo ©2004 Tania Schnapp. Makeup by Una DeChellis. Hair by Jon Paul Prunier for Mechanique, Inc. Jacket by Cayson Designs. Rouge branding concept and design: Sametz Blackstone Associates, Boston; *www.sametz.com*

Interior photo credits: Photos ©2004 Tania Schnapp; ©2000 Corbis Corporation; ©Banana Stock Ltd.; ©1995 PhotoDisc, Inc.

Joe Yonan

To our mothers,

the first chefs we met—and by far the most fearless

Andy Husbands

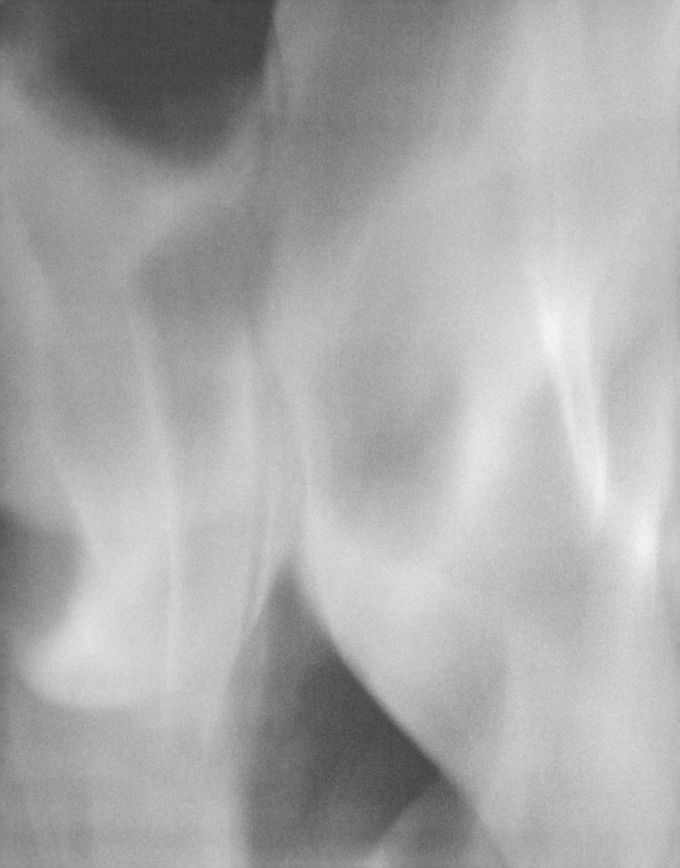

table of contents

acknowledgments

Andy would like to thank . . .

Gretchen, Sage, Sorel, Grandma Odinov, and Mom and Dad for the love and support.

Jason Santos and Matt Audette for their dedication to Tremont 647 and for deftly handling all our requests for ingredients and testing support.

Testers Nancy Kohl and Kirsten Mikalson for the meticulous hard work.

Michael Staub, Richard Perlmutter, Paul Sowizral, and Dennis Quilty for their guidance.

Also: the Harts; the Rosenbergs; the Perrotts; Peter White; Chris Schlesinger; Doc; Nick and Deanna; the staffs of the Franklin and Silvertone; Ken Oringer; Sauces 'n Love; Steve at Yale Electric; Marc Orfaly; Ed Doyle; Lisa Ekus; Courtney Nolan and Adams Media; John Delpha; Rachel Kelso and Sametz Blackstone; Buff and Johnnie; Share Our Strength; Operation Frontline; the supercool Tania Schnapp; Billy Barlow; beverage czar Matt Ryan; Joy Richard; Michelle Vernier; Tsering Dongshi; and everyone else on the hardworking and dedicated staffs of Tremont 647, Sister Sorel, Rouge, and Kestral; and Fat Ram and the girls of Gardner Street: Jenna, Sandra, and Moe.

And Joe for having patience with my lack of patience, and for his hard work, excellent writing, and his ability to put into words what I'm trying to say.

Joe would like to thank . . .

The women and men in my family who helped shape how I cook and think about food: my mother, who taught me never to beat the cream too long or it would turn to butter; my sister Rebekah, who makes her own everything and who bakes the finest pie (rhubarb); my sister Teri, who taught me gracious table manners over fried chicken and biscuits; my brother Michael, who first taught me how to divine "real" Texas chili (no beans, no tomatoes); my sister Julie, who always eats with gusto and glee; my late sister Bonny, who knew how to laugh over a wok; and my late father, whose stories of his Assyrian mother's *khoufta* made me proud of my heritage.

Friends, for their never-ending patience when I would answer yet another social invitation with, "I can't; I'm working on the cookbook," especially Rebekah and Peter, Christopher and Edouard, Allen, Amy and Tina, Deb and Nell, Karin and Bill, and members of the JP Bookgroup, some of whom also helped test recipes, either by making them or eating the results, or both.

Nancy Kohl and Kirsten Mikalson, whose good-natured yet tough and thorough recipe testing served as a much-needed reality check throughout this process.

Courtney Nolan, our editor at Adams Media, for keeping us on track with such enthusiasm.

Lisa Ekus, our agent, for her unwavering support and level-headedness.

Tania Schnapp for her gorgeous photos.

Colleagues at the *Boston Globe* who have supported my food and travel writing, which has greatly informed my approach to this book: Mark Morrow, John Yemma, Fiona Luis, Wendy Fox, Sheryl Julian, Alison Arnett, Amy Graves, Ellen Clegg, Helen Donovan,

Marty Baron, Julie Dalton, Anne Fitzgerald, Keren Mahoney-Jones, and Tom Haines.

Roberta Dowling of the Cambridge School of Culinary Arts, who with a mere twinkle in her eye and chuckle in her voice showed me firsthand the joys of a life spent cooking and teaching.

And mostly to Andy, without whom none of this would have happened, for his infectiously boundless energy and drive, his insistence on always looking ahead (even when I didn't want to), his goofy sense of humor, his instinctive abilities as a chef and a businessman, and, most of all, his friendship.

FOREWORD by Chris Schlesinger

IN 1985, MY PARTNER CARY WHEATON AND I OPENED THE EAST COAST GRILL, a small storefront restaurant in the Inman Square neighborhood of Cambridge. Our goal was to create a fun, exciting restaurant, with food that was neither fussy nor boring, and a staff that treated all of our guests with genuine hospitality.

We also were determined to exhibit exactly none of the characteristics of our respective former bosses in the restaurant business. This ambition led to many group discussions among the staff that in turn created a tight-knit work environment and many of the dynamics of a (slightly dysfunctional) family. Cary and I played Mom and Dad, while on our staff we had the crazy uncle (Smiley) and the absent-minded grandmother (Miriam). It was a relatively peaceful family existence. That is, of course, until Andy Husbands showed up on the scene. Tattooed, pierced, sporting hair that changed color weekly, Andy was energetic, talented, and wildly irreverent—perfectly suited for the role of the rebellious teenage son on our little restaurant sitcom. Sometimes funny, sometimes moody, he was always there as a reminder that somehow, something along the way had gone off-kilter, and that as the staff parents, it must be our fault.

Qualities that are difficult enough in a son are even more so in a young and inexperienced (though certainly not in his own mind) cook.

I found Andy engaging and even compelling, partly because he reminded me of myself at that age. But as a boss and a chef, I found him a constant challenge. Because every time I was too tired to explain to him exactly why I wanted a dish done a certain way, or why a policy needed to be articulated the way I wanted it to be—in other words, every time I wanted him to just be quiet and do it my way—I remembered all the bosses over the years whom I had successfully irritated to the point of their screaming at me. So I refused to give Andy the satisfaction of driving me to that point. This is not to say that I was totally successful all the time, and it is not to say that I didn't enjoy the game; in fact, I was constantly amused at the lengths to which Andy would go to be distracting.

But Andy had high-class kitchen skills. He was first hired as a line cook, a position that calls for unique abilities, and not every cook (not even some great chefs) can do it successfully. It takes a slightly bent personality (just read Tony Bourdain's *Kitchen Confidential*) and a distorted but distinct sense of pride. Andy excelled at this job; he was fast, precise, and unfazed by the intensity of busy Saturday nights. His unorthodox lifestyle, quasi-refusal to recognize authority, and advanced sense of humor not only were characteristic of the quintessential line cook, but also made Andy a popular teammate.

At that point Andy had the raw skills and the drive to be a thoughtful cook, but something was lacking. The turning point in the process of his development might have been the long afternoon that I spent explaining to him why strawberries didn't work in a paella. For some reason that particular session seemed to turn Andy's attention toward the areas in which he needed to grow. He began to read books and magazines, to eat out often at other interesting restaurants, and to become involved in various chef organizations. He even started to use his growing expertise to guide younger cooks just as he had been guided in the past, taking time to explain and teach. In a surprise to everyone, perhaps most of all to himself, Andy the rebellious youth, the skillful line cook, had turned into a responsible member of the profession.

A CHEF.

Of course, the change was not that complete. He was also still the tattooed and pierced chef with green or purple hair, he still loved to question and challenge authority at every turn, and he could never resist a joke at my expense. But that was Andy, and just as his personality had a particular style, so his food became his own as he warmed to the opportunity to express himself more fully through his cooking. Building on what he had learned at the Grill as well as in his reading and travels, he began with the international nature of modern American food and took it one step further. In the process, Andy created his own personal repertoire of dishes that are imaginative without being silly, brightly flavored without being overly aggressive, and simple without being simple-minded.

Andy left East Coast Grill in 1995 to open his own restaurant. Andy had worked for me for three years, and for two of them he was the chef responsible for all kitchen operations. He had done an outstanding job, and his legacy was a combination of clearly seasoned food, clean walk-ins, and a smiling crew.

Now Andy and cohort Joe Yonan have written a cookbook to try to teach a harried public how to re-create Andy's food at home. Having worked with Andy as long as I did, I already have a great deal of respect for Joe, and I cannot imagine anyone better suited to filter

Andy's intensity. A longtime fan of Andy's cooking, a culinary school graduate, and an accomplished home cook in his own right, Joe brings the clarity and inquisitiveness of a journalist to this project.

The result is a book that will be welcomed by casual folks young and old who like to entertain and have sophisticated palates, but do not have a lot of time on their hands. They want good ideas, explained well. Already, I've enjoyed reading this book and even—don't tell Andy—cooking some of the dishes. I know you will, too.

—Chris Schlesinger

FEARLESS *introduction*

WHY **COOK**, ANYWAY?

You probably don't have to. You probably live right around the corner from a decent pizza place, maybe a fab little taqueria, perhaps an early-morning-to-late-night coffee shop with pastries to die for. If you're lucky, you might even live within walking distance of one of your favorite restaurants. You know the place: You've been there so often you could probably bus your own table and nobody would blink. The food is interesting, consistent, and reasonably priced, and you know all the waitstaff, most of the other customers, and maybe even the owners. You feel almost at home there.

Almost. And that, ultimately, is why you cook. Because sometimes—actually, probably a lot of the time—you'd rather be in your own space. And sometimes you want to know exactly what you're eating: where those vegetables and that chicken came from, and how they were put together. If you're alone, maybe you just want to be able to throw together a fun salad and scarf it down in front of the TV. If you're entertaining, it's because maybe you want to share your home, your life, with friends—that new CD you found, the new wine you're excited to try, an intriguing recipe from a new cookbook, or perhaps just your tried-and-true favorites.

Sometimes, whatever the reason, you want to create your own vibe. And more than anything, of course, that includes your food. You want to find the best raw ingredients and combine them in a way that highlights what's unique about each one. You want to serve dishes that excite and soothe and entice and amuse. You want to know that a recipe is going to work the first time you try it, and yet you want ideas about how to put your own stamp on it. You want to come home from the farmer's market, the butcher, or the supermarket, and not feel confused and anxious as you unpack the leeks, the lamb, and the buttermilk, but undaunted. You want to feel confident that you can clean, chop, sauté, braise, and reduce those raw foods into something that will make your friends say, "Where did you learn to make that? And can you teach me?"

You want to be, in a word, fearless.

We think we can help, because, really, we're not so different from you. Sure, we probably have more culinary training and experience—one of us is a restaurant chef, after all—but we each also spend hours every week cooking at home for ourselves, for family, and for friends, without fancy restaurant equipment or hard-to-find ingredients. Just like you do.

That means we've had to learn some shortcuts, some easy ways to create bold-flavored dishes without access to a Fryolator or wood-fired brick oven, and in these recipes we pass those lessons along, while also giving you plenty of ways to tweak the ingredient list and make the dish your own. We've taken the mission of Andy's restaurants—the idea of "adventurous American cuisine," influenced by the flavors of the world—and filtered it through the time-restricted realities of today's home cooks, who don't have sous-chefs, expediters, and waitstaff at the ready.

With our help, you see, you won't need them. You can create your own vibe, your own food, without fear. And you can go out to eat another night.

Prep Work

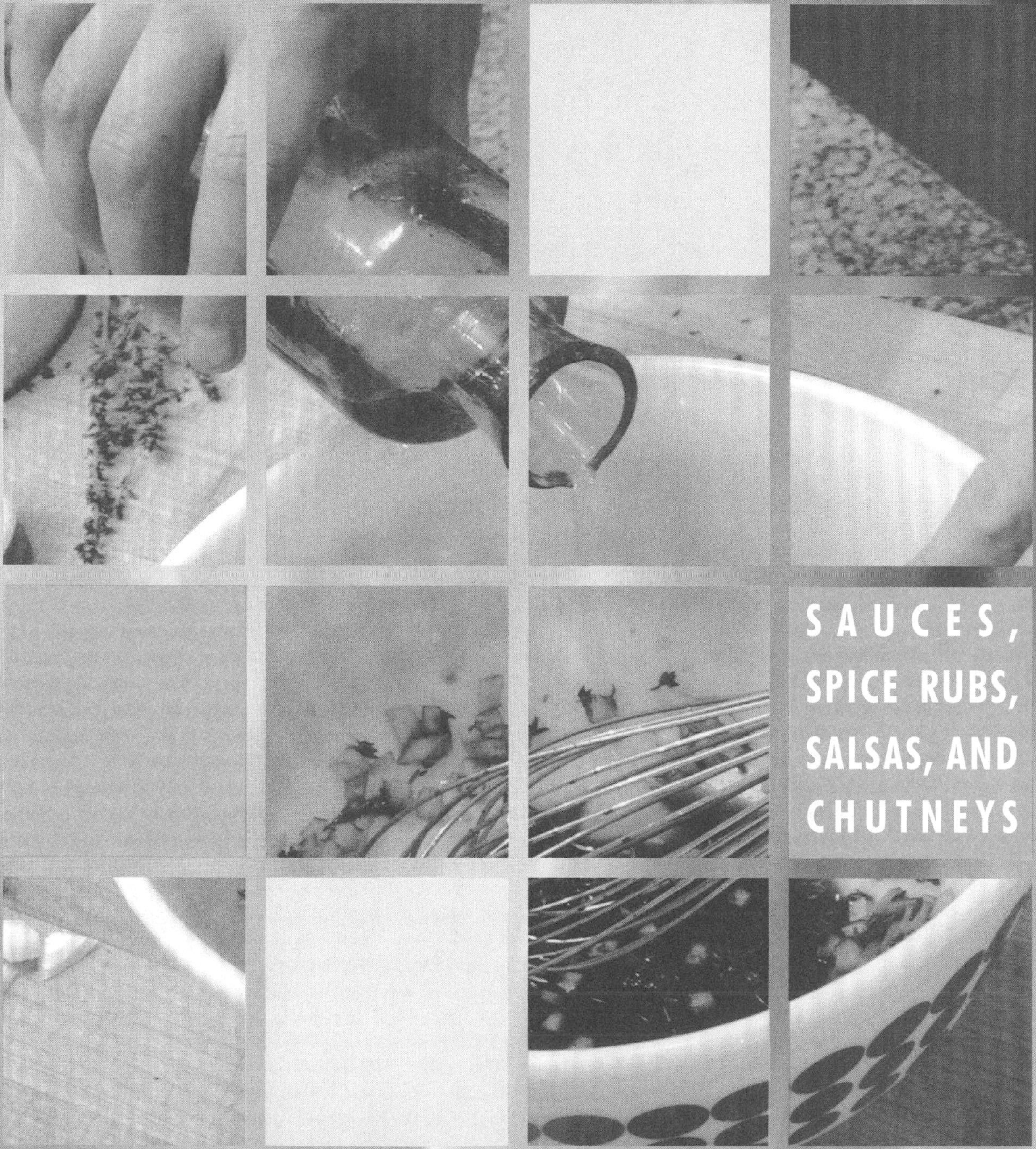

SAUCES, SPICE RUBS, SALSAS, AND CHUTNEYS

WHERE DID **SAUCES** COME FROM? One theory that gets tossed around is that the French created their rich butter sauces to mask unrefrigerated meat or fish that had passed its prime. The problem is, many culinary historians dismiss that theory and instead say that as early as ancient Rome, sauces were probably used to add flavor. (The French word for "sauce," in fact, is derived from Latin's *salsus,* meaning salted.) Whatever the truth, one thing's for sure: Even in today's age of Sub-Zeroes, too many sauces cover up food instead of enhancing it.

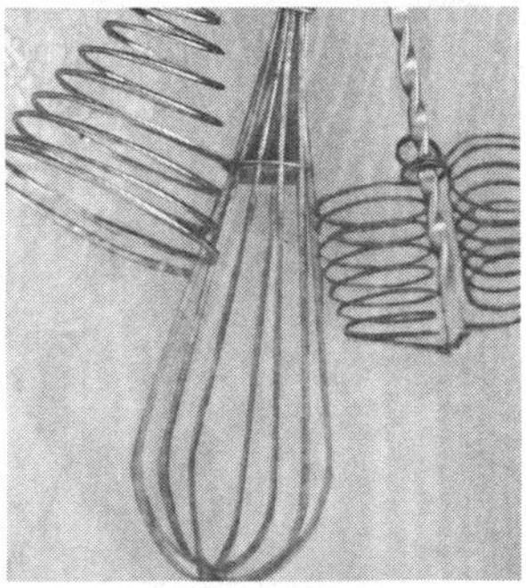

Sauces should be used in small quantities, and their flavor should be **intense**—like an exclamation point, complementing the food or serving as a counterpoint. Meats, poultry, and fish have mild flavors, so a **bold** sauce can make them sparkle.

As delicious as a smooth stock- or cream-based sauce can be, there are plenty of other ways to go. Try a **chutney**—a combination of sweet, sour, savory, and spicy flavors (think peach, lime, parsley, and cumin). Or a **salsa**, from one made with simple peppers or fruit to a cool and calming one like a cucumber salsa.

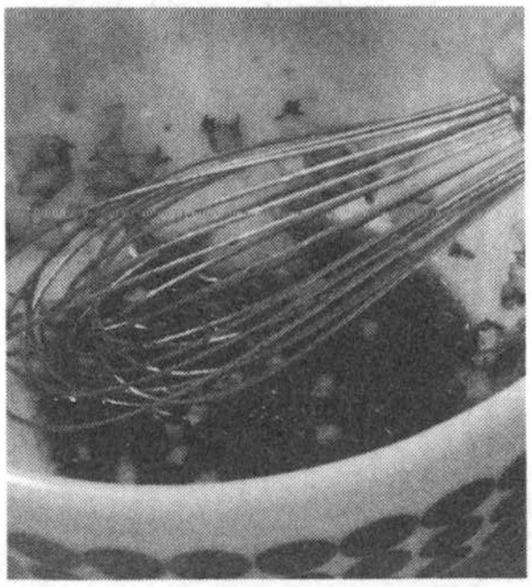

Dry **spice rubs** are one of our favorite ways to add the same kind of punch that a sauce can. From straight chili powder on a fish fillet to a more complicated barbecue rub on pork ribs, this technique can give a powerful first impression that leaves space for the rich simplicity of the food underneath.

You can also go the very wet route, by **marinating** or **brining**. A basic brine, a sugar-salt-water combination, was once used for preservation, but now we use it to add flavor as well as help meat stay **juicy**. A brined piece of meat tastes seasoned from the inside out. Pork—which is much leaner, and therefore drier, than it used to be—and chicken are by far the most common meats we brine, but smoked tuna, fried turkey, and salmon fillets can turn out well with brines, too. Of course, the brine can be tailored to the cuisine; add lemongrass, star anise, and fish sauce for a Southeast Asian touch.

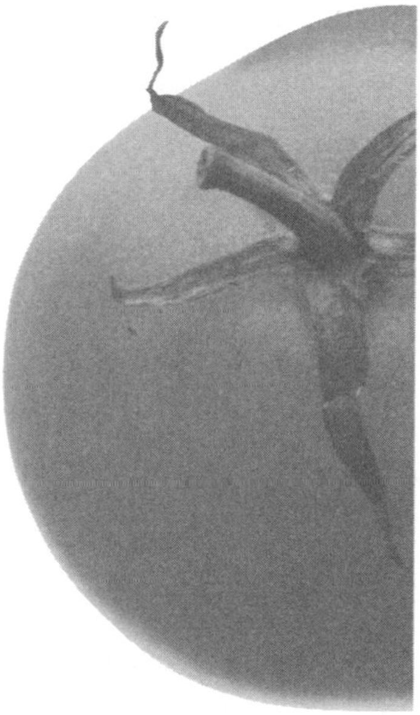

None of these techniques should be used in a vacuum. You can brine a chicken, rub it with spices, roast it, and then serve it with a chutney or salsa. Be sure you're working with the natural flavors of the meat—not covering them up.

THE EASIEST WAY to give someone a taste of Bourbon Street flair, aside from hanging purple, gold, and green beads around their neck, is to serve them something made with this spice mix. Use in such dishes as Southern Clam Chowder (page 110), Red Beans, Sausage, and Rice (page 125), Blackened Salmon with Lemon-Scallion Butter (page 188), and Buttermilk Fried Chicken with Green Onion Gravy (page 220). It's also great for grilling steak or fish, pickling okra, sautéing with corn in butter, and even thrown into a Bloody Mary. **NOW THAT'S NEW ORLEANS.**

CREOLE SEASONING

Makes approximately ½ cup

2 tablespoons dry thyme
2 tablespoons dry basil
2 tablespoons paprika
1 tablespoon gumbo filé powder
1 tablespoon cayenne
1 teaspoon chili powder
1 bay leaf, ground or finely chopped

Combine all the ingredients in a small bowl and mix thoroughly. The rub will stay fresh for up to 3 months, stored in an airtight container in a cool, dark place.

ETHIOPIAN SPICE MIX

ALLSPICE, GINGER, clove, and cinnamon: Sound familiar? Nope, it's not an apple pie, but the beginnings of a spice mix that evokes Ethiopia. Apply judiciously; the flavor is intense. Use in Seared Ethiopian Lamb Chops with Pear-Orange Compote (page 38), Braised Lamb Shanks with Eggplant and Chickpeas (page 217), and Eggplant Chutney (page 167). Sprinkle on steak or chicken before grilling, or add to your favorite meat before stewing or braising (in either method, use 1 tablespoon per pound of meat). Or add ½ teaspoon per cup of hummus, baba ganoush, or puréed roasted root vegetables.

Makes ¾ cup

½ cup dried basil
2 tablespoons whole cloves
½ tablespoon allspice berries
¼ cup ground ginger
2 tablespoons ground fenugreek
1 (2-inch) stick cinnamon
1 tablespoon cayenne

Combine all the ingredients in a coffee grinder or mortar and pestle, and grind until smooth. Will keep for about 3 months, stored in an airtight container in a cool, dark place.

NORTH AFRICAN SPICE MIX

FROM TAGINES to preserved lemons to couscous, the tastes of Morocco are captivating. This spice mix brings home the mysteries of Casablanca like nothing since, well, *Casablanca*. Use it in North African Hummus (page 130), Lamb Tagine with Sesame-Almond Garnish (page 115), and on any grilled red meat or chicken.

Makes ¼ cup

1 tablespoon cumin seeds, toasted and ground
1 tablespoon coriander seeds, toasted and ground
2 teaspoons ground cinnamon
½ tablespoon ground fenugreek
1 teaspoon ground ginger
½ tablespoon red pepper flakes

In a small bowl, combine all the ingredients and mix well. The spice mix will keep, covered tightly, for up to 1 month.

BASIC BARBECUE RUB

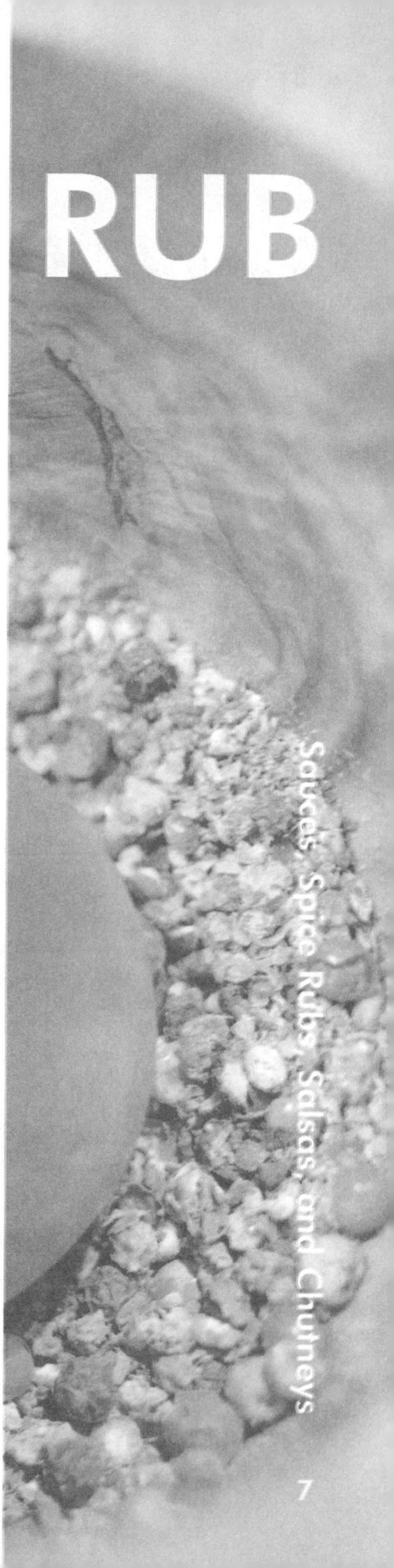

When I say **"BARBECUE,"** I mean slow-cooking by smoky, indirect heat, not grilling. If you don't have a smoker, try this rub for slow-roasting meat in the oven. (Avoid using it for direct-fire grilling or broiling because the spices and sugar in the rub will burn.) As a general rule, use ¼ cup per pound of meat, and let it rest about 30 minutes before cooking.

Makes about 1 cup

2 tablespoons granulated sugar
2 tablespoons brown sugar
2 tablespoons ground cumin
2 tablespoons chili powder
2 tablespoons salt
2 tablespoons freshly ground black pepper
1 tablespoon cayenne
4 tablespoons paprika

Mix together all the ingredients thoroughly. Will keep for several months stored in a cool, dark place in an airtight container.

If you've ever wondered which plant **CURRY** comes from, it's time you learned that curry isn't a spice at all, but merely a term for a spice mix as unique as the cook who makes it. Adding to the confusion is the Indian herb known as curry leaf, but that's another entity altogether. In India, cooks prepare their own curries from scratch, customizing them to suit their taste and the recipe at hand. Use in Tomato-Ginger Chutney (page 29), Curried Butternut Squash Soup with Mint Oil (page 99), Curried Thai Chicken and Mushroom Soup (page 112), Curried Basmati Rice with Almonds and Golden Raisins (page 142), and Braised Pumpkin with Curry (page 165).

TREMONT 647 CURRY

Makes 1 cup

1/4 cup cumin seeds
1/4 cup coriander seeds
2 teaspoons cardamom seeds
2 teaspoons fenugreek seeds
2 1/2 tablespoons commercial CURRY powder
1 tablespoon turmeric
2 teaspoons ground cinnamon
1 tablespoon cayenne pepper

1. In a small, heavy-bottomed sauté pan or cast-iron skillet, toast the cumin and coriander seeds over medium heat for about 5 minutes, until fragrant and slightly darkened. Take care not to burn them.

2. Transfer the seeds to a clean coffee grinder (working in batches if necessary) or mortar and pestle. Grind to fine powder.

3. Add the remaining ingredients and grind the mixture to a fine powder.

BASIC BRINE

SOAKING lean pork and poultry in a sugar-salt solution seasons it throughout, adds moisture, and makes it harder to overcook. With all those benefits, why not brine?

Makes 1 quart

2 cups kosher salt
1 cup brown sugar (for pork) or white sugar (for poultry)
1 quart cold water
Handful whole peppercorns, unpeeled garlic cloves, star anise, bay leaves, juniper berries, or a combination, smashed (optional)
1 pork roast or 1 whole chicken (no more than 6 pounds)

1. Dissolve the salt and sugar in water in a large bucket or stockpot. Add the spices.

2. Immerse the pork or chicken in the mixture and refrigerate for about 3 hours. Remove from brine, rinse thoroughly in cold water, and dry well.

ALL-PURPOSE FIRE

THIS SAUCE has a little sweetness, a little saltiness, and a hell of a lot of heat, but it's meant to augment other dishes, not stand on its own. Add to rice (in the water before cooking), slather on a steak before grilling, or create an instant chutney by adding to a store-bought jam or jelly.

Makes approximately 2 cups

1 lightly packed cup parsley leaves
3 cloves garlic
2 habanero peppers, seeded and roughly chopped (or milder serrano chilies, if you prefer)
½ cup olive oil
½ cup lemon juice (about 2 lemons)
1 tablespoon chili powder
1 tablespoon salt
1 tablespoon granulated sugar

1. Combine the parsley, garlic, and chilies in a food processor or blender; process until finely chopped.

2. Add the oil, lemon juice, chili powder, salt, and sugar; process until smooth. Will keep for 3 or 4 days if refrigerated in an airtight container.

HOT, HOTTER, & HOTTEST

There are hundreds of varieties of chili peppers. Here are the most common:

Habanero: Closely related to the Scotch bonnet, this is the hottest pepper around, with a musky flavor. Use sparingly.

Serrano (a.k.a., "The Green Bullet from Hell"): These are very hot, with crisp, almost bitter bell pepper flavor.

Jalapeño: Hot to very hot, with a fruity flavor. The most common chili pepper in the United States, found pickled on nachos, stuffed as jalapeño poppers, in sauces, and more.

Chipotle (smoked and dried jalapeño): Hot to very hot, found dried or, more commonly, canned in *adobo* sauce, with a unique smoky flavor.

Poblano: Heat varies, but usually mild, with a rich flavor that makes them popular for use in chili rellenos, a fabulous stuffed and deep-fried pepper dish.

Ancho (dried poblano): Mild, with a slightly fruity flavor that adds smoke and earthiness to a dish without the heat of the chipotle.

AIOLI

MAYONNAISE is as old as classical French cooking itself, and the French have been adding garlic to it virtually from its invention, giving that creaminess a welcome bite. If time is of the essence, and you don't want to make your own mayonnaise, buy Hellmann's (sold as Best Foods west of the Rockies), and add garlic to it. But try this recipe at least once, and I bet you bring out the Hellmann's a lot less often than you used to.

Makes 1¼ cups

1 large egg
1 tablespoon fresh lemon juice
2 cloves garlic, peeled and roughly chopped
2 teaspoons Dijon mustard
1 cup canola oil
Salt and freshly ground black pepper

1. Put the egg, lemon juice, garlic, and mustard in a food processor or blender; purée.

2. Slowly drizzle the oil into the food processor until the mixture is smooth, thick, and shiny. Season with salt and pepper. Refrigerate for up to 1 week, covered.

YUCATAN CHILI SAUCE

This sauce makes slow-cooked meats like Yucatan Roasted Pork (page 210) taste as if they were cooked in an earth pit on the coast of Mexico.

Yields 1 1/2 cups

1/4 cup annatto seeds
1/4 cup whole black peppercorns
1 1/2 tablespoons toasted cumin seeds
1 teaspoon whole allspice berries
1 cup peeled garlic cloves
1/4 lightly packed cup fresh oregano leaves
2 tablespoons kosher salt
3/4 cup orange juice
1/4 cup dry white wine
1 tablespoon red pepper flakes

1. Grind the annatto seeds, peppercorns, cumin seeds, and allspice in a spice grinder and set aside.
2. In a food processor, finely chop the garlic and oregano along with the salt.
3. Add the orange juice, wine, and red pepper flakes; blend until fairly smooth. Add the ground spices and process until fully incorporated.
4. Refrigerate, covered, until ready to use.

For Color & More

Annatto seeds, also known as achiote seeds, are a popular seasoning in regional Mexican cooking and have also been used for decades to color commercial butter and margarine. Available in good Latin markets, some general-interest supermarkets, and online, these hard-as-a-rock red seeds are musky in flavor. We use them to impart their **color and flavor** to an oil that goes into a salad dressing, and as part of pastes and spice rubs.

SOY SAKE SAUCE

EVERY SUSHI LOVER KNOWS: That ubiquitous soy sauce can be heavy and way too salty. Add sake and water, though, and it's light and flowery. Use as a dipping sauce for Tibetan Momos (page 36), fresh vegetables, and grilled meat and fish. Or marinate chicken or steak strips for 30 minutes in it before skewering and grilling, for an elegant twist on teriyaki.

Makes 2 cups

½ cup soy sauce
½ cup sake
1 cup water
1 scallion, white and light green parts, thinly sliced
2 teaspoons red pepper flakes

In a small mixing bowl, combine all the ingredients and mix well. Keeps for up to 1 week refrigerated in an airtight container.

ROUGE'S NEW ORLEANS BARBECUE SAUCE

AT ROUGE, we have a passion for all things Southern, which is why we love this sauce. We slather it on our wildly popular Rouge's Barbecued Shrimp with Hominy (page 33). Be warned: This sauce is as intense as the New Orleans blues.

Makes about 1 cup

1 lemon, peeled and quartered
4 cloves garlic, peeled
Shells from 1 pound cocktail-sized shrimp (optional), reserved from Rouge's Barbecued Shrimp with Hominy (page 33)
1 tablespoon black peppercorns
1 cup Worcestershire sauce
1 cup Louisiana hot sauce
1 bay leaf
1 sprig fresh thyme

Combine all the ingredients in a small saucepan over medium-high heat. Bring to a boil and reduce by half. Strain and set aside. Will keep refrigerated for up to 7 days in an airtight container.

PULL ON THE LATEX

When I was at East Coast Grill, I was responsible for the ever-popular "Hotter Than Hell" nights, when the menu is peppered, literally, with chilies. I spent days working with fiery habaneros and even adding straight capsaicin oil (the substance that makes peppers hot) to dishes. I didn't use gloves, but I washed my hands obsessively, so no problem, right?

Wrong! I found that out the first time I went to the bathroom. Yow-wee. It's a good thing I didn't rub my eyes.

Here's the moral of the story: The oils in chilies—found mostly in the seeds and veins—do not easily wash off in soap and water. So when you're seeding chili peppers (which you should for most recipes), wear latex gloves. If you don't have any, and are too stubborn to heed my advice and go buy some, clean the chilies under running water, and don't just wash your hands; scrub them. Hard. Then scrub under the nails. Then soak your hands for several minutes in warm salt water. Then scrub them again.

After you do all that—or if you forget, and touch yourself in a delicate place—believe me, you'll go out and buy some latex gloves.

UFO Social Club Barbecue Sauce

No, I haven't been fraternizing with aliens, although at barbecue competitions in New England and across the nation, it sometimes seems like it. This sauce is named for my barbecue team, which is in turn named for the UFO brew made by Harpoon, our sponsor. It's a primary ingredient in Baked Barbecue White Beans (page 132), but its best use is simply on barbecued meat. Slather it on right before serving, serve on the side, or use as a dipping sauce.

Makes about 5 cups

2 tablespoons vegetable oil
1 large yellow onion, chopped
1 (14.5-ounce) can tomato purée
1 (14.5-ounce) can tomatoes, with juice
½ cup white vinegar
2 packed tablespoons dark brown sugar
2 tablespoons granulated sugar
1 tablespoon salt
1 tablespoon freshly cracked black pepper
1 tablespoon paprika
1 tablespoon chili powder
2 tablespoons molasses
¼ cup Basic Barbecue Rub (page 7)
½ cup orange juice
4 tablespoons yellow mustard
1 (12-ounce) bottle dark beer

1. Heat the oil in a large, heavy-bottomed saucepan over medium-high heat. Add the onion and sauté, stirring frequently, until golden brown, about 10 minutes.
2. Add the remaining ingredients and bring to boil. Reduce heat to very low and simmer gently for 2 hours. Stir the sauce occasionally, scraping the bottom of the pot to prevent scorching.
3. Transfer the sauce to a food processor or blender and purée in 2 batches. Transfer to a clean glass jar and store for up to 7 to 10 days in the refrigerator.

Marinate, Don't Cook

When I was in ninth grade, I went on a kebab-grilling kick. I would cut steak into cubes, pour a salad dressing on top, and let it sit a day or two—the longer the better, right? Then I would thread it onto skewers and grill it over charcoal reeking of lighter fluid.

These days, we wouldn't marinate a steak for longer than 3 or 4 hours, because we want the steak to taste like steak, not like marinade, and not like lighter fluid, either. (For fish, we marinate it for even less time, 1 to 2 hours. Most marinades include an acid such as vinegar or lime juice, and if the fish sits too long in the acid it will start to "cook," as in ceviche.)

One other tip: Drain the meat and pat the excess marinade off before grilling or sautéing, to avoid burning the exterior before cooking the inside.

Vietnamese Cilantro Dipping Sauce

THIS SAUCE is perfect for dunking grilled shrimp, pork, or beef skewers, and as a marinade for just about any meat or fish—anything you want to give a Southeast Asian flair. Use in Shrimp-Stuffed Squid (page 202) and Lemongrass Rice with Lamb (page 140).

Makes about 1 cup

¼ cup freshly squeezed lime juice (about 2 limes)
2 cloves garlic, peeled
2 tablespoons fish sauce
3 tablespoons brown sugar
1 tablespoon minced chives
1 teaspoon red pepper flakes
½ cup roughly chopped cilantro leaves

Put all the ingredients in a food processor or blender and purée. The sauce will taste good for 2 to 3 days (refrigerated in an airtight container), but it is much prettier when freshly made and the cilantro is still bright green.

SPICY ROASTED YELLOW PEPPER CURRY

USE AS A DIPPING SAUCE for grilled shrimp or lamb or pork cubes for a fun appetizer, or as an ingredient in Pork Soup with Yellow Pepper Curry and Pecans (page 114). In fact, this can be the base for any curry stew; for 4 people, just sear 2 pounds of cubed chicken thighs or lamb, add ½ cup of this paste plus ½ cup water, simmer until done, and serve over rice.

Makes about 3 cups

5 yellow bell peppers
1 tablespoon vegetable *or* olive oil
About 2 tablespoons salt
¼ cup roughly chopped onion
¼ cup sweetened, shredded coconut, toasted
3 cloves garlic, peeled
1 jalapeño, seeded and roughly chopped
2 tablespoons red wine vinegar
1 tablespoon Tremont 647 Curry (page 8)
1 tablespoon brown sugar
1 teaspoon caraway seeds, toasted and ground
1 teaspoon dry mustard

1. Preheat oven to 450°F.

2. Put the peppers on a foil-lined baking sheet, drizzle with the oil, and sprinkle with the salt. Roast until the peppers are soft and the skins are slightly blackened in spots, 20 to 30 minutes, turning occasionally.

3. Transfer the peppers to bowl, and cover tightly with plastic wrap. Let stand until the peppers are cool enough to handle, about 15 minutes. Remove the skin and seeds from peppers.

4. Place the cleaned peppers in a food processor or blender and purée until smooth. Add the remaining ingredients and process again until smooth. Will last for up to 1 week refrigerated in an airtight container.

THIS IS A FINE EXAMPLE of the **HOT-SOUR-SALTY-SWEET** combination that makes Southeast Asian dishes so addictive. Use as a dip for Curried Chicken Skewers (page 41), or serve warm or cold with roasted or grilled chicken, shellfish, or red meat.

Makes approximately 3 cups

2 tablespoons canola oil
1 onion, cut into ¼-inch dice
2 tablespoons peeled and minced ginger
3 cloves garlic, peeled and minced
3 mangoes, peeled and cut into ¼-inch cubes
1 cup canned mango juice
3 tablespoons chili-garlic paste
¼ cup freshly squeezed lime juice (about 2 limes)
¼ cup fish sauce
Salt and freshly ground pepper, to taste

1. In a heavy-bottomed sauté pan, heat the oil on medium-high. Add the onions and cook, stirring occasionally until softened, about 5 minutes. Turn heat to low and add the ginger and garlic. Cook, stirring occasionally, until the onions are lightly caramelized, about 15 minutes.

2. Add the mangoes and mango juice; bring to simmer. Cook, stirring occasionally to keep the mixture from scorching, until the mangoes collapse, about 10 minutes. Remove from heat and stir in the chili-garlic paste, lime juice, fish sauce, and salt and pepper; mix well.

FIERY VIETNAMESE MANGO JAM

RED ONION VINAIGRETTE

THE COMBINATION of sweet onion and tangy vinegar makes this a keeper. Use it on salads or as a marinade, or add a spoonful to lightly seared spinach leaves for a burst of flavor. Warmed up, it's great over sliced prosciutto and grilled asparagus; add some grilled brioche, and you've got the makings of an incredible sandwich.

Yields 2½ cups

½ medium-size red onion, peeled and roughly chopped
3 large garlic cloves
1 tablespoon roughly chopped fresh parsley
1 tablespoon finely minced fresh rosemary
½ tablespoon roughly chopped fresh sage
1 tablespoon Dijon mustard
¼ cup balsamic vinegar
¼ cup red wine vinegar
1 teaspoon kosher salt
½ teaspoon freshly cracked black pepper
1½ cups olive oil

1. In a food processor or blender, combine the onion, garlic, and herbs; pulse until finely chopped.
2. Add the mustard, both vinegars, and salt and pepper, processing briefly to blend.
3. With the machine running, add the oil through the feed tube in a thin stream until the dressing is well blended.
4. To serve warm, finely chop the onions, garlic, and herbs, and whisk together all the ingredients in a small stainless steel saucepan over low heat. The dressing will keep, covered and refrigerated, for up to 2 weeks.

BLUE CHEESE VINAIGRETTE

THE CHAMPAGNE VINEGAR—no, it doesn't have bubbles—is so light it lets the flavors of the pungent blue cheese and the musky thyme come through. The obvious use is on a salad, but there are others: Use as a dipping sauce with Polenta Fries (page 52), or drizzle over a grilled or broiled steak right before serving.

Makes a little over 1 cup

- 1/4 cup champagne vinegar
- 1/4 cup crumbled blue cheese
- 3/4 cup olive oil
- 1/4 cup roughly chopped Italian parsley leaves
- 2 tablespoons thyme leaves
- Salt and freshly ground black pepper, to taste

Combine all the ingredients in a food processor or blender and purée. Refrigerate. Stir well immediately before use.

Something Tastes Fishy

Fish sauce, which is made from salted and fermented fish, is a wonderfully pungent condiment ubiquitous in Southeast Asian cooking. You can find it in any Asian market and these days in many good general supermarkets, too. Our favorite thing about it, besides the fabulous taste: no refrigeration required. Our least favorite thing: the smell, which definitely takes some getting used to.

Vietnamese Vinaigrette

THIS VERSATILE Southeast Asian dressing, similar to *nuoc cham*, is great to have on hand. Use it over salad (such as Mango, Cabbage, and Toasted Peanut Salad, page 65) or over cold soba noodles, or add to chili-garlic paste for a tasty spring roll dipping sauce. You can even use it as a quick marinade for fish, but don't leave the fish in it too long or you'll be on the road to ceviche.

Yields about 2½ cups

1 cup hot water
¼ cup granulated sugar
½ cup Vietnamese *or* Thai fish sauce (*nuoc nam* or *nam pla*)
½ cup lime juice (about 4 limes)
1 carrot, peeled and grated
2 large cloves garlic, peeled and minced
½ tablespoon ginger, peeled and minced

1. Stir together the hot water and sugar in a medium-size stainless steel bowl until the sugar dissolves.
2. Add the remaining ingredients and store in an airtight container. Refrigerate until cool. The dressing will last for 2 weeks.

A CLASSIC CONDIMENT made *muy picante* (that's "very spicy," for the English-only crowd) by the addition of cumin, chipotle, and, of course, lime. Serve straight up with chips and salsa, or with grilled or roasted chicken, grilled shrimp, or any Latin-style dish, such as Chicken Chicharrones with Fresh Oregano (page 34), Shrimp Taquitos with Chili Dipping Sauce (page 56), Beer-Poached Shrimp with Tomatillo Cocktail Sauce (page 58), or Corn, Turkey, and Tomato Quesadillas (page 40).

LIMED SOUR CREAM

Makes about ½ cup

½ cup sour cream
Juice of 1 lime (about 2 tablespoons)
½ teaspoon cumin seeds, toasted and ground
1 dried chipotle pepper, rehydrated and minced (or squeezed of extra liquid if canned)
Salt and freshly cracked black pepper, to taste

Combine all the ingredients in a small mixing bowl and stir thoroughly. Will keep for about 1 week refrigerated in an airtight container.

PARSLEY PURÉE

THIS WAS INSPIRED by *chimichurri*, that great Argentinian accompaniment to grilled meat, but it's simpler and not as spicy. But be forewarned: It changes drastically after only a couple of hours, and not for the better, so make it fresh every time you want it. Serve with any grilled meat or fish.

Makes about 3/4 cup

1 1/2 loosely packed cups parsley leaves
3 cloves garlic, peeled
1/4 cup freshly squeezed lime juice (about 2 limes)
1/4 cup olive oil
2 teaspoons kosher salt
2 teaspoons freshly ground black pepper

Combine all the ingredients in a food processor and purée until smooth. Serve immediately. Will keep for up to 6 hours in an airtight container and refrigerated.

SALSA 101

SALSA hasn't been exotic in years; it's more popular than ketchup. Too many people, though, eat it out of a jar, not realizing that nothing compares to a fresh salsa. What's the upside to that? Even though it's simple to make, your guests will be instantly impressed.

Makes about 2 cups

1 large ripe tomato, cut into ¼-inch dice
½ cup minced red onion
½ cup chopped cilantro
1 jalapeño, seeded and minced
2 tablespoons freshly squeezed lime juice (about 1 lime)
1 tablespoon extra-virgin olive oil
Salt and freshly ground black pepper, to taste

In a medium-size mixing bowl, combine all the ingredients. The salsa will keep for up to 1 week, refrigerated.

FIERY THREE-ONION SALSA

USE ON TACOS or burritos, alongside chips, or with Birria (page 216), a rustic Mexican stew. Try charring the yellow onions over a grill before chopping, or adding 1 cup of diced mangoes, pineapples, and/or Granny Smith apples. Of course, if it's too fiery for you, use a milder chili pepper than that (wonderfully) evil habanero.

Makes approximately 2 cups

3 scallions, chopped
1 yellow onion, peeled and chopped
1 red onion, peeled and chopped
1 habanero chili, seeded and finely minced
½ cup chopped cilantro leaves
3 tablespoons freshly squeezed lime juice (about 1½ limes)
1 tablespoon extra-virgin olive oil
Salt and freshly ground black pepper, to taste

In a medium-size mixing bowl, combine all the ingredients. Best used fresh, when the different onion flavors are distinct, but will keep for 1 week, covered and refrigerated.

BACK TO LIFE

Dried chilies need to be rehydrated before use. Here's how to do it:

1. Heat about ¼ inch of oil in a sauté pan and add the dried chilies. Cook on both sides for only about 20 to 30 seconds. They'll get brighter red—be careful not to burn them.
2. Transfer to a small bowl and cover with hot water for about 5 to 10 minutes until the chilies are soft. Remove, and squeeze out extra water.
3. Wearing latex gloves (see "Pull on the Latex," page 14) and/or working under running water, slit open the chilies to remove the seeds and scrape off visible veins from the inside, and proceed with use.

LIKE CHINESE sweet-and-sour dishes? You'll love this Southeast Asian twist, a glaze that turns shrimp, pork, chicken, or beef into sticky, fabulous party food like the Fiery Thai Sticky Shrimp (page 39).

Yields 1 cup

1 tablespoon sesame oil
2 teaspoons peeled and minced fresh ginger
½ cup apricot preserves
¼ cup fish sauce
2 tablespoons chili-garlic paste

1. In a heavy saucepan, heat the oil over medium-high heat. Add the ginger and sauté, stirring frequently, until the ginger gives off intense perfume and starts to brown, about 2 minutes.
2. Add the remaining ingredients and reduce heat to low. Simmer, stirring occasionally, until the preserves are melted and the sauce ingredients are incorporated, about 4 minutes, stirring occasionally.
3. Transfer to a small bowl to cool. The sauce will keep, covered and refrigerated, for up to 1 week.

APRICOT THAI GLAZE

SOY-CURRY GLAZE

THIS GLAZE is deep and mysterious, both in flavor and color: dark brown with a golden glow. Use in Hunan Glazed Chicken with Asian Vegetables (page 89), and Atlantic Cod in Banana Leaves (page 182), to glaze vegetables such as Deep-Fried Green Beans (page 170), red meat, or fish, or toss into lo mein noodles (served hot or cold).

Makes about 1 cup

2 tablespoons sesame oil
2 tablespoons peeled and minced garlic
¼ cup hoisin
¼ cup honey
¼ cup soy sauce
¼ cup sherry
2 tablespoons curry powder
1 tablespoon chili-garlic paste
Juice and zest of 1 large orange
¼ cup fermented black beans, rinsed with hot water and chopped

In a small (1-quart) saucepan, combine the oil and garlic. Place the pan over medium-high heat and cook, stirring frequently, until the garlic is light brown and fragrant. Add the remaining ingredients and bring to a boil. Adjust the heat to a simmer and cook, stirring occasionally, until thickened, 6 to 8 minutes. Remove from heat. The glaze will keep for up to 2 weeks refrigerated in an airtight container.

A DELICIOUS MISNOMER

Fermented black beans are fermented, but they're not black beans—well, not the turtle beans that we normally think of when we hear that term, anyway. Also called Chinese black beans, they're actually preserved, salted, fermented black soybeans. They are sold in cans or plastic bags in good Asian markets, and they last for up to a year in the refrigerator. As with salt cod or anchovies, make sure you rinse them before using, or their rich, dark flavor won't be a mysterious addition as much as an overpowering presence.

PEKING IN

Hoisin, also known as Peking sauce, is a sweet, spicy mixture of soybeans, garlic, chili peppers, and spices, in a ketchup consistency. Found in Asian markets and good general-interest supermarkets, it's a wonderful glaze for roasted meat—such as the classic Peking duck—as well as a stand-alone dipping sauce or condiment in wrapped-up dishes like mu shu. For particularly festive Chinese dinners, retire the salt and pepper shakers for the night and instead put out little dishes of hoisin, chili-garlic paste, chopped peanuts, and soy sauce.

THIS VERSATILE, dynamic sauce, similar to hoisin but more complex, has become a staple in my kitchen; I've used it for more than 15 years to dress hot or cold noodles and glaze vegetables, meats, and fish. Use it in Sweet Potato, Cabbage, and Pecan Salad (page 84), Asian Chicken and Rice Salad (page 149), and Sweet-and-Spicy Lo Mein (page 61). When grilling or pan-frying with the glaze, use it at the end of cooking, or it will burn.

Makes about 3 1/3 cups

1/3 cup sesame oil
1 tablespoon peeled and minced garlic
1 tablespoon peeled and minced ginger
1 cup light molasses
1/2 cup soy sauce
1/4 cup brown sugar
1/4 cup any fruit vinegar
1/4 cup cider vinegar
1/4 cup rice vinegar
1/4 cup sherry
1 tablespoon chili-garlic paste
2 tablespoons cornstarch, dissolved in 1/4 cup water

1. In a saucepan over medium-high heat, heat the sesame oil. Add the garlic and ginger, and cook until fragrant, stirring frequently, about 2 to 3 minutes.

2. Add the molasses, soy sauce, brown sugar, vinegars, sherry, and chili paste, and bring to a gentle boil. Whisk in the cornstarch slurry and simmer, stirring occasionally until thickened, about 5 minutes. Best used within 2 weeks but will keep for up to 3 months refrigerated in an airtight container.

SWEET-AND-SPICY SOY GLAZE

Sweet & Sour . . . and Sticky

Tamarind, also called the Indian date, grows as a large pod, but it's the sweet-and-sour, tarlike paste inside that is used for flavoring in Asia, Africa, India, and the Caribbean. It's what helps give Worcestershire sauce its distinctive tang. You'll find it in Asian or Latin markets as a brick, which is the best-tasting form but requires the most prep; you have to soak it in hot water or vinegar to separate it from the seeds buried within. You can also find it in jars, with the seeds removed, but the taste isn't as fresh.

Tomato-Ginger Chutney

Designed as a jazzed-up ketchup to go on burgers, this chutney works just as well on all sorts of grilled meat, such as Nectarine and Lamb Kebabs (page 226), or on beef and pork. Spread it on just before serving or serve on the side.

Makes approximately 2 cups

2 tablespoons canola oil
1 medium-size onion, cut into 1/4-inch dice
1/2 cup minced ginger (4- to 5-inch piece)
3 cloves garlic, peeled and minced
1 (14.5-ounce) can whole tomatoes, with juice
1 tablespoon tamarind paste
2 tablespoons Tremont 647 Curry (page 8)
2 tablespoons brown sugar
1/4 cup freshly squeezed lime juice (about 2 limes)
1/4 cup chopped cilantro
Salt and freshly ground black pepper, to taste

1. In a heavy-bottomed sauté pan, heat the oil over medium-high heat. Add the onions and cook, stirring occasionally, until softened, about 5 minutes. Turn the heat to low, and add the ginger and garlic. Cook, stirring occasionally, until the onions are lightly caramelized, about 15 minutes.

2. Add the tomatoes, tamarind, curry, and brown sugar; stir well to combine, breaking up the tomatoes as you go. Simmer for 10 to 15 minutes, stirring occasionally, until the mixture is about as thick as mashed bananas.

3. Remove from heat and add the lime, cilantro, salt, and pepper. Serve immediately, or allow to cool to room temperature. Will keep for 3 to 5 days, refrigerated in an airtight container.

A Toast to Flavor

Why do we call for so many whole spices to be toasted? Because it brings out the flavor of the spices, especially cumin, coriander, and caraway seeds. Here's how to toast them:

1. Heat a sauté pan over low heat, and add spices. Slowly shake them until you notice smoke rising up, about 3 to 4 minutes. Be careful not to burn them.

2. Remove pan from heat, and immediately remove the spices from the pan, pouring them into a small dish to cool before using.

Summer Peach Chutney

THIS CHUTNEY, much chunkier and tastier than traditional barbecue sauce, doesn't just say summer; it screams it. Use on smoked or grilled meats such as Basil-Rubbed Pork Medallions (page 43). Just be sure your peaches, or any farm-fresh ripe stone fruit you want to substitute, are juicy and in season.

Makes about 2 cups

2 tablespoons canola oil
1 large onion, diced
2 tablespoons peeled and chopped garlic
2 large, ripe peaches, cut into small chunks
1/4 cup cider vinegar
1/2 tablespoon Dijon mustard
2 tablespoons Worcestershire sauce
1/4 packed cup brown sugar
1 1/2 teaspoons cumin seeds, toasted and ground
1/4 teaspoon red pepper flakes
Up to 1 1/2 cups orange juice, as needed

1. In heavy-bottomed sauté pan, heat the oil on medium-high. Add the onions and cook, stirring occasionally, until softened, about 5 minutes. Turn heat to low and add the garlic. Cook, stirring occasionally, until the onions are lightly caramelized, about 15 minutes.

2. Add the peaches, vinegar, mustard, Worcestershire, brown sugar, cumin, red pepper flakes, and cook on medium-low heat for 30 minutes, stirring occasionally. Add orange juice only as needed, 1/4 cup at a time, to keep the mixture from scorching or becoming too thick (less orange juice will be needed if peaches are nice and juicy). Cool and refrigerate until ready for use. Will keep in an airtight container, refrigerated, for 4 to 6 days.

First Things First

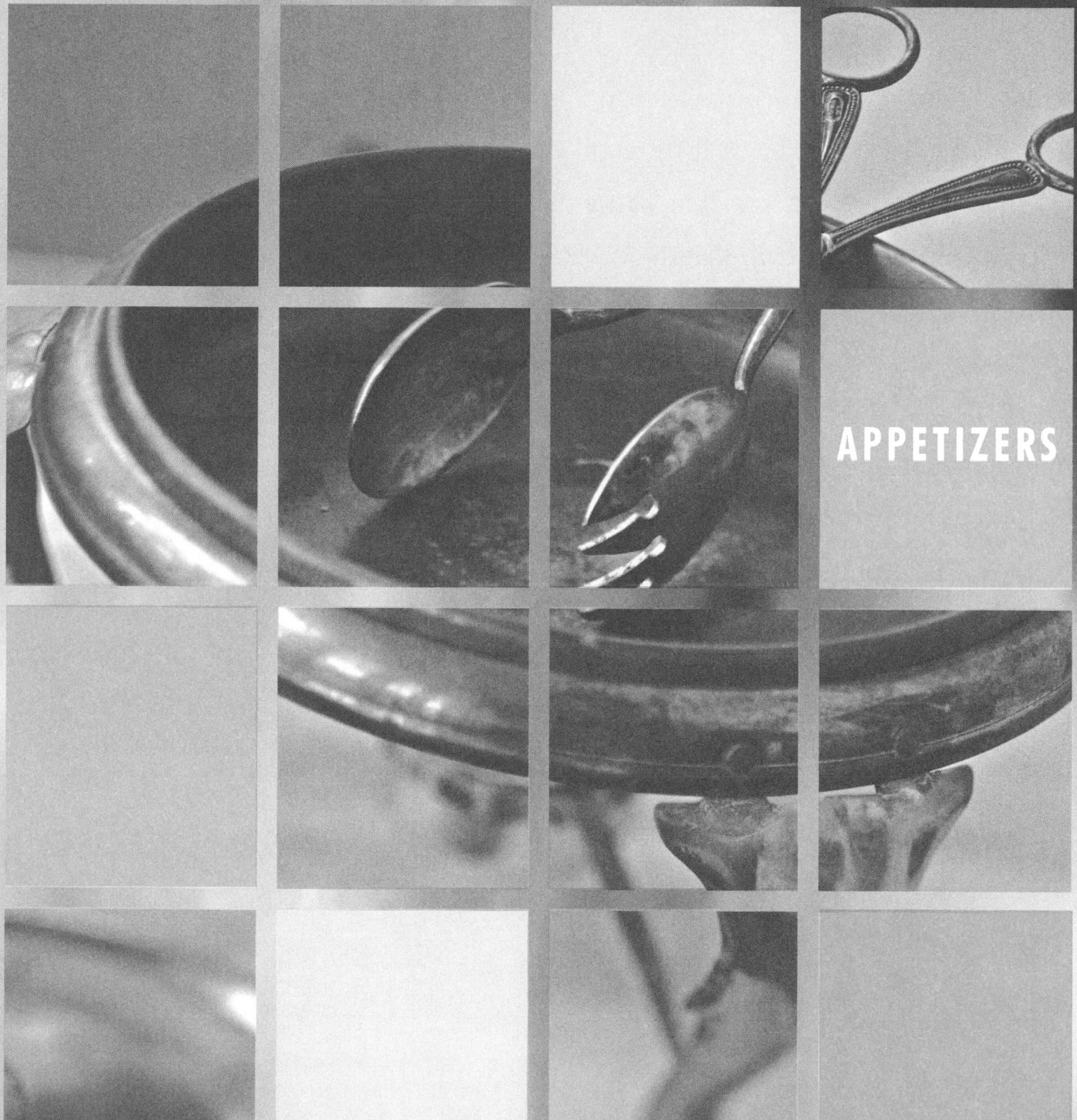

APPETIZERS

A GOOD **APPETIZER** IS LIKE THE STARTER'S GUN at a track meet, like the ". . . and they're off!" of a horse race, like a warm-up band for your favorite act. It should be groovy, fun, exciting. It should say, "You think this is good? Just you wait."

Why do we like appetizers so much? Perhaps it's about our short attention span; we like appetizers because we like sound bites, movie trailers, and short stories. Or perhaps it's because in their communal friendliness, they remind us of a party (tapas), or of lazy Sunday mornings (dim sum).

Appetizers can go one of two ways: simple, like stinky cheese and bread, or layered with flavors, like Tibetan Momos (page 36) dipped in a mild soy sauce and then a hot sriracha (Thai chili sauce). Either way, they should do what the French call "amuse bouche" (amuse the mouth), making it smile at the taste it just had—and salivate at the thought of what's to come.

amuse bouche

ROUGE'S BARBECUED SHRIMP WITH HOMINY

IF YOU'VE BEEN to **N'AWLINS** (New Orleans), you know it's the land of big, pungent flavors (not to mention all manner of indiscreet behavior), and this is in that spirit. Don't worry: If you don't have hominy, fresh corn kernels, okra, or red bell peppers are tasty substitutes. Serve with Stacy's Spicy Corn Bread (page 239), or with toasts made from Butter Bread (page 250).

Serves 4 to 6

2 tablespoons olive oil
2 cloves garlic, peeled and minced
1 pound cocktail-sized shrimp, peeled and deveined (reserve shells for sauce)
1 (14.5-ounce) can hominy, drained
4 scallions, cut into 1-inch pieces
½ cup Rouge's New Orleans Barbecue Sauce (page 14)
2 tablespoons cold unsalted butter, cubed
¼ cup roughly chopped flat-leaf Italian parsley

1. Heat the oil in a large, heavy sauté pan over medium-high heat. Add the garlic and cook, stirring frequently, for 30 seconds. Add the shrimp and sear for 30 seconds.

2. Turn the shrimp. Add the hominy, scallions, and barbecue sauce. Reduce heat to medium and cook for 3 to 5 minutes, until the shrimp are firm.

3. Remove pan from heat. Add the cold butter, one piece at a time, stirring until each is melted before incorporating more. Garnish with parsley. Serve immediately.

CHICKEN CHICHARRONES WITH FRESH OREGANO

THESE LITTLE NUGGETS of crispy-moist chicken are best eaten scooped up in a warm tortilla and drizzled with Limed Sour Cream (page 22). The secret to the texture lies in the high heat; the meat comes awfully close to burning, so be prepared to act quickly.

Serves 4 as an appetizer or 2 as an entrée

¼ cup olive oil
1½ pounds skinless, boneless chicken thighs, cut into 3-inch squares
Kosher salt and freshly cracked black pepper, to taste
¼ cup peeled and minced garlic
1 tablespoon chili powder
1 tablespoon cumin seeds, toasted and ground
1 tablespoon coriander seeds, toasted and ground
1 tablespoon roughly chopped fresh oregano
⅓ cup white vinegar
½ lime, cut into wedges

1. In a heavy-bottomed skillet over medium-high heat, heat oil until it is hot but not smoking.

2. Season the chicken with salt and pepper, and add it to the skillet. Cook until it turns golden brown and starts to fall apart, 7 to 10 minutes, stirring occasionally and scraping as it sticks to the bottom of the pan.

3. Add the garlic and cook 2 more minutes, stirring constantly so the garlic doesn't burn. Add the chili powder, cumin, coriander, and oregano; cook for 1 minute. Stir in the vinegar and cook until the chicken is glazed, about 1 minute more. Remove from heat. Season with salt and pepper.

4. Squeeze the fresh lime over the chicken and serve hot with warm tortillas, Salsa 101 (page 24), and Limed Sour Cream (page 22).

TAPAS TIME

The term tapas has emigrated to English, and has come to be known as any collection of small plates. Eating this way is perfect for a party because it fosters camaraderie, with people milling about, reaching, tasting, and talking.

How do you decide which small dishes to put out on a tapas table? You can compare or contrast, going either for dishes that are similar in flavor and texture, or playing up the differences.

For example: Go Latin, Asian, or Mediterranean. Or mix ethnicities but not ingredients, choosing all seafood. **To contrast:** Include some milder dishes and some spicier ones, some rustic ones alongside some elegant ones.

JASON SANTOS, whose mood we can track by the shade of blue dye in his hair, worked his way up from lowly bread boy to **EXECUTIVE CHEF** at Tremont 647 and now Kestral, where he keeps things running at a smooth clip. I was skeptical when he brought me this dish, and then I took a bite. The spicy cherries sealed the deal with their flavor and color, although from Jason I admit I expected something, well, bluer.

Serves 4 to 6 as an appetizer or 2 as an entrée

1 cup dried cherries (or dried cranberries)
½ cup warm water
¼ cup Tabasco
¼ cup Aioli (page 11)
1 tablespoon maple syrup
1½ pounds large sea scallops
Salt and freshly ground black pepper, to taste
2 tablespoons canola oil
¼ cup roughly chopped flat-leaf Italian parsley

SCALLOPS WITH CHERRIES

1. In a small bowl, combine the cherries, water, and Tabasco. Allow the cherries to soak for at least 20 minutes.
2. In a small mixing bowl, combine the aioli and maple syrup; mix thoroughly. Set aside.
3. Season the scallops with salt and pepper. Heat the oil in a heavy-bottomed sauté pan over high heat. Carefully place the scallops in the pan, and reduce heat to medium-high. Sear the scallops until they have developed a golden-brown crust on each side, about 2 to 3 minutes per side.
4. Strain the cherries and discard the liquid. Place the scallops in the center of each plate. Sprinkle the cherries on top. Use a spoon to drizzle the maple aioli in a crisscross pattern over the cherries. Garnish with parsley and serve immediately.

AT TREMONT 647 these delectable momos are such a popular signature dish that we have had a momo chef, Tsering Dongshi, cranking out hundreds of them every night; in our first five years, we sold a cool million of them. Tsering is from Tibet, where he says they make and eat versions of these little dumplings that are not so little, but we prefer them bite-sized. That way, you can easily be eating one while you dip the next one into the Soy Sake Sauce (page 13).

Makes about 25 bite-sized momos

For the filling:

½ pound ground pork or turkey
1 tablespoon peeled and minced fresh ginger
1 tablespoon peeled and minced garlic
2 tablespoons soy sauce
2 tablespoons peeled and finely chopped red or white onion
¼ cup finely chopped fresh cilantro leaves
1 teaspoon red pepper flakes

For the dough:

2 cups all-purpose flour
½ teaspoon salt
¾ cup warm water

TIBETAN MOMOS

1. In a large bowl, combine the filling ingredients and mix until fully combined. Cover and refrigerate until needed.

2. When ready to shape the momos, make the dough: In a large bowl, mix together the flour and salt. Gradually add just enough warm water until the dough comes together in a soft, not sticky, ball. Transfer the dough to a lightly floured work surface. Use a sharp knife to cut off about 1/4 of the dough; cover the remaining dough and set aside. Roll the piece of dough between your hands to form a 2-inch-wide log, and cut the log into sections about as big as a small walnut.

3. Flatten one small piece of dough with the heel of your hand, then use a rolling pin to form it into a 4-inch disk. Rotate the disk counterclockwise after each roll to keep it circular, rolling from the center out and making the edges as thin as possible.

4. Turn your left hand palm up and lay the circle of dough across your slightly bent fingers. With your right hand, scoop about 1 tablespoon of filling into the center of the dough. Press your left thumb gently on top of the filling and hold it there while you shape the dough with your right hand.

5. Think of the disk of dough as the face of a clock. Use your right thumb and first two fingers to pinch together one edge of the dough firmly at 3 o'clock. Draw in the dough from the 2 o'clock position, and pinch it tightly against the first pinch to make two adjacent folds in the dough. (This is the beginning of what will look like a drawstring bag.) As you draw in the third pinch of dough (from 1 o'clock), rotate the dumpling toward you slightly, so the pinched folds stay in the 3 o'clock position. Don't forget to keep your left thumb lightly pressed on top of the filling.

6. As you continue to add tight folds, the dough will start to enclose your left thumb. When you can't pinch any more folds, take your thumb out, gently grasp the top of the folds with the tips of your fingers, and twist lightly to seal the dumpling and accentuate the swirl design.

7. Repeat with the remaining circles of dough. Try to keep your folds small and neat. Don't give up if they aren't perfect right away; your momos will get prettier with practice. (If you just cannot get the hang of forming these dumplings, form them into half-moons instead.) Filled momos will keep, covered and refrigerated, for up to 1 day, but they are best steamed right away.

8. When all the momos have been formed, spray the insides of a large steamer basket with nonstick cooking spray (or lightly oil the surface). Arrange the momos in the basket in a single layer, side by side but not touching. Place the steamer over, not in, a pan of boiling water (the water should not touch the momos), and cover tightly. Steam until the momos have swelled and the dough is firm and no longer tacky to the touch, about 15 minutes. Serve with Soy Sake Sauce (page 13), chili-garlic paste, sriracha, or your favorite hot sauce.

GLISTENING dried fruit atop pristine pieces of lamb makes this perfect for an elegant dinner party, especially if you ask your butcher to "French" the rack, trimming the fat and meat from around the rib bones to expose them. Then, instead of mere lamb chops, you'll serve perfect little lamb lollipops glazed with jewel-like compote, and your guests may want to become boarders.

PEAR-ORANGE COMPOTE

Makes about 2 cups

1 cup water
½ cup honey
1 large orange, peeled, sectioned, seeds removed
Juice of 1 lemon (about ¼ cup)
6 ounces very firm dried pears, sliced into ½-inch strips (about 2 cups)
2 tablespoons finely chopped fresh sage
2 tablespoons finely chopped fresh mint
1 teaspoon coriander seeds, toasted and ground

1. Combine the water and honey in a heavy-bottomed 2-quart saucepan over high heat. When the mixture comes to a boil, add the orange segments, lemon juice, and pears. Lower heat and simmer, stirring occasionally, until the fruit is plump and tender, about 20 minutes.

2. Remove from heat and stir in the herbs and coriander. Let the compote cool to room temperature, cover, and refrigerate. Serve chilled or at room temperature.

ETHIOPIAN LAMB CHOPS

Serves 4

4 (½-inch-thick) lamb sirloin steaks or 1 lamb rack, cut into chops (about 1 pound)
¼ cup canola oil
¼ cup Ethiopian Spice Mix (page 5)
Salt and freshly ground black pepper, to taste

Rub the chops with oil, and season with the spice mix, salt, and pepper. Grill over a hot fire or pan-sear to desired doneness, about 2 to 3 minutes per side for medium-rare. Serve with the Pear-Orange Compote.

STANDING OR SITTING?

One of the most crucial decisions in your choice of appetizer revolves around whether you want finger food or not. This, in turn, should reflect whether people will have room to sit, even if it's a buffet and not a formal sit-down, or whether they'll be standing and mingling.

It may sound obvious, but we've all been to parties where we had to juggle a plate, a drink, and a plate of messy noodles. Who can eat those standing up?

If folks aren't sitting, give them things they can pick up and nibble on. And that doesn't have to mean little crustless sandwiches. Almost anything in this chapter can be turned into finger food if it's slathered onto little crostini or served with big leaves of soft, buttery Boston lettuce for grabbing hold of.

SEARED ETHIOPIAN LAMB CHOPS WITH PEAR-ORANGE COMPOTE

Heat and Then Some

If we only want to add heat, we throw in some jalapeños or, if feeling particularly sadistic, habaneros. But when we want a more flavorful spiciness, particularly in Chinese dishes, we reach for something we always keep around: chili-garlic paste. This Chinese condiment, which consists of garlic, chilies, vinegar, and sometimes fava beans and flour, is commonly found in Asian markets and good general-interest supermarkets. We sometimes spoon it, sparingly, atop grilled meat or fish, and often use it to make close-to-instant spicy peanut sauce, by combining to taste with peanut butter, then thinning with water if necessary.

Fiery Thai Sticky Shrimp

Sweet apricot, sour lime, then the slow burn of chili-garlic paste. No wonder it's one of my favorites; this was on my first restaurant's first menu, and it makes a cameo now and again to this day. Substitute pork or chicken for the shrimp if you'd like. For an entrée, serve over steamed rice.

Serves 4 to 6 as an appetizer or 2 as an entrée

1 tablespoon vegetable oil
1 pound cocktail-sized shrimp, peeled and deveined, tails left on
½ tablespoon peeled and minced garlic
¼ pound snow pea pods, trimmed
1 red bell pepper, seeded and cut into 1-inch squares
4–6 scallions, washed and sliced into 1-inch pieces (about 1 cup)
4 tablespoons Apricot Thai Glaze (page 26)
¼ cup peeled and shredded carrots
6 lime wedges

1. In a large skillet, heat the vegetable oil on medium-high. Add the shrimp and sear for 1 minute.
2. Quickly turn the shrimp, add the garlic, snow peas, red pepper, and scallions; sauté 30 seconds more.
3. Add the Apricot Thai Glaze, and cook, stirring until the sauce thickens to a glaze and the shrimp turn from translucent to opaque, about 1 minute more. Remove from heat. (Note: If the shrimp give off much liquid, transfer them to a serving platter as done and reduce the sauce to a stickier glaze.)
4. Transfer the shrimp to a serving dish and garnish with the carrots and lime wedges. Serve immediately.

CORN, TURKEY, AND TOMATO QUESADILLAS

I USE THESE when I teach a Kids Up Front class, which as part of the nonprofit Share Our Strength shows at-risk kids how to make quick, nutritious snacks. After all, even my stepson Sage gets tired of PBJs every now and then. The toasted fresh corn is a must, but ground pork or beef work well instead of turkey, as do Chicken Chicharrones with Fresh Oregano (page 34).

Serves 4 as an appetizer or 2 as an entrée

2 tablespoons olive oil
1½ cups fresh corn kernels (about 3 large ears of corn)
½ pound ground turkey
Salt and freshly ground black pepper, to taste
2 teaspoons peeled and minced garlic
4 (8-inch) flour tortillas
1 cup grated Monterey jack cheese *or* queso fresco
2 ripe tomatoes, cored, halved, and cut into ¼-inch-thick slices
4 teaspoons canola oil, divided

1. Heat the olive oil in a 10- or 12-inch cast-iron skillet or heavy-bottomed sauté pan over high heat. When the oil begins to smoke, test it with a piece of corn: It should sizzle loudly when it hits the pan. Carefully add the corn to the pan and cook, stirring constantly while the corn sizzles and pops, until it is evenly toasted and golden brown, 1 to 2 minutes. Add the turkey and continue to stir, breaking up the turkey with a spoon and cooking until no longer pink, 3 to 5 minutes more. Add the garlic and cook for 1 minute; remove pan from heat. Season with salt and pepper, and transfer the turkey mixture to a bowl. Wipe out the sauté pan.

2. Line up the tortillas on a work surface, and divide the cheese among them. Spread out the cheese so it covers the bottom half of each tortilla. Top the cheese on each tortilla with a generous ½ cup of turkey filling, and then with tomato slices. Fold the top half of each tortilla over the filling, pressing gently.

3. Return the sauté pan to medium heat, and drizzle about 1 teaspoon canola oil in the pan. When the oil is hot, carefully lift 1 quesadilla, holding the edges closed with your fingers, and place it in the pan. Cook until the bottom is golden brown and crisp, 2 to 3 minutes. (Check its progress after 1 minute by lifting it with a spatula.) Carefully turn the quesadilla over and toast the second side. Transfer to a cutting board and cut into 3 wedges. Repeat with the remaining quesadillas. Serve hot with Fiery Three-Onion Salsa (page 25) and Limed Sour Cream (page 22).

Curried Chicken Skewers

GOOD OLD MEAT-ON-A-STICK makes for a perfect passed appetizer because of that built-in handle. Try pork tenderloin, flank steak, shrimp, or a combination instead of, or in addition to, the chicken. If it's grilling season, by all means, take these (and the entire party, for that matter) outside—but make sure to soak the skewers for at least 3 hours beforehand so they don't catch fire. You want to keep the party lively, not dangerous.

Serves 4

1 pound boneless, skinless chicken breast, cut lengthwise into ½-inch strips
20 (about 8-inch) wooden skewers
2 tablespoons Tremont 647 Curry (page 8)
Salt and freshly cracked black pepper, to taste
2 tablespoons canola oil

1. Thread the chicken strips on the wooden skewers, and sprinkle with the spice rub, salt, and pepper. Pat skewered chicken pieces together to evenly spread coating. Set aside.

2. Heat the oil in a large sauté pan over medium-high heat. Arrange the chicken skewers in the pan in a single layer. (Work in batches to avoid crowding pan, using a little more oil if necessary.) Cook until the chicken is golden brown on bottom, 1 to 2 minutes; turn and cook on the second side. Transfer to a serving platter, and serve hot with Fiery Vietnamese Mango Jam (page 18).

DELPHA'D EGGS

ONE OF MY FAVORITE CHEFS is a devilish teddy bear named John Delpha, who invented these. They're really little deconstructions of salad niçoise, perfect for passed appetizers at a swanky soiree. If you don't do raw tuna, these would also be great with cooked crabmeat, sliced lobster tail, or shrimp.

Serves 6

6 eggs
½ cup Aioli (page 11)
Splash of Tabasco
1 tablespoon minced chives
1 tablespoon capers, drained well
1 tablespoon black olives, pitted and minced (preferably niçoise)
1 pound sushi-quality tuna, cut into tiny cubes
1 tablespoon fresh lemon juice
1 tablespoon extra-virgin olive oil
1 tablespoon chopped fresh chervil (or dill if chervil is hard to find)
Salt and freshly ground black pepper, to taste

1. Place the eggs in a 2-quart saucepan. Cover with cold water to at least ½ inch above the eggs. Bring to a boil over high heat. Once the water boils, reduce heat and simmer gently for 10 minutes. Transfer the eggs to a bowl of ice water until cool.

2. While the eggs are cooling, in a small bowl combine the aioli, Tabasco, chives, capers, and black olives; mix well. In another bowl, combine the tuna, lemon juice, olive oil, and chervil. Toss until well mixed, and season with salt and pepper. Cover and refrigerate both bowls until ready to use.

3. Peel the cooled eggs, and halve them lengthwise. Carefully remove the yolks and put them in a mixing bowl; mash with a fork. Arrange the whites on small serving platter and set aside.

4. Add half of the aioli mixture to the yolks and mix well. Add as much of the remaining aioli as needed to reach the desired consistency. With a small spoon, scoop the yolk mixture into the egg whites. Top with tuna and serve immediately.

BASIL-RUBBED PORK MEDALLIONS WITH SUMMER PEACH CHUTNEY

SEND THESE PUPPIES around while you're sweating at the grill to keep your backyard partygoers enthralled while you work your next bit of magic. Either slather on the chutney beforehand, or cut the pork into chunks after cooking and let people dip their own. If you have a hankering for beef, this is outstanding with flank steak, too. Just be careful: With an opening like this, the bar is raised for the entrée.

Serves 4

1/2 cup roughly chopped basil
1/4 cup olive oil
Juice of 1 lemon (about 1/4 cup)
1 teaspoon paprika
1/4 teaspoon red pepper flakes
2 teaspoons Basic Barbecue Rub (page 7) *or* 1 teaspoon cumin seeds, toasted and ground
1/4 teaspoon salt
1/4 teaspoon black pepper
1 pound pork tenderloin, cut crosswise into 1/2-inch-thick medallions
2 cups Summer Peach Chutney (page 30)

1. In a glass pie plate, combine all the ingredients *except* the pork; mix well. Place the pork slices in the mixture to coat, cover with plastic wrap, and marinate in the refrigerator for 1 to 4 hours.

2. Remove the pork slices from the marinade and gently pat them dry. Grill or broil to an internal temperature of at least 150°F, 2 to 3 minutes per side. (Or, film a heavy-bottomed sauté pan with canola oil and place over high heat. When very hot, pan-fry the slices until slightly pink, working in batches if necessary to avoid crowding the pan.) Serve with Summer Peach Chutney.

FLANK STEAK AND FRESH MOZZARELLA SALAD

FLANK AND SKIRT STEAKS, previously underrated, have started to get popular because of the unbeatable combination of high-end flavor and low-end price. Don't you love it when that happens? The hearty meat makes a nice base for this creamy, spicy salad. The key is to make sure to slice it against the grain—and very thinly—after cooking.

Serves 4 as an appetizer or 2 as an entrée

5 tablespoons balsamic vinegar
3 tablespoons extra-virgin olive oil
1 tablespoon minced shallots
2 teaspoons kosher salt
2 teaspoons freshly ground black pepper, plus more, to taste
1 pound flank steak, trimmed of most of the fat
1 pint cherry or grape tomatoes, stems removed, washed, and cut in half
3/4 pound fresh mozzarella, cut in 1/4-inch slices
1/4 cup roughly chopped basil leaves
2 tablespoons roughly chopped chervil or parsley leaves

1. Mix the vinegar, oil, shallot, salt, and pepper in a small bowl. Place the steak in a shallow glass dish and pour half of the marinade over it. After 15 minutes, turn over the meat and marinate for 15 minutes more.

2. Heat a large, heavy sauté pan or cast-iron skillet over high heat. Remove the steak from the marinade and pat dry with paper towels.

3. Add the flank steak to the pan, reduce heat to medium-high, and sear for 4 minutes on each side. Remove from pan, let cool to room temperature on a cooling rack sitting on a sheet pan. When cool enough to handle, add the juices to the bowl of reserved marinade.

4. Slice the meat against the grain, 1/8 to 1/4 inch thick. Divide evenly among serving plates. Layer the tomatoes and then mozzarella on top of the steak, drizzle with the reserved marinade, and sprinkle with the chopped herbs and more freshly ground black pepper to taste.

GLORIA'S CRAB DIP
WITH GARLIC CROSTINI

IN HIGH SCHOOL, I worked for Gloria Hart, mother of my best friend Chris, at Beacon's in Walpole, where she sold pounds upon pounds of this every night as an appetizer. To the less garlicky-inclined, it's a triple threat; to garlic lovers, it's a triple treat. If you don't want to make the crostini, this dip is also perfect with Sesame Flatbread (page 237).

Serves 4

For the crostini:

1 small, crusty French baguette
1 tablespoon olive oil
1 tablespoon butter
2 garlic cloves, peeled and sliced into very thin chips
Kosher salt and freshly cracked black pepper, to taste

For the crab dip:

½ cup Aioli (page 11)
1 stalk celery, finely diced
Garlic from the crostini, finely chopped
1 small shallot, finely diced
1 tablespoon finely grated fresh horseradish
1 tablespoon chopped flat-leaf Italian parsley
1 teaspoon fresh thyme leaves
1 tablespoon Dijon mustard
½ teaspoon red pepper flakes
2 tablespoons fresh-squeezed lemon juice (about ½ lemon)
Salt and freshly ground black pepper, to taste
½ cup fresh crab or chopped lobster meat
½ cup fresh bread crumbs

1. Preheat oven to 450°F.

2. Slice the bread into ¼-inch-thick coins and place on a baking sheet. In a small, heavy sauté pan, heat the oil, butter, and garlic over medium-high heat. Stir frequently until the butter has melted and the garlic chips are light brown.

3. Remove from heat, let cool for 2 minutes, and strain the garlic from the oil. Set aside the garlic for the dip. Lightly brush the bread with the oil-butter mixture and season with salt and pepper. Place in the oven and bake for approximately 5 to 7 minutes or until golden brown. (These can be served warm or kept in an airtight container for the next day.)

4. Place the aioli, celery, the garlic from the crostini, the shallot, horseradish, parsley, thyme, mustard, red pepper flakes, lemon juice, and salt and pepper in a mixing bowl; stir to combine well. Using a spatula, lightly fold in the crab (or lobster).

5. Transfer the dip to a 6-inch cast-iron skillet, glass loaf pan, soufflé dish, or other casserole dish. Sprinkle the bread crumbs on top, and place in the oven. Bake for 10 to 15 minutes until the top is light brown. Serve hot with the crostini.

MINI-BRUSCHETTA WITH GREEN OLIVE RELISH

WITH PIQUANT FLAVORS packed into such small bites, these make a glamorous addition to any cocktail party. Substitute the optional blue cheese with tiny cubes of fresh mozzarella if desired. Be careful not to pack too much relish on these, or they get plenty messy—and there goes the glamour.

For the mini-bruschetta:
1 baguette, cut into 1/4-inch-thick slices
Olive oil
1 large garlic clove, peeled and cut in half
About 3 tablespoons kosher salt
1 large ripe tomato, cored and cut in half
1/4 cup crumbled blue cheese (optional)
1/4 cup coarsely ground almonds (optional)
Very small basil leaves, for garnish

Serves 8

For the green olive relish (makes about 1 cup):
1/2 cup pitted and roughly chopped green olives (Greek are best)
1 clove garlic, peeled and minced
2 tablespoons peeled and finely diced red onion
2 tablespoons seeded and finely diced red bell pepper
1 teaspoon minced fresh rosemary
2 mint leaves, minced
2 tablespoons roughly chopped fresh basil leaves
1 tablespoon capers, rinsed
1 1/2 teaspoons minced anchovy fillet
1 tablespoon extra-virgin olive oil
1 tablespoon balsamic vinegar or juice from 1 lemon
2 teaspoons freshly cracked black pepper

1. Combine all the relish ingredients in a bowl and mix well. Refrigerate until needed. (The relish can be made 1 to 2 days in advance.)

2. Preheat oven to 450°F.

3. Place the bread slices on a baking sheet. Brush the top of each piece lightly with olive oil, and rub with the cut piece of garlic. Sprinkle sparingly with salt, and bake until light golden brown, 6 to 8 minutes.

4. As the toasts bake, slice the tomato into 1/4-inch-thick half-moons. When the toasts are ready, top each with a tomato slice and about 2 teaspoons of the relish. If using, sprinkle blue cheese and almonds on top. Garnish with fresh basil and serve immediately.

MISO COD WITH CABBAGE AND PEPPERS

MOST OF US know miso from the soup we have before sushi. Nobody says "Pass the miso," at least not around here—yet. Maybe that will change, especially after you try combining its uniquely wonderful musty flavor with good old buttery cod.

Serves 6 to 8

¼ cup white miso
1 tablespoon peeled minced fresh ginger
2 tablespoons soy sauce
1 teaspoon red pepper flakes
1 tablespoon honey
1 tablespoon sesame oil
1 tablespoon lime juice (about ½ lime)
1-pound skinless cod fillet, cut into 4 pieces
2 tablespoons canola oil
2 cups shredded Napa cabbage
1 red bell pepper, cored, seeded, and julienned
Kosher salt, to taste
1 lime, quartered
1 tablespoon toasted sesame seeds

1. Preheat oven to 350°F.
2. Combine the miso, ginger, soy sauce, red pepper flakes, honey, oil, and lime juice in a small bowl. Add the cod, coat with marinade, cover, and refrigerate for 1 hour.
3. Heat the canola oil over medium-high heat in a nonstick pan. Remove the fish from the marinade, reserving the marinade, and pat dry.
4. Add the fish to the pan and cook for 2 minutes or until golden brown on one side. Remove from the pan, and add the cabbage and bell pepper to the pan. Top with leftover marinade, and stir to incorporate.
5. Place the fish on top of the vegetables, and put the pan in the oven for 3 to 5 minutes or until the fish is slightly firm to the touch and just opaque throughout. Remove from the oven.
6. Divide the vegetables onto 6 to 8 appetizer plates and top each with a piece of cod, or serve on a large platter. Season with salt. Squeeze lime over dish, and garnish with sesame seeds. Serve immediately.

Mussel Magic

Mussels are delicious, but they require special care because of safety concerns, since they filter seawater through their bodies, and can pick up toxins along with nutrients. Here's how to stay safe:

1. When buying mussels, avoid ones that feel too heavy or ones that feel loose when shaken, and avoid those that are cracked or do not close when you tap them.

2. Try to cook mussels on the day of purchase, and keep them in a bowl of lightly salted cold water in the refrigerator for at least 2 hours or until ready to use. If you need to cook them the next day, add 1 tablespoon flour to the salted cold water, and soak them overnight in the refrigerator.

3. To clean and debeard mussels, use a small sharp knife to scrape barnacles off the outside of each shell, and with your thumb against the knife blade, pull out and detach from the hinges any hair-like "beards." Then use a stiff brush under cold running water to scrub each shell briskly.

4. Again scrutinize them, discarding the mussels that are cracked or stay open even when tapped. Also discard any that stay shut when cooked.

Spicy Mussels and Salsa

FLAVORFUL doesn't have to mean difficult. These could hardly be easier, and the fresh fire of a just-made salsa mingles delightfully with the briny flavor of mussels. Try to find Prince Edward Island mussels, my favorite, or substitute (pound for pound) cockle clams, littleneck clams, or shrimp. And make sure to have lots of crusty bread on hand for the inevitable sopping.

Serves 4 as an appetizer or 2 as an entrée

1 large tomato, roughly chopped
1 tablespoon roughly chopped cilantro
½ small red onion, cut into ¼-inch dice
1–2 tablespoons finely diced jalapeño pepper
3 tablespoons fresh lime juice (about 1½ limes)
1 tablespoon extra-virgin olive oil
Salt and freshly ground black pepper, to taste
1½ pounds fresh mussels, soaked in bowl of lightly salted cold water for at least 2 hours, and scrubbed and debearded
2 limes, quartered, for garnish

1. In a small bowl combine the tomato, cilantro, onion, jalapeño, lime juice, olive oil, and salt and pepper; mix well.

2. In a large, heavy, straight-sided sauté pan or cast-iron skillet, heat the salsa over medium heat. When it begins to boil, add the mussels and cover. Cook for 5 to 7 minutes or just until all the mussels are open. Serve immediately, garnished with lime wedges.

SPANISH-STYLE PAN-ROASTED CLAMS

YOU KNOW how people love hanging out in the kitchen when you're cooking? Put a steaming skillet of these on your countertop, especially with big croutons or bread for sopping, and they can pick at the clams while you work. For an instant entrée, serve over your favorite pasta.

Serves 4 as an appetizer or 2 as an entrée

2 tablespoons extra-virgin olive oil
16 littleneck clams, washed well to remove all sand
4 shallots, peeled and minced
1 tablespoon peeled and minced garlic
½ cup sherry
½ cup dry white wine
4 tablespoons butter
Kosher salt and freshly ground black pepper, to taste
¼ cup flat-leaf Italian parsley leaves, washed and dried
1 lemon, cut into 8 wedges

1. Preheat oven to 400°F.
2. Heat the oil in a cast-iron pan or heavy sauté pan over medium-high heat. Add the clams and swirl in the pan for 1 minute. Add the shallots and garlic; cook for 1 minute.
3. Carefully pour in the sherry so the fumes don't ignite. Cook for 30 seconds, then add the wine and butter; place the pan in the oven.
4. Cook for 6 to 8 minutes, until all the clams have opened. Remove from the oven, season with salt and pepper, and garnish with parsley and lemons. Serve hot, right in the skillet.

Caramelized Onion and Green Apple Tart

THIS TART IS a perfect brunch dish; it's wonderful served hot, fantastic served cold. Substitute half of the goat cheese with your favorite blue for some extra punch, or sprinkle some sharp Cheddar on top for that classic apple-Cheddar combination.

Serves 6 to 8

6 slices bacon, minced
1 tablespoon extra-virgin olive oil
2 medium-size red onions, peeled and sliced into ⅛-inch rings
¼ cup red wine vinegar
2 tablespoons granulated sugar
2 teaspoons salt
1 tablespoon peeled and minced garlic
2 green apples
Juice of 1 lemon (about ¼ cup)
8 ounces goat cheese
1 (9- to 10-inch) tart shell, made with Savory Herbed Pie Dough (page 257) and prebaked according to the recipe
½ cup roughly chopped flat-leaf Italian parsley

1. Preheat oven to 425°F.
2. In a heavy-bottomed sauté pan, preferably nonstick, cook the bacon, stirring frequently until browned and crunchy, 6 to 8 minutes. Drain on paper towels. Discard the bacon drippings and wipe out the pan.
3. Add the olive oil to the pan over medium heat. Add the onions, vinegar, sugar, and salt; cook, stirring occasionally, until golden brown, about 15 minutes. (Lower the heat toward the end of cooking to prevent scorching.) Add the garlic and cook for 2 minutes. Set aside the onions to cool.
4. While the onions are cooking, peel, core, and slice the apples into thin wedges. Toss with the lemon juice and set aside.
5. Spread the goat cheese evenly in the tart shell, then top with the apple slices, overlapping them in concentric circles. When the onions are cool, spread them evenly on top of the apples. Sprinkle the bacon on top. Bake until warmed through, about 10 minutes. Garnish with parsley and serve immediately.

PAN-SEARED QUAIL WITH SQUASH AND PEARS

I WAS SURPRISED at how rarely I see quail in home kitchens—until I tried to find it in supermarkets. If you have access to a big Asian market, you're all set; if not, ask a good butcher to order quail for you if it's not in stock. Once you get your hands on these little birds, you'll love the rich flavor, which combines with squash, fruit, nuts, and calvados to take the chill off a fall night.

Serves 4

4 (5- to 6-ounce) semiboneless quail, cut into quarters
Salt and freshly ground black pepper, to taste
2 tablespoons chestnut *or* all-purpose flour
3 tablespoons canola oil
1 cup peeled and 1/4-inch diced butternut squash
1 medium-size pear, peeled, cored, and cut into 1/2-inch dice
1/4 cup golden raisins
2 cloves garlic, peeled and minced
1/4 cup roughly chopped walnuts
1 1/2 teaspoons chopped fresh rosemary
1/2 cup calvados
3 tablespoons sherry vinegar
2 tablespoons cold butter, cut into cubes

1. Pat the quail pieces dry with paper towels and season with salt and pepper. Place them in a shallow bowl and sprinkle with the flour, tossing to coat.

2. Heat the oil in a large, heavy-bottomed sauté pan over high heat. Lift the quail pieces out of the flour, patting off any excess, and add them to the pan, skin-side down. Sear without turning until golden brown on the bottom, about 2 minutes.

3. Turn the quail pieces over and scatter the squash around them. Cook, stirring frequently, until the squash starts to caramelize, 2 to 3 minutes. Add the pear, raisins, garlic, walnuts, and rosemary. Cook, stirring constantly, until fragrant, about 1 minute.

4. Lower heat to medium and add the calvados and sherry vinegar. Cook, stirring frequently, until the liquid has reduced and thickened, 2 to 3 minutes.

5. Remove from heat. Scatter the butter in the pan and stir gently until melted. Season with salt and pepper, and serve immediately.

WHEN TO SEAR

As a young chef, I was always taught that we pan-seared to lock in the juices. Of course, later I realized that it doesn't really do that. How could the juices actually get locked in? The seal created by a sear is certainly not impenetrable.

Why do we do it, then? To get a form of caramelization known as the Maillard reaction, where sugars and proteins produce a flavorful browning. It's the same thing that happens when you roast meats, but here, you're replicating it in the pan because we want it to happen quickly. If we cooked scallops in the oven, for instance, by the time we got the caramelization the scallops would be overcooked in the center.

By pan-searing, we get the crunchy exterior and creamy interior we want. For something that we want barely cooked inside, it's an unbeatable technique.

Fry, Fry Again

When I was in fourth grade, I decided to make doughnuts for a how-to project in school. Of course, I didn't know anything about oil temperatures and frying principles, so the doughnuts were just soaked with grease. Doused in powdered sugar, they were fine—to a fourth-grade palate. Now, thankfully, we know how ethereal and light correctly fried food can be.

It's all about the oil temperature and purity. When the oil is 350°F before the food goes in, a moisture barrier keeps the oil from soaking into the food. That is, if the oil is fresh. Oxygen, water, and food particles can cause oil to deteriorate, and then this moisture barrier doesn't work, and the fat rushes in.

Keep the oil at 350°F using a candy thermometer, and don't reuse oil. Your fries, your doughnuts, and your arteries will appreciate it.

POLENTA FRIES

SERVE THESE creamy-crunchy fries at a party, and your guests may forget there's such a thing as a potato. This polenta, by the way, is a much sturdier recipe than the rich, creamy sort you would want to serve on its own. As such, it can be made up to 3 or 4 days ahead, as can the Blue Cheese Vinaigrette (page 20), so perfect for dipping them into.

Serves 8

3 tablespoons butter, divided
½ red bell pepper, seeded and finely diced
1 tablespoon peeled and minced garlic
1 tablespoon minced fresh sage leaves
1 cup buttermilk
5 cups water
2 cups cornmeal
Canola oil, as needed for frying
Flour, as needed for dredging
Salt, to taste, *or* finely grated Parmesan cheese and freshly ground black pepper

POLENTA FRIES continued

1. Grease an 11" × 17" rimmed baking sheet with 1 tablespoon of the butter. Set aside.

2. In 3- or 4-quart saucepan, heat the remaining 2 tablespoons butter over medium-high heat. Add the bell pepper, garlic, and sage; cook, stirring frequently with a wooden spoon, until the garlic is golden and the butter starts to brown, about 4 to 6 minutes.

3. Add the buttermilk and water, and bring to rolling boil. (Note: The mixture will curdle, but don't be alarmed; it will smooth out when the polenta is added.) Gradually shake in the cornmeal, stirring constantly to prevent lumps.

4. Reduce heat to medium and continue stirring as the polenta thickens, adjusting the heat so the mixture bubbles but does not burn. Cook until the bottom of the pan is visible as you stir and the polenta looks thick and dry, about 10 minutes. (Note: The polenta should hold its shape when mounded, and settle slowly.) Remove from heat.

5. Spread the polenta in an even ½-inch-thick layer in the prepared pan. (*Hint:* A slightly wet spatula makes spreading easier.) Refrigerate until thoroughly cool; chilled polenta can be covered with plastic wrap and refrigerated for up to 4 days.

6. Add canola oil to a depth of 1 inch in a heavy, 3-inch-deep skillet. Heat over medium-high heat to 350°F. To test the temperature, drop a small scrap of polenta into the oil; it should sizzle immediately and vigorously, rising to the surface. If it doesn't rise to the surface, or if it bubbles lazily, the oil is not hot enough. If it burns quickly, it's too hot; reduce heat slightly and test again after a few minutes. Meanwhile, cut the chilled polenta into ½-inch-thick, 3-inch-long "fries."

7. Working with about 10 pieces at a time, dredge the fries very lightly in flour, knocking off any excess, and drop into the hot oil; stir often to keep them from sticking together. Fry until deep golden brown, about 5 minutes, and transfer to paper towels to drain. Season immediately with salt *or* Parmesan cheese and pepper.

GRILLED SALMON SALSA WRAPS

WRAP IT UP, and they'll take it—especially if the salmon is tossed in a fresh salsa, the tortillas are warm, and a smoky, tangy sour cream pulls it all together.

Serves 8 as an appetizer or 4 as an entrée

1 large, ripe tomato, cored and diced (about 1 cup)
½ red onion, peeled and diced (about 1 cup)
½ red bell pepper, seeded and diced (about ¾ cup)
½ green bell pepper, seeded and diced (about ¾ cup)
2 tablespoons chopped cilantro
Juice of 1 lime (about 2 tablespoons)
½-pound boneless salmon fillet
1 tablespoon canola oil
Salt and freshly ground black pepper, to taste
4 (6-inch) flour tortillas
4 tablespoons Limed Sour Cream (page 22)

1. Combine the tomato, onion, red and green peppers, cilantro, and lime juice in a bowl and mix well.

2. Lightly coat the salmon with oil and season generously with salt and pepper. Grill the fish, skin-side up, over a hot fire until well seared on the bottom, 2 to 3 minutes. Turn and grill just until the fish is warmed through but dark pink and creamy inside, 2 to 3 minutes longer. Remove the skin and let the fish cool slightly. Working over the bowl of salsa, use your fingers to break the fish into chunks; gently fold the salmon into the salsa. Adjust seasoning with salt, pepper, and lime juice.

3. Grill each tortilla, flipping regularly until warm and ever-so-slightly browned. Spoon ¼ cup salmon salsa and 1 tablespoon Limed Sour Cream down the center of one tortilla. Fold one end in, and roll up tightly. Cut in half. Repeat with the remaining tortillas, and serve immediately.

PAN-SEARED CHICKEN LIVERS

IF LIVER IS YOUR THING, you'll love this dish. Find a free-range or natural chicken liver by a company like Bell and Evans; the lack of chemical additives in the feed makes a big difference in the flavor of the livers even more than the rest of the meat. I prefer to serve chicken livers still rosy inside, but cook throughout if you prefer.

Serves 4 as an appetizer or 2 as an entrée

2 tablespoons olive oil
1 pound chicken livers, trimmed of fat and patted dry
Salt and freshly ground black pepper, to taste
2 garlic cloves, peeled and cut into slices as thin as possible
1 teaspoon fennel seeds, toasted and ground
½ red onion, peeled and sliced into ⅛-inch rings
1 bunch arugula, washed well
¼ cup balsamic vinegar
1 tablespoon sunflower seeds, toasted in a dry skillet until fragrant

1. In a large, heavy-bottomed sauté pan, heat the oil on high. Season the livers with plenty of salt and pepper, and add to the pan. Sear without turning until golden brown on bottom, 2 to 4 minutes. Add the garlic, fennel, and onions; cook 1 minute more.

2. Turn the livers over and continue cooking until the onions start to soften, stirring occasionally, 1 to 2 minutes. Scatter the arugula on top of the livers, and pour the vinegar over the top. Add the sunflower seeds, and toss to combine. Cook until the liquid is reduced slightly. Season with salt and pepper, and serve hot.

WHEN WE PUT LITTLE TACOS on our menu, they outsell everything except our perennially popular Tibetan Momos (page 36). One bite of these, and you'll see why. Instead of the shrimp, try minced pork or ground turkey. (Incidentally, plenty of folks might call these flautas because of their rolled shape, but purists will tell you that a true flauta should be as thin as the flute for which it is named.)

SHRIMP TAQUITOS WITH CHILI DIPPING SAUCE

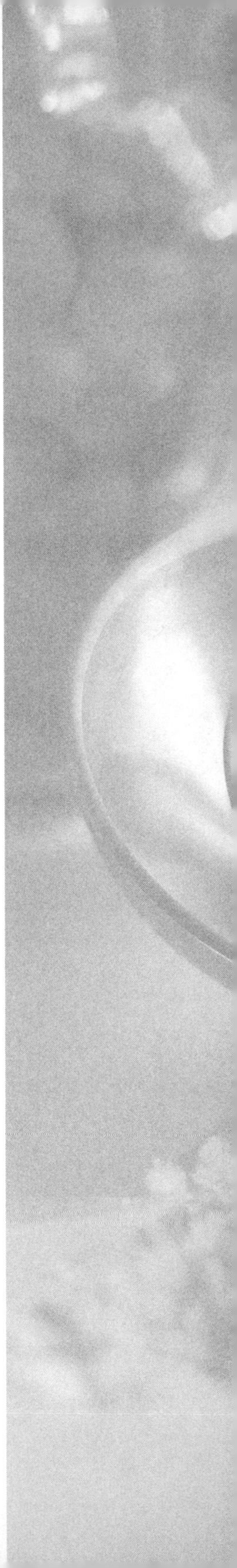

FOR THE SHRIMP TAQUITOS:

Serves 4 to 6

2 tablespoons olive oil
3 garlic cloves, peeled and minced
¼ pound shrimp, peeled, deveined, and roughly chopped
1 cup shredded Savoy cabbage
1 medium-size carrot, peeled and shredded
1½ teaspoons cumin seeds, toasted and ground
1½ teaspoons coriander seeds, toasted and ground
Juice of 1 lime (about 2 tablespoons)
¼ cup chopped cilantro leaves
Salt and freshly ground pepper, to taste
6 (6-inch) flour tortillas
2 cups canola oil

1. Heat the olive oil in a medium-size sauté pan over medium-high heat. Add the garlic and sauté until fragrant, 1 to 2 minutes. Add the shrimp, cabbage, and carrot; sauté, stirring frequently,

SHRIMP TAQUITOS—continued

until the vegetables start to soften, about 3 minutes. Add the cumin and coriander; cook for 1 minute more and transfer to mixing bowl. Add the cilantro, lime juice, and salt and pepper. Let cool to room temperature.

2. Spread out the tortillas on a work surface. Divide the filling evenly among them, arranging the filling in a straight line on the bottom third of each tortilla. Roll up tightly like a cigar, securing each with toothpick.

3. In an 8-inch sauté pan, add the canola oil to a depth of at least ½ inch. Place the pan over medium-high heat. When the oil is hot (a shred of cabbage will sizzle quickly on the surface), arrange 3 taquitos in the oil, toothpick-side down. Cook until golden brown, 1 to 2 minutes per side. Use tongs to transfer the taquitos to paper towels to drain, and season with salt and pepper. Repeat with remaining taquitos, and serve hot with Limed Sour Cream (page 22) and Chili Dipping Sauce, following.

FOR THE CHILI DIPPING SAUCE:

Makes about ½ cup

½ cup apricot preserves *or* orange marmalade
Juice of 1 lime (about 2 tablespoons)
1 teaspoon red pepper flakes
1 teaspoon coriander seeds, toasted and ground
1 teaspoon salt

Combine all the ingredients in a heavy-bottomed sauté pan over medium heat, stirring frequently until smooth and hot. Remove from heat and serve hot.

BEER-POACHED SHRIMP WITH TOMATILLO COCKTAIL SAUCE

THIS IS SUCH A distant cousin to the shrimp cocktail that I doubt they'd even recognize each other at a family wedding. It doesn't matter; I know which one I'd rather hang out with.

FOR THE TOMATILLO SAUCE:

5–6 tomatillos, husked and washed
2 tablespoons grated fresh horseradish
½ small red onion, diced
2 tablespoons roughly chopped parsley
1 large tomato, roughly chopped
Juice of 1 lime (about 2 tablespoons)
1 tablespoon olive oil
2 dashes Tabasco
Kosher salt and freshly ground black pepper, to taste

FOR THE SHRIMP:

1 (12-ounce) bottle light- to medium-bodied ale
¼ cup water
10 whole peppercorns
1 pound cocktail-size shrimp, peeled and deveined
1 lemon or lime, cut into 8 wedges
Kosher salt and freshly ground black pepper, to taste

Serves 4 as an appetizer or 2 as an entrée

1. Preheat oven to 350°F.
2. Place the tomatillos on a baking sheet and roast for 10 to 12 minutes, until slightly softened. Remove and allow to cool, then roughly chop.
3. Combine the tomatillos with the remaining sauce ingredients in a medium-size mixing bowl and stir to combine thoroughly.
4. Bring the beer, water, and peppercorns to boil in a large saucepan. Add the shrimp to the boiling mixture and remove from heat; let poach for about 4 to 6 minutes, or until the shrimp has turned pink and firm.
5. Remove the shrimp and immediately place in a bowl of ice water until cool. Drain well and refrigerate until ready to serve with the tomatillo sauce and lemon or lime wedges. Season with salt and pepper, if desired, and serve.

LORETTA'S PAPUSAS WITH SPINACH AND GOAT CHEESE

ONE OF MY FIRST sous-chefs was Loretta Huguez, who developed this recipe as a vegetarian appetizer before she went on to open El Pelon Taqueria in Boston's Fenway neighborhood. Besides being fun and easy to make, these crunchy little Salvadoran purses can handle all sorts of fillings. Change the cheese to queso fresco, Monterey jack, or sharp Cheddar, or add ground and seasoned turkey, pork, beef, or the Chicken Chicharrones with Fresh Oregano (page 34)—about 1 tablespoon per papusa. Serve with Limed Sour Cream (page 22) and/or Salsa 101 (page 24).

Makes 8 papusas

FOR THE DOUGH:

2 cups instant masa
1½ cups warm water
1½ teaspoons salt

FOR THE FILLING:

1 tablespoon olive oil
½ pound fresh spinach, stems removed, thoroughly washed, and roughly chopped
4 ounces goat cheese
Salt and freshly ground black pepper, to taste
2–3 cups canola oil, for frying

1. To make the dough, combine the masa, water, and salt in a medium-size bowl; mix until the water is evenly blended in and the dough is smooth. Reserve a pinch of dough for testing. Divide the remainder into 8 balls, cover with damp towel or plastic wrap, and set aside while making the filling.

2. Heat the olive oil in a large sauté pan over high heat. Add the spinach and sauté until it wilts and the moisture evaporates. Transfer the spinach to a mixing bowl and stir in the goat cheese. Season to taste with salt and a generous amount of pepper. Divide the filling into 8 portions.

3. To form papusas, break one ball of dough in half. Place one of the halves in the palm of your hand and flatten it to form a broad, shallow cup about ¼ inch thick. (If the dough is very moist, spread a bit of oil in your palm first; if it seems dry, wet your hands with water.) Spoon a portion of spinach filling into the dough cup, and set aside. Form the second shallow cup with the other half of dough. Place the second cup on top of the first cup and pinch together the "rims" of the cups to seal in the filling. Gently flatten the papusa between your palms, sealing the dough all around. Repeat to form 7 more cakes.

4. Pour the canola oil into a large, heavy-bottomed sauté pan to a depth of ¼ inch, and heat on medium-high. When the oil is sizzling hot (test by dropping in a pinch of dough), carefully add the papusas and fry until golden brown on the bottom, 2 to 3 minutes. Carefully turn over and brown the second side. Drain on paper towels.

SWEET-AND-SOUR LOBSTER TAILS

SOME LIKE THE CLAW, but I'm partial to lobster tails, which have the crunch of shrimp but a sweetness all their own. Make sure you buy the lobster fresh out of a tank; either ask your fishmonger to remove the tail for you, and save the claws and bodies for Corn and Lobster Bisque (page 106), or follow my easy-kill method below—much easier to stomach than the knife method. To turn this into an entrée, add broccoli spears to the pan with the lobster tails, and serve with steamed rice.

Serves 4 as an appetizer or 2 as an entrée

2 (1½-pound) live lobsters *or* 2 (6- to 8-ounce) lobster tails in the shell, cut in half lengthwise
¼ cup cornstarch
3 tablespoons peanut *or* canola oil
3 tablespoons fresh lime juice (about 1½ limes)
2 tablespoons soy sauce
2 packed tablespoons brown sugar
2 tablespoons cold water
1 tablespoon toasted sesame oil
1 tablespoon peeled and minced ginger
3 scallions, cut into 1-inch pieces
¼ cup roughly chopped unsalted, roasted peanuts
¼ loosely packed cup cilantro leaves
1 lime, cut into wedges

1. Preheat oven to 425°F.

2. If working with whole lobsters, bring a large stockpot of water to a boil and plunge the lobsters headfirst into the boiling water. After 2 minutes, remove to bowl of ice water to stop the cooking. When cool enough to handle, tear tails from lobster bodies, leave tails in shells, and cut in half lengthwise. Reserve lobster claws and bodies for another use.

3. Dredge the lobster tails in cornstarch, patting off excess. Meanwhile, heat the oil in a medium-size, heavy-bottomed sauté pan over high heat. Add the lobster tails, flesh-side down, and sear until golden brown on bottom, 3 minutes. Flip the tails over and put the pan in the oven; roast for 3 minutes.

4. While the lobster is roasting, combine the lime juice, soy sauce, brown sugar, and water; mix well. Set aside.

5. Transfer the pan from the oven to the stove and heat on medium-high. (Be careful: The pan handle will be very hot. Use an oven mitt.) Add the sesame oil and ginger; cook, stirring frequently, for 1 minute. Add the lime juice mixture, scallions, and peanuts, stirring and turning the lobster tails in the liquid until well combined and slightly thickened, another 2 minutes.

6. Transfer the lobster tails to a serving dish, cut-side up, and pour the scallion mixture on top. Garnish with cilantro leaves and lime wedges, and serve immediately.

Sweet-and-Spicy Lo Mein

LO MEIN doesn't have to be a greasy mess; with lightly cooked vegetables, it can be downright healthy and bright, almost like a lo mein primavera. My take on it is a purely veggie dish, but you carnivores can get your fix by adding about 1 pound of leftover (or freshly grilled) meat or shrimp. Other possibilities: Add 2 to 3 tablespoons chopped Thai basil, chopped cilantro, or a hot pepper.

Serves 4 as an appetizer or 2 as an entrée

2 tablespoons sesame oil
1 tablespoon peeled and minced fresh ginger
2 stalks celery, washed and thinly sliced on the bias
1 small carrot, peeled and julienned
1 red bell pepper, seeded and julienned
1 green bell pepper, seeded and julienned
½ pound fresh lo mein noodles, blanched to barely tender (or use linguine)
1 cup Sweet-and-Spicy Soy Glaze (page 28)
½ cup sesame seeds, toasted

1. Heat the oil in a large sauté pan over medium-high heat. Add the ginger and cook, stirring, until it starts to brown, 2 minutes. Add the celery, carrots, and peppers; continue to cook, stirring often, until the vegetables start to soften, about 4 to 6 minutes.

2. Reduce heat to medium and add the noodles and sauce. Use tongs to toss together the vegetables and noodles until well mixed and heated through, 1 to 2 minutes. Serve hot or cold, garnished with sesame seeds.

A Toss-Up

SALADS

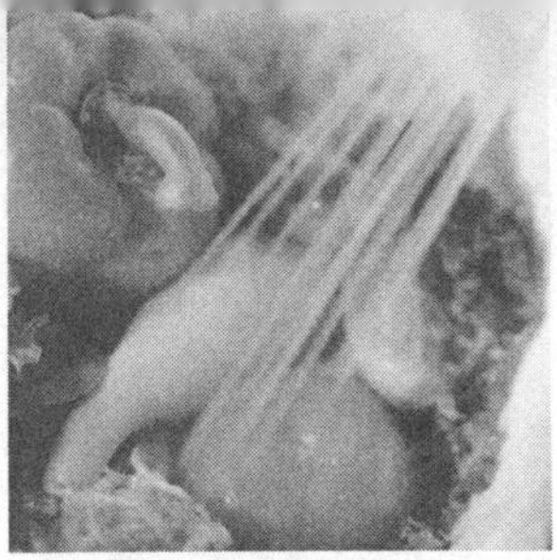

WHEN SHOULD YOU EAT A **SALAD?** In America we've grown up with the notion that the order goes appetizer, soup, salad, entrée, dessert. Europeans, though, eat their salads at the end of the meal to cleanse the palate; the French say it helps digestion.

Either approach, I think, can pigeonhole the poor salad, which really is much more flexible than we seem to think. It can go on the side of the entrée, can serve as a bed for it—or can even be the entrée.

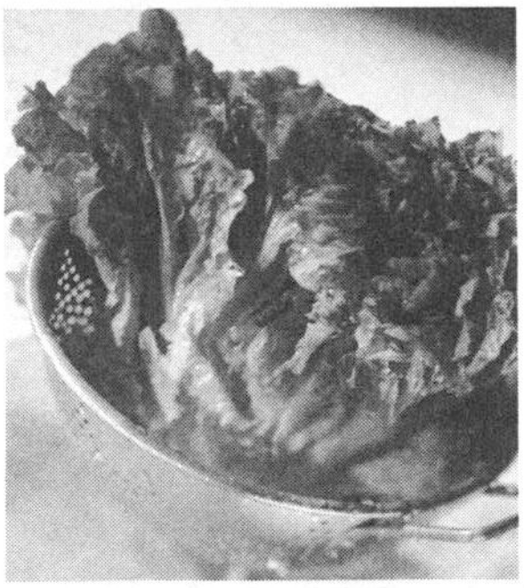

Salads are often overlooked, and that's too bad. When done right, they can be one of the most interesting parts of the meal: crisp and light or hearty and mysterious, simple or complex. More than any other part of the meal, though, they should represent the season. There's nothing like local tomatoes in August or spicy greens in the winter.

Of course, I love to twist the classics like Caesar salad, coleslaw, or Cobb salad. Try it: Add an element, replace an ingredient, and spice it up. Look beyond the greens-plus-tomatoes-plus-dressing idea, start playing with other flavors and textures, and for goodness' sake, set your salad free. You'll be surprised where it can lead you.

salads *a toss-up*

MANGO, CABBAGE, AND TOASTED PEANUT SALAD

JUICY MANGOES, crisp cabbage, and crunchy peanuts in a tangy sweet-and-sour dressing—this is a perfectly delightful and light summer salad, a much livelier slaw than the mayo-heavy glop we're used to. Change the flavors to suit your taste with Thai basil, fresh mint, or hot peppers—or turn this into an entrée by adding grilled chicken, pork, or shrimp.

Serves 4

½ large *or* 1 small head Napa cabbage, halved, cored, and sliced crosswise into ¼-inch strips
2 ripe, firm mangoes, peeled and diced
1 red bell pepper, seeded and diced
1 green bell pepper, seeded and diced
¼ cup roughly chopped fresh cilantro
6 scallions, green and white parts, cut on an angle into 1-inch pieces
1 cup Vietnamese Vinaigrette (page 21)
1 cup chopped roasted peanuts
Salt and freshly ground black pepper, to taste

In a large salad bowl, combine the cabbage, mangoes, peppers, cilantro, and scallions; toss until well mixed. Add the dressing and toss again. Sprinkle with peanuts, season with salt and pepper, and serve.

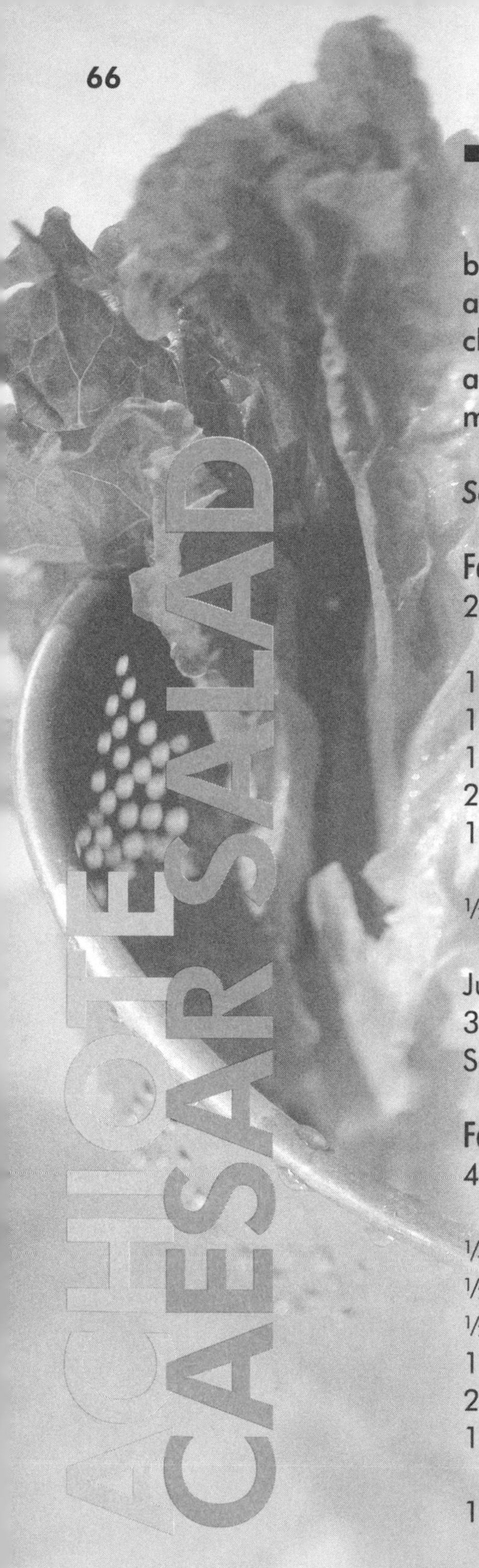

ACHIOTE CAESAR SALAD

THERE'S NOTHING WRONG with a good old-fashioned Caesar salad, but spicy corn bread croutons, Spanish manchego cheese, and achiote—a light and musky Latin spice—give the classic a kick in the **PANTALONES**. Make it a meal for two by adding 1 pound grilled pork marinated in ½ cup Yucatan Chili Sauce (page 12).

Serves 4

For the dressing:

2 tablespoons whole achiote (annatto) seeds, *or* 1 tablespoon ground
1 cup olive oil
1 egg yolk
1 tablespoon Dijon mustard
2 garlic cloves
1 teaspoon cumin seeds, toasted and ground, *or* ½ teaspoon ground cumin
½ tablespoon anchovy paste *or* 2 anchovies, mashed
Juice of 1 lemon (about ¼ cup)
3 dashes (*or* to taste) Tabasco
Salt and freshly ground black pepper, to taste

For the croutons:

4 cups Stacy's Spicy Corn Bread (page 239), cut into ¾-inch cubes
¼ cup canola oil
½ teaspoon coriander seeds, toasted and ground
½ teaspoon cayenne pepper
1 teaspoon kosher salt
2 tablespoons roughly chopped fresh cilantro
1 head Romaine lettuce, washed, dried, and cut into 1-inch pieces
1 cup grated manchego cheese • • •

1. Preheat the oven to 400°F.

2. In a small, heavy-bottomed saucepan, heat the achiote seeds and olive oil over medium heat. Bring to a simmer and cook gently for 5 minutes. Strain the oil into a mixing bowl and bring to room temperature. Discard the seeds. (If using ground achiote, bring the oil and achiote to a simmer, remove from heat, and let steep for 10 minutes. Pour the oil into a small bowl, leaving the sediment behind.)

3. In a food processor or blender, combine the egg yolk, mustard, garlic, cumin, anchovy paste, lemon juice, and Tabasco. Blend well, and with the machine running, slowly add the cooled achiote oil through the feed tube in a thin stream. The dressing will thicken to a mayonnaise consistency. Season with salt and pepper, and refrigerate until ready to use.

4. Spread the corn bread on a rimmed baking sheet. In a small bowl, whisk together the oil, coriander, cayenne pepper, salt, and cilantro; drizzle the mixture evenly over the bread. Using your hands, very gently toss the bread cubes to coat them with the dressing. Bake for 5 to 10 minutes, until the bread begins to turn golden brown. Cool to room temperature.

5. To serve, place the lettuce and croutons in a serving bowl, and pour the dressing over them. Toss until the lettuce is well coated, add the cheese, toss again, and serve immediately.

GET THE GRIT OUT

Ever been excited to dig into a delicate, beautiful salad, only to feel the crunch of grit between your teeth during a bite? There goes your appetite.

Unless they're hydroponically grown (in a pool of water), greens can get pretty sandy from being so close to the soil. Spinach is the biggest culprit. Their leaves, particularly if organically grown, also seem wonderfully attractive to all manner of insects, which are even less appetizing than dirt.

Wash your greens up to three times to make sure they're debris-free. Here's how to do it:

1. With a sharp knife, quickly trim off the core, roots, and stems. Immerse the greens in very cold water, with at least twice the amount of water as greens, and delicately swish them around.

2. Pull them out of the water carefully, pour out the water, and rinse out the bowl; repeat this process twice.

3. Transfer to a salad spinner to dry. (If you don't have a salad spinner, use the tried-and-true pillowcase method. Drain the greens in a colander, put them in an immaculately clean pillowcase, and spin it over your head so the water flies into the fabric.) When storing, pack lightly in a container and top with a paper towel to keep fresh. Greens are best used the day they are washed.

GIANT SUMMER SALAD WITH ROASTED VEGETABLES

WAIT UNTIL the height of summer to make this, when you can get locally grown lettuces and other greens; try a combination of green leaf, red leaf, and romaine, or add something spicy like mustard greens. If you don't have easy access to farm stand greens, you might think about moving. While you're house hunting, go ahead and buy a mesclun mix from your supermarket; the flavor varies considerably depending on where the greens are grown, so shop around until you find one you like.

Serves 4

1 medium-size summer squash, washed and halved lengthwise, then cut into 1/4-inch half-moons
1 medium-size zucchini, washed and halved lengthwise, then cut into 1/4-inch half-moons
1 yellow pepper, washed, cored, and julienned
1 red pepper, washed, cored, and julienned
1 bunch scallions, cut into 1-inch pieces
1 tablespoon minced fresh basil
1/2 teaspoon minced fresh sage
1/2 teaspoon minced fresh oregano
3 tablespoons extra-virgin olive oil
2 teaspoons kosher salt
2 teaspoons freshly ground black pepper
1/2 pound of your favorite greens or combination, washed, thoroughly dried, and torn into bite-sized pieces
1/2 pound ripe tomatoes, cut into wedges
1/3 cup Red Onion Vinaigrette (page 19)

1. Preheat oven to 425°F.

2. Place the squash, zucchini, peppers, scallions, herbs, olive oil, salt, and pepper in a large mixing bowl and toss to combine well.

3. Place the vegetables on a sheet pan or roasting pan, and roast for about 15 minutes, or until the vegetables are tender but still retain some bite. Let cool to room temperature.

4. Put the greens and tomatoes in a large serving bowl, drizzle with vinaigrette, and toss lightly. Garnish with the roasted vegetables and season to taste with salt and pepper. Serve immediately.

GREEK TOMATO AND HERB SALAD

MY FRIEND Mark Orfaly, chef at Boston's Pigalle restaurant, reinvented Greek salad for a fundraiser I hosted, replacing the lettuce with fresh herbs and turning the focus to tomatoes. It's a keeper. Use a variety of heirloom tomatoes if you have access to them; if not, go for the best tomatoes you can find, in season.

Serves 4 to 6

¼ cup red wine vinegar
¼ cup extra-virgin olive oil
1 tablespoon honey
1 tablespoon kosher salt
2 pounds assorted heirloom or other best-quality ripe tomatoes, washed, cored, and diced
½ cup pitted and roughly chopped kalamata olives
1 medium-size red onion, peeled and diced
2 tablespoons peeled and minced garlic
1 red bell pepper, cored, seeded, and cut into ¼-inch dice
¼ cup roughly chopped fresh basil leaves
1 tablespoon roughly chopped fresh oregano
¼ cup roughly chopped fresh chervil
¼ cup roughly chopped fresh mint
½ cup crumbled feta
Salt and freshly ground black pepper, to taste

1. In a large mixing bowl, combine the vinegar, olive oil, honey, and salt; mix thoroughly.
2. Add the tomatoes, olives, onions, garlic, and red pepper; toss to combine well, and let sit for at least 1 hour.
3. Right before serving, toss with the basil, oregano, chervil, and mint, and garnish with feta. Season with salt and pepper and serve immediately.

IF I HAD TO GO without hothouse tomatoes or those imported from warmer climes the entire rest of the year just so I could taste the glorious fruits of summer in their prime from a local farm, I think I'd do it. Sure, you could use any ripe tomato for this salad, but the real delight is in the color, size, and taste variations that come with using Cheyenne, peach, green, or other types of heirloom tomatoes, now widely available, in whatever combination strikes your fancy.

Serves 4

6 tablespoons olive oil (*not* extra-virgin)
2 teaspoons chili powder
1 teaspoon red pepper flakes
1 tablespoon prepared mustard
2 tablespoons white vinegar
1 clove garlic
1 teaspoon cumin seeds, toasted and ground
1 tablespoon honey
2 tablespoons freshly squeezed lime juice (about 1 lime)
1/4 cup cilantro leaves
1–1 1/2 pounds ripe assorted heirloom tomatoes
1/4 cup chopped herbs, for garnish (parsley, cilantro, basil, chervil, or a combination)
Salt and freshly ground black pepper, to taste

1. In a small saucepan, heat the oil, chili powder, and red pepper flakes over medium heat; cook for about 3 to 5 minutes, or until the oil starts to bubble. Remove from heat, strain, and let cool to room temperature. Set aside.

2. Place the mustard, vinegar, garlic, cumin, honey, lime, and cilantro in a blender, and purée. Slowly drizzle in the chili oil to emulsify until thick, shiny, and smooth. Season with salt and pepper.

3. Cut the tomatoes into different shapes—some in wedges, some in slices, some diced—to play up the varieties.

4. In a large mixing bowl, gently toss the tomatoes with the dressing. Garnish with chopped herbs and season with salt and pepper. Serve immediately or refrigerate; the salad will keep well for 1 day.

HEIRLOOM TOMATO SALAD WITH CHILI OIL

JEFE ENSALADA

THIS IS A LATIN take on a chef's salad. *Jefe,* for all you gringos out there, is Spanish for "boss"; in a multicultural kitchen like mine, where the Spanglish flies as fast as the orders, it means "chef."

Serves 4 to 6

½ cup white vinegar
½ cup granulated sugar
1 teaspoon kosher salt
1 tablespoon paprika
3 teaspoons chili powder, divided
1 medium-size red onion, peeled and sliced into very thin rings
3 tablespoons freshly squeezed lime juice (about 1½ limes)
1 habanero, serrano, or jalapeño pepper, seeded and minced
¼ cup, plus 2 tablespoons extra-virgin olive oil
1 tablespoon dark molasses
Salt and freshly ground black pepper, to taste
½ cup canola oil
3 6-inch corn tortillas, cut into ½-inch strips
1 medium-size red bell pepper, cored, seeded, and julienned
1 medium-size yellow bell pepper, cored, seeded, and julienned
1 medium-size green bell pepper, cored, seeded, and julienned
¼ pound arugula, washed and thoroughly dried

1. To make the pickled onions, combine the vinegar, sugar, salt, paprika, and 1 teaspoon of the chili powder in a small saucepan over medium heat, stirring until the sugar is dissolved, about 2 to 4 minutes. Let the mixture cool to room temperature, and pour over the onions in a small bowl. Let sit for at least 20 minutes.

2. To make the vinaigrette, combine the lime juice, chili pepper, olive oil, molasses, the 2 remaining teaspoons chili powder, and salt and pepper in a small mixing bowl and whisk to thoroughly combine. Set aside.

3. Heat the canola oil in an 8- to 10-inch cast-iron skillet or heavy sauté pan over medium-high heat. When the oil is hot, fry the tortilla strips for 3 to 5 minutes or until slightly golden and crisp, turning with tongs frequently. Work in batches if necessary to avoid overcrowding the pan. Remove the strips from the oil immediately and drain on paper towels. Season immediately with salt.

4. Combine the bell peppers and arugula in a large bowl. Give the dressing a last whisk, pour it over the salad, and toss to coat well.

5. Garnish each serving with the pickled onions (discard pickle liquid) and crispy tortilla strips. Serve immediately, while the tortillas are still crunchy.

Don't Hold the Mayo

Mayonnaise is by far a favorite condiment; it's hard to imagine sandwiches without it. When I was a kid, I put it on peanut-butter sandwiches, while Joe made entire sandwiches out of just mayo (about an inch thick). We didn't even know each other, but we were kindred spirits even then, at least when it came to mayonnaise.

Mayo is the eighth wonder of the world. Who knew that one egg could hold all of that oil? When made properly, it's one of the most stable emulsions around, much more so than a vinaigrette.

While we want to sing the praises of a homemade mayonnaise like the Aioli (page 11), we also have to admit that Hellmann's (called Best Foods west of the Rockies) is darn good, too. In fact, if you're too pressed for time to make aioli for any of the recipes in this book, here's how to jazz up Hellmann's so that it tastes homemade. Combine 1 cup Hellmann's, 2 cloves peeled and chopped garlic, 1 to 2 tablespoons fresh-squeezed lemon juice, a pinch of salt, and a few turns of freshly ground black pepper in a food processor or blender; process until smooth.

Latin-Style Coleslaw

This crisp, crunchy, spicy slaw makes a nice counterpoint to any braised or roasted meat. Or, roll it up in a tortilla with some lime-grilled chicken (or leftover pot roast) and sliced hot peppers.

Serves 4 to 6

½ cup Aioli (page 11)
1–2 teaspoons hot red pepper flakes
¼ cup fresh cilantro leaves
1 teaspoon cumin seeds, toasted
2 tablespoons fresh lime juice (about 1 lime)
2 tablespoons light molasses
4 cups shredded green cabbage
Raw kernels cut from 1 large ear of corn (about ½ cup)
1 small red bell pepper, seeded and julienned
2 whole scallions, cut crosswise into ¼-inch pieces
Salt and freshly ground black pepper, to taste

1. Put the aioli, red pepper flakes, cilantro, cumin, lime juice, and molasses in a food processor or blender and purée until smooth.

2. In a large mixing bowl, combine the cabbage, corn, red pepper, and scallions. Toss with the dressing, and season with salt and pepper.

UFO SOCIAL CLUB COLESLAW

WE DON'T JUST serve this slaw at our competitions; we also eat it in pulled-pork sandwiches while we're waiting for the judges' decision. You can use it to the same effect in Barbecued Chicken Sandwiches (page 224).

Serves 4 to 6

½ cup Aioli (page 11)
2 tablespoons granulated sugar
2 tablespoons lemon juice *or* juice from a jar of dill pickles
1 tablespoon yellow mustard
2 teaspoons celery salt
1½ teaspoons Basic Barbecue Rub (page 7)
4 cups shredded white, green, *or* Savoy cabbage
1 cup shredded red cabbage
1 large carrot, peeled and grated
1 small red onion, peeled and julienned (or thinly sliced)
Salt and freshly ground black pepper, to taste

1. In a small bowl, combine the aioli, sugar, lemon *or* pickle juice, mustard, celery salt, and barbecue rub; mix well.

2. In a large bowl, toss together the cabbages, carrot, and onion. Just before serving, add the dressing and toss until thoroughly mixed.

CHOW-CHOW

ANIMAL LOVERS, relax: Chow-chow is a sweet-and-sour relish, and it has absolutely nothing to do with that breed of dog. Purists might take issue with my recipe, which doesn't use mustard, but there's no arguing that it's downright delicious, especially in the heat of the summer, and that it looks as good as it tastes. Serve with Billy's Crispy Pork Chops with Maple Chili Glaze (page 212).

Serves 4 as a side salad

¼ cup diced kosher pickle (about ½ large pickle)
2 tablespoons pickle juice
½ cup fresh raw corn kernels (about 1 large ear of corn)
1 small red bell pepper, cored, seeded, and diced
½ small red onion, peeled and diced
1 cup shredded green cabbage
1 tablespoon olive oil
2 tablespoons roughly chopped parsley leaves
Salt and freshly ground black pepper, to taste

In a medium-size bowl, combine all the ingredients and mix well. Season with salt and pepper. Chow-chow can be left unrefrigerated for several hours. It will keep when refrigerated for several days, becoming more homogenous in flavor.

PEA TENDRILS mean SPRING. When the pea stalks start sending out their curly shoots, and other spring produce and soft-shell crabs are right around the corner, it's my favorite time to be a chef. For a lively, light spring meal, pair this salad with grilled scallops or shrimp and Curried Basmati Rice with Almonds and Golden Raisins (page 142).

SEARED MADRAS PEA TENDRILS

Serves 4

- ¼ cup freshly squeezed lime juice (about 2 limes)
- 2 teaspoons seeded and minced hot chili pepper, such as habanero, Scotch bonnet, *or* serrano
- 3 tablespoons brown sugar
- 1 teaspoon curry powder
- 1 teaspoon turmeric
- 1 teaspoon cumin seeds, toasted and ground
- 2 teaspoons salt
- 2 tablespoons canola oil
- 2 red bell peppers, cored, seeded, and julienned
- 1 pound pea tendrils, washed, tough stems removed
- ¼ cup almond slivers, toasted
- ½ cup diced pineapple

1. Blend the lime juice, chili pepper, brown sugar, curry, turmeric, cumin, and salt thoroughly in a blender or food processor. (This dressing will last for up to 4 days covered and refrigerated.)

2. In a large sauté pan, heat the oil over medium-high heat. Add the red peppers and cook for 1 minute, stirring frequently. Add the pea tendrils, stirring frequently for 1 to 2 minutes more, until slightly wilted.

3. Drizzle the dressing onto the pea tendrils and mix completely. Remove from heat, and transfer to a serving bowl. Garnish with the almonds and pineapple, and serve immediately.

MOM'S RICE SALAD

MY MOM'S such a great cook, coming up with such hits as the Summer Peach Chutney (page 30) and this rice salad, which I've loved ever since she packed it in my lunch for a hiking trip. To turn this into a single-dish meal, vegetarians can add tofu and leave out the fish sauce, while we carnivores can spice it up with leftover shrimp, lobster, chicken, or pork.

Serves 4 to 6

1 tablespoon fresh lime juice (about ½ lime)
2 tablespoons rice wine vinegar
1 tablespoon soy sauce
1 tablespoon fish sauce
1 tablespoon sesame oil
1 tablespoon canola oil
2 cups cooked white rice
½ pint cherry tomatoes, washed, stems removed, and halved
2 scallions, white and light green parts, cut into ¼-inch slices
1 small red bell pepper, cored, seeded, and cut into ¼-inch dice
¼ cup cilantro leaves
1 teaspoon red pepper flakes

1. In a small mixing bowl, combine the lime juice, vinegar, soy and fish sauces, and sesame and canola oils. Set aside. (This keeps in the refrigerator, in an airtight container, for 3 to 4 days.)

2. In a large mixing bowl, combine the rice, tomatoes, scallions, red pepper, cilantro, and red pepper flakes. Toss with the dressing, and serve.

IN A WORLD with so much hunger, waste is downright irresponsible. Don't throw away that leftover baguette or country-style loaf; use it for French toast, bread pudding, or this salad, whose Catalan touches of nuts, dried fruit, sherry, and manchego turn it into something so delectable there won't be a trace left—not even for the compost pile.

Serves 4

4 cups day-old firm, crusty bread, cut into 1/2-inch cubes
1 tablespoon extra-virgin olive oil
1 teaspoon salt
1 teaspoon freshly ground black pepper
3/4 cup golden raisins
1/4 cup toasted and very coarsely chopped almonds
1/2 cup green olives, pitted and sliced
1/2 medium-size red onion, peeled and diced

For the dressing (makes about 1 1/2 cups):

3 very ripe plum tomatoes, puréed and pressed through a fine-mesh sieve (to yield about 1 cup purée)
1/4 cup parsley leaves
2 cloves garlic, peeled
1/2 teaspoon lemon zest
1/2 teaspoon saffron threads
1 tablespoon sherry vinegar
1 tablespoon Dijon mustard
1/2 tablespoon sherry
3 tablespoons extra-virgin olive oil
Salt and freshly ground black pepper, to taste
1/2 cup grated manchego cheese

1. Preheat oven to 450°F.

2. Put the bread cubes in a bowl and drizzle with the olive oil, tossing to coat. Season with the salt and pepper, and spread the cubes on a baking sheet. Bake until lightly toasted, 4 to 6 minutes. Transfer the bread cubes to a bowl to cool. Add the raisins, almonds, olives, and onion; mix well.

3. In a food processor or blender, combine the tomato purée, parsley, garlic, lemon zest, saffron, vinegar, mustard, and sherry. With the machine running, slowly drizzle in the oil until the dressing emulsifies.

4. Pour the dressing over the salad, tossing to coat. Season with salt and pepper. Sprinkle with the cheese just before serving. Can be served immediately, with the bread still crunchy, or can sit as long as overnight refrigerated, letting the bread absorb moisture from the rest of the salad.

OLD BREAD AND NEW CHEESE SALAD

POTATO SALAD WITH PICKLES, CARAMELIZED ONIONS, AND ROSEMARY

EVERYBODY loves a good potato salad, but the classic could use some revving up. For extra color, substitute roasted red bell pepper for the onion. Should you want a more traditional version, leave out the onions and rosemary altogether—but try it at least once like this. You'll make it again, we promise.

Serves 4 to 6

1½ pounds Yukon gold potatoes, washed with skin left on, cut into ½-inch dice
2 tablespoons kosher salt
2 tablespoons canola oil
1 large yellow onion, peeled and diced
1 cup diced kosher pickles
2 tablespoons pickle juice
1 cup Aioli (page 11)
1 tablespoon Dijon mustard
2 stalks celery, washed and diced
2 teaspoons peeled and minced garlic
1½ teaspoons chopped fresh rosemary
Salt and freshly ground pepper, to taste

1. Place the potatoes over high heat in a saucepan filled with just enough cold water to cover the potatoes. Add kosher salt. When the water begins to boil, reduce heat, and simmer the potatoes until they are fork-tender, about 15 minutes.

2. While the potatoes are cooking, heat the oil in a heavy-bottomed sauté pan or cast-iron skillet over medium heat. Add the onions and cook, stirring frequently, for 10 to 15 minutes or until golden brown. Remove the onions from the pan and let cool to room temperature.

3. When the potatoes are done, strain, and run cold water over the potatoes until cool. Drain thoroughly and set aside.

4. In a large mixing bowl, toss together the potatoes, onions, and remaining ingredients, seasoning generously with salt and pepper. Chill thoroughly before serving. Will keep for up to 4 days refrigerated in an airtight container.

RADICCHIO AND GREAT HILL BLUE CHEESE SALAD

SINCE IT'S SO BITTER, radicchio is often just punctuation to an otherwise mild salad; if it does take center stage, it is often grilled or heated to soften its bite. But what if you like the bite? This salad has a bitter base that gives way to a creamy, pungent sweetness from Massachusetts' own Great Hill blue cheese, one of my favorites.

Serves 4 to 6

1 small yellow onion, peeled and sliced into 1/8-inch rings
2 tablespoons balsamic vinegar
1 tablespoon extra-virgin olive oil
2 tablespoons granulated sugar
1 teaspoon kosher salt
1 medium-size head radicchio, core and outer leaves removed
1 carrot, peeled and grated
1/4 pound Great Hill blue cheese (or other good-quality blue), crumbled
Freshly cracked black pepper, to taste

1. Place the onion, vinegar, oil, sugar, and salt in a small mixing bowl; toss well to combine and set aside for 20 minutes.

2. Cut the radicchio in half lengthwise and shred by cutting into 1/8-inch strips.

3. Divide the radicchio onto plates. Evenly sprinkle the carrots on top. Divide the pickled onions on top of the carrots and drizzle some of the onion dressing over each salad. Top each salad with blue cheese, and season with black pepper. Serve immediately.

SEARED GREENS WITH BACON AND CORN

YOU COULD hardly find an easier summer salad. This is also a good use for farm-fresh greens that, unlike their supermarket counterparts, often look less than perfect but more than make up for it in flavor.

Serves 4

2 teaspoons extra-virgin olive oil
4 strips bacon, cut into matchsticks
2 cloves garlic, peeled and minced
Kernels from 4 large ears of corn (about 2 cups)
1 pound hearty greens (mustard, beet, turnip, collards, chard, or a combination), cut into strips, tough stems removed
1 tablespoon sherry vinegar
Salt and freshly cracked black pepper, to taste

1. In a large sauté pan, heat the oil over medium heat. Fry the bacon until crisp, stirring frequently.

2. Add the garlic and cook for 30 seconds, until the garlic is aromatic but not browned. Add the corn, stirring frequently, and cook for 2 minutes more.

3. Add the greens and toss thoroughly to coat completely. Cook until wilted, about 2 minutes. Add the vinegar and season with salt and pepper. Serve immediately.

Compose Yourself

A tossed salad is the easy way: Put it all in a bowl, pour on the dressing, give a quick toss, and serve. Nothing wrong with that.

But sometimes you want something more chi-chi, with an elegant presentation, or you want the textures and flavors to be even more distinct. That's when a composed salad comes in. You create a little masterpiece on each plate, layering and arranging artistically so the thing looks as good as it will taste.

There's a pitfall: underseasoned or dry elements. Dress and/or season to taste each element separately before you put them together. If there's a creamy sauce on the bottom and greens on top, that's fine, but the greens need to be glistening with at least a simple lemon-oil dressing, with salt and pepper in it. If tomatoes are going on top, make sure to season them, too.

Why? Because some diners may grab just one element in the salad and eat it by itself. If everything is seasoned, the salad will taste good no matter how it's eaten.

SMOKED TROUT WITH BABY LETTUCE

LONG BEFORE refrigeration, ingenious cooks invented smoking and curing as ways to preserve meats, and for that, I'm grateful. Where would we be without prosciutto or smoked fish? This salad makes use of the glorious saltiness of smoked trout, such as that made by Maine's Ducktrap River Fish Farm, combining it with a tart dressing and light, tender baby lettuce.

Serves 4

½ cup plain yogurt
1 clove garlic, peeled and minced
¼ cup minced chives
2 teaspoons minced fresh sage
Salt and freshly ground black pepper, to taste
2 tablespoons fresh-squeezed lemon juice (about ½ lemon)
1 tablespoon extra-virgin olive oil
½ pound baby lettuce, washed and dried
1 medium-size red onion, peeled and sliced into very thin rings
½ pound smoked trout

1. In a small bowl, combine the yogurt, garlic, chives, and sage. Season with salt and pepper. (You can do this 1 day in advance, as long as you keep it sealed in the refrigerator.)
2. In a large bowl, combine the lemon juice and olive oil, whisking briefly. Add the lettuce and toss gently.
3. Plate the salads individually. Spread about 1 tablespoon yogurt dressing on each plate. Divide the greens into 4 equal portions, and mound in the center of each plate. Scatter some onion rings on each. Evenly flake the trout on top of the lettuce and onions. Garnish with more freshly ground black pepper, and dollop the remaining dressing in dots around the edge of the plates.

SMOKY, SPICY FRUIT SALAD

WE RUN A brisk catering business, and we're always in demand to provide what we call a Latin Summer Fiesta, which includes Mojitos (page 281), a pig roast, and this salad. It also makes a perfectly addictive addition to much less ambitious spreads, such as any summer brunch or barbecue table.

Serves 4 to 6

1 small dried chipotle pepper, rehydrated in hot water, stem and seeds removed, and finely chopped (or 1 canned chipotle, squeezed of extra liquid and finely chopped)
¼ cup fresh lime juice (about 2 limes)
2 tablespoons dark rum (such as Gosling's)
1 golden pineapple, peeled, cored, and cut into ½-inch cubes
2 ripe mangoes, peeled, pitted, and cut into ¼-inch cubes
2 ripe papayas, peeled, seeded, and cut into ¼-inch cubes
2 green apples, peeled, cored, and cut into ¼-inch cubes

1. In a small bowl, combine the chili, lime juice, and rum; stir to mix well. Set aside.

2. Place the fruit in a serving bowl and toss with the dressing. Serve chilled.

SPINACH, CAPICOLA, AND MOZZARELLA SALAD

THIS ITALIAN-STYLE SALAD has an irresistible combination of creamy and crunchy textures and sweet and peppery flavors. Look for loose spinach in bunches or, better yet, baby spinach leaves. And if you can get mozzarella *di bufala*, made from water-buffalo milk and usually imported from Italy, it's worth the price difference for the extra-rich flavor.

Serves 4 to 6

2 tablespoons olive oil
½ pound sweet capicola or prosciutto, thinly sliced (about 20 pieces)
1 pound spinach, stems clipped, double-washed and dried, or about ½ pound baby spinach leaves
20 fresh large basil leaves, washed and dried
1 pint cherry tomatoes, washed, stemmed, and halved if large
½ cup Red Onion Vinaigrette (page 19)
8 ounces fresh mozzarella, diced
Freshly ground black pepper, to taste

1. Heat the oil in a heavy-bottomed sauté pan over high heat. Fry the capicola or prosciutto slices for 30 seconds on each side. Divide among serving plates.

2. In a large mixing bowl, combine the spinach, basil, and tomatoes. Toss with vinaigrette, and divide among the plates of capicola. Garnish with mozzarella and black pepper, and serve immediately.

GROUND RULES

When we go out to a restaurant, we're the guys who never say "when" when the waiter is grinding fresh pepper on our salads. We love the pepper's bite to offset sweet greens.

Pepper, like any spice, loses flavor the minute it's ground. That chalky superfine ground pepper we saw in restaurants as kids is thankfully rare now. We much prefer a coarse grind, so the pepper still has some texture with its flavor.

In my restaurants, I like to use 10-mesh pepper, which is a reference to the grind size; it's also known as butcher's pepper. Home cooks, of course, can't set the grind size so exactly, but you can make sure your grinder is set to the coarsest grind possible, so that when you're seasoning you always turn out the biggest chunks your mill can manage.

If you're having a big party, try grinding a bunch of pepper in a coffee grinder (make sure to clean out the coffee residue first!) or in a mortar and pestle; then, have ¼ cup sitting alongside a container of kosher salt right at your work area, so your wrist doesn't get sore from all that pepper-mill twisting.

SWEET POTATO, CABBAGE, AND PECAN SALAD

SERVED COLD, it's still got some crunch, but this salad is also good warmed up (and made softer) in the microwave. It can also serve as a versatile base for leftovers such as grilled chicken, shrimp, broccoli, or asparagus.

Serves 4 to 6

- 2 medium-size sweet potatoes (about 1 pound total), peeled and cut into ½-inch dice
- 1 tablespoon salt
- 4 cups shredded Napa *or* Savoy cabbage
- ½ cup toasted and very coarsely chopped pecans
- 2 scallions, cut crosswise into 1-inch pieces
- 1 red *or* green bell pepper, seeded and julienned
- 1 cup Sweet-and-Spicy Soy Glaze (page 28)
- 1–2 tablespoons of your favorite hot chili paste (optional)

1. Put the sweet potatoes in a saucepan, add enough cold water to cover them, and heat on medium-high. When the water boils, add the salt and reduce heat to a simmer. Cook the potatoes until just tender, 10 to 15 minutes (be careful not to overcook). Drain and let the potatoes cool.

2. Transfer the cooled potatoes to a large bowl and add the remaining ingredients; toss gently to combine. The salad will keep for up to 4 days in an airtight container, refrigerated.

ICEBERG WEDGE WITH BUTTERMILK DRESSING

ICEBERG has been treated like the ugly stepsister of the lettuce family since the '80s, when those glamorous mesclun greens showed up at the ball. But when it's fresh (and, better yet, from a farmer's market), iceberg lives up to its name, which is why it's so many people's guilty pleasure.

Serves 6

½ pound bacon, minced
1 carrot, peeled and cut into chunks
1 stalk celery, cut into pieces
¾ cup Aioli (page 11) or Hellmann's (or Best Foods) mayonnaise
½ cup buttermilk
½ tablespoon garlic powder
½ tablespoon onion powder
Salt and freshly ground black pepper, to taste
1 head best-quality iceberg lettuce, outer leaves removed, cored, and cut into 6 wedges

1. In a heavy-bottomed sauté pan over medium heat, cook the bacon, stirring frequently, until crisp, about 6 to 8 minutes. Drain on paper towels. (Makes about ½ cup bacon bits.)

2. To make the dressing, process the carrot and celery in a food processor until finely minced. Transfer to a small mixing bowl and add the aioli (*or* mayonnaise), buttermilk, garlic powder, and onion powder; mix well. Season to taste with salt and pepper. (Makes 2 cups.)

3. Put a wedge of iceberg on each of 6 salad plates. Ladle ¼ cup dressing over each wedge, and garnish with bacon bits. Serve immediately.

TRIPLE-BEET SALAD WITH PANCETTA

BEETS are meaty, earthy, sweet, and versatile—and that's just the root vegetable part. The greens are no slouch, either; they're hearty and gorgeous, with red veins running through deep-green leaves. This salad keeps those colors together and uses the plant three ways: with the greens as the base, the root vegetable puréed in the dressing and pickled in the garnish. Using golden or candy stripe beets would make for another look entirely, but the taste is just as good.

Serves 4 to 6

3 large bunches beet greens
4 golf ball–size red beets
1 tablespoon olive oil
¼ pound pancetta, finely chopped
3 tablespoons white vinegar
2 tablespoons granulated sugar
1 clove fresh garlic, peeled
½ tablespoon Dijon mustard
3 tablespoons plain yogurt
3 tablespoons grapefruit juice
5 tablespoons extra-virgin olive oil
1 tablespoon sesame oil
Salt and freshly ground black pepper, to taste
2 tablespoons sesame seeds, toasted until golden brown

1. Preheat oven to 400°F.
2. Separate the beets, stems, and greens, discarding the stems. Wash and dry the beets and greens well. Tear the greens into bite-size pieces, removing the tough center ribs from each leaf and discarding, and refrigerate in a mixing bowl until needed. (4 cups torn greens are needed.)
3. If the greens came with more than 4 golf ball–sized beets, save extra for another use. Rub the beets with oil and roast on a small, foil-lined baking sheet until fork-tender, about 40 minutes. Set aside until cool enough to handle, and slip off the skins.
4. While the beets are roasting, cook the pancetta in a heavy-bottomed sauté pan over medium-high heat, stirring frequently until crisp and browned, about 5 minutes. Drain on paper towels.
5. Dice the peeled beets, reserving 1 for the dressing. Put the remaining beets in a small, stainless steel bowl and add the vinegar and sugar, tossing to coat. Set aside to pickle for at least 20 minutes, or until serving time.
6. Put the reserved beet in a food processor along with the garlic, mustard, yogurt, grapefruit juice, sesame oil, and olive oil; process until smooth and emulsified. Season with salt and pepper.
7. To serve, toss the greens with the dressing and divide between serving plates. Remove the pickled beets from the vinegar mixture and drain. Garnish the greens with the pickled beets, sesame seeds, and pancetta.

Warm Turnip Greens with Chicken and Parsnips

When winter hits New England, I dust off my snowboard. That's the upside to the onset of cold weather; the downside is the lack of local produce. Thankfully, some vegetables are as hardy in the cold as I am. These spicy turnip greens, combined with chicken thighs and sweet, creamy parsnips, will get you ready for the slopes. Double your serving, add some rice, and you've got a meal.

Serves 2 to 4

2 tablespoons canola oil
¼ pound boneless, skinless chicken thighs (about 1 large thigh), trimmed of fat and cut into ¼-inch-wide strips
1 large yellow onion, peeled and cut into thin half-moons
2 large parsnips, peeled and cut into ½-inch dice
2 cloves garlic, peeled and sliced as thin as possible
½ pound turnip greens, tough ends trimmed, greens washed well and cut crosswise into 2-inch-wide strips
1½ teaspoons Basic Barbecue Rub (page 7) *or* 2 teaspoons cumin seeds, toasted and ground
Juice of 2 lemons (about ½ cup)
Salt and freshly ground black pepper, to taste

1. Heat the oil over high heat in a large, heavy-bottomed sauté pan (preferably cast iron) until it starts to smoke. Season the chicken with salt and pepper, and add it to the pan. Cook, stirring frequently and scraping the bottom of the pan, until the chicken is golden brown, about 4 to 6 minutes. Remove the chicken and set aside.

2. Lower the heat to medium and add the onion, parsnips, and garlic to the pan. Cook, scraping the bottom of the pan occasionally, until the parsnips are just tender, about 4 minutes.

3. Raise the heat to medium-high and add the greens, browned chicken, barbecue spice (or cumin), and lemon juice. Cook, stirring often, until the greens are fully wilted and most of the liquid has evaporated, about 4 to 6 minutes. Season with salt and pepper, and serve.

WARM ASPARAGUS WITH PARMESAN AND GARLIC

ASPARAGUS, especially when it's locally grown, is as exciting as the much-awaited onset of spring that it heralds. It's one of the most versatile vegetables around, but rather than messing too much with it, we prefer to treat it gingerly, letting its grassy flavor come through loudly.

Serves 4 to 6

1½ pounds asparagus, ends trimmed
2 tablespoons extra-virgin olive oil
2 tablespoons peeled and minced garlic
2 tablespoons sherry vinegar
¼ cup freshly grated Parmigiano-Reggiano cheese
Salt and freshly ground black pepper, to taste

1. Bring 2 quarts of salted water to boil in a saucepan. Blanch the asparagus for 3 to 4 minutes or until bright green and barely crisp. Immediately remove from water and place in a stainless steel bowl full of ice water, to stop the cooking process. Drain and set aside.

2. In a heavy-bottomed sauté pan or cast-iron skillet, heat the oil on medium-high. Add the asparagus and garlic, and cook for 2 to 3 minutes, stirring frequently, until the garlic is golden brown. Remove from heat.

3. Add the vinegar and cheese, and toss to combine thoroughly. Season with salt and pepper and serve immediately.

Going Kosher

Why do we have iodized salt? Iodine was originally put in salt to stem an epidemic of thyroid goiters in the 1920s, when people weren't getting enough potassium iodine. It worked; the epidemic was wiped out.

These days, most Americans eat enough seafood to get the iodine we need without the supplement in iodized table salt, and that's a good thing, because iodized salt has a bitter, metallic element to its flavor.

Sea salt, especially the wonderful French fleur de sel (for "flower of the salt"), can be expensive, but it's wonderful to use as a last-minute crunchy garnish on a salad. For everyday cooking, it's hard to beat kosher salt, which is cheaper than sea salt and sweeter. It's also easier to measure (because it's easier to pinch) and flakier than regular table salt, making it easier to blend.

Hunan Glazed Chicken with Asian Vegetables

Apply the soy-curry magic to chicken thighs for a dynamic starter, good when served cold for scooping up with lettuce leaves or served hot with a thimble of steamed rice (more, of course, if you're making a meal of it). It's also good with leftover meat instead of the chicken thighs. Earthy crunchy types: Try it with tofu.

Serves 4 as an appetizer or 2 as an entrée

2 tablespoons canola oil
1 pound boneless and skinless chicken thighs, cut into ½-inch strips
Salt and freshly ground black pepper, to taste
1 large carrot, peeled and julienned
1 red bell pepper, seeded and julienned
1 green bell pepper, seeded and julienned
1 daikon radish (about ½ pound), julienned
1 cup snow peas or sugar snap peas, strings removed
½ cup Soy-Curry Glaze (page 27)
Steamed rice (if served hot)
8 large leaves Boston lettuce (if served cold)

1. In a large, heavy-bottomed sauté pan, heat the oil over high heat. Season the chicken with salt and pepper, and add it to the pan. Cook, stirring occasionally, until golden brown, 4 to 6 minutes. Add the carrot, peppers, daikon, and snow peas; stir-fry until crisp-tender, about 3 minutes. Stir in the Soy-Curry Glaze and heat thoroughly, about 1 minute.

2. Serve hot with steamed rice or cold with lettuce leaves.

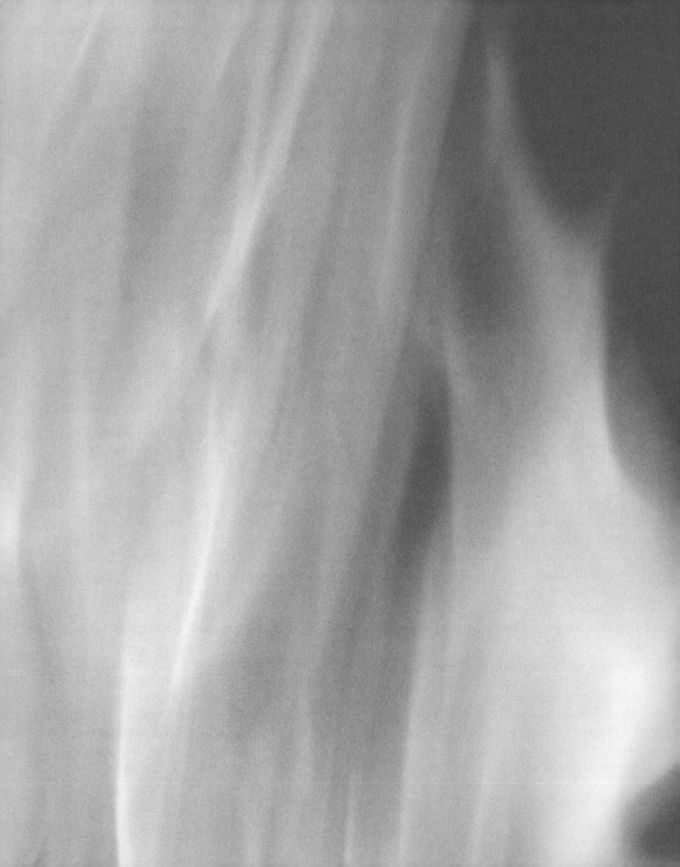

Bowled Over

SOUPS

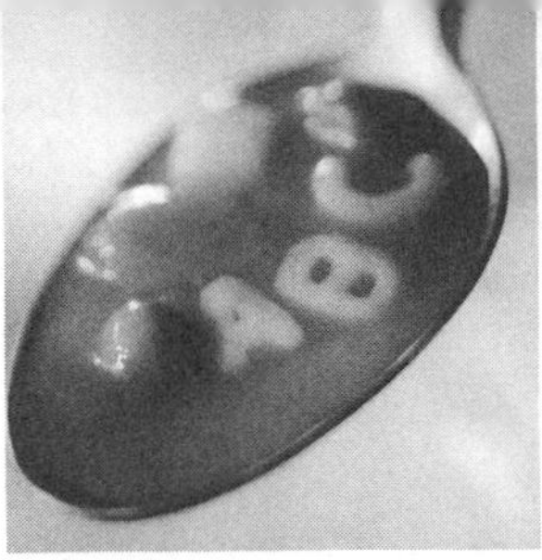

JUST THE SIGHT OF A **STEAMING BOWL** OF **SOUP** makes me think of staying home from school, watching *Gilligan's Island* reruns while my mom would take care of me. (For Joe, it was *Mary Tyler Moore*, but that's another story.) Even today, the smell can take both of us right back to those warm childhood couches.

Long before Campbell's Chicken Noodle, of course, were stews, tagines, and chowders. People have been cooking meats and vegetables in a pot with liquid ever since they had, well, a pot and liquid.

Soups, God love 'em, are so easy to manipulate—a little more lemongrass here, a lot fewer peanuts there. Many of them can be made ahead of time, and freeze well. In fact, plenty of soups, like a good chowder, taste even better once they sit for a day and their flavors meld. A good chili is fine right away, but really comes to life after three days. (Some, though, like a crisp Thai soup, should be served just as soon as you combine the broth and other ingredients.)

How do we like to jazz up a soup? Well, one of our favorite ways is to focus on the garnish: parsley and a squeeze of lemon at the end, or toasted nuts with coriander and hot pepper.

But the best additions to any soup, in our book, are a blanket and a remote control.

SOUPS

bowled over

SPICY CHARRED T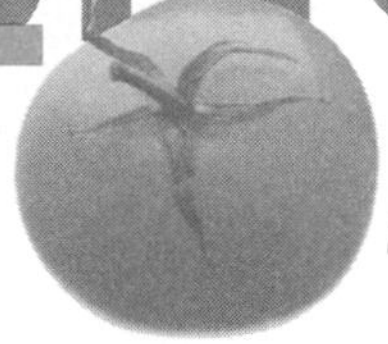MATO SOUP

WE COULDN'T RESIST giving some much-needed *oomph* to the classic tomato-basil soup. Here, the tomatoes get charred under the broiler, red pepper flakes add a kick, and the basil does garnish duty, making this soup the kind of fun-loving dish you'll want to serve at a summer celebration.

Serves 4

3 tablespoons extra-virgin olive oil, divided
6 plum tomatoes, cored
1 medium-size red onion, peeled and roughly chopped
1 large carrot, peeled and roughly chopped
1 medium-size yellow onion, peeled and roughly chopped
2 stalks celery, roughly chopped
4 cloves garlic, peeled
1 cup canned tomato juice
1 cup water or Vegetable Stock (page 120)
2 cups heavy cream
2 teaspoons red pepper flakes
8 large fresh basil leaves, minced
½ cup sour cream
Juice of 1 lemon (about ¼ cup)
Salt and freshly ground black pepper, to taste

1. Preheat broiler to high.
2. In a cast-iron skillet or oven-safe baking dish, toss together 1 tablespoon olive oil, plum tomatoes, and red onions. Place under the broiler for 10 to 15 minutes, stirring occasionally until the tomatoes and onions are slightly blackened. Set aside.
3. Meanwhile, heat the remaining 2 tablespoons olive oil in a 4-quart saucepan over medium-high heat. Add the carrot, onion, celery, and garlic; cook for 8 to 10 minutes, stirring frequently, until the vegetables brown. Add the tomato juice, water (or stock), heavy cream, and red pepper flakes. Bring to a boil, reduce heat to low, and simmer for 30 minutes.
4. Add the charred tomatoes and onions, along with any juices that have accumulated, and simmer for 10 minutes more.
5. Purée the soup using an immersion blender or in batches in a food processor or blender (returning each batch to a clean saucepan). Season with salt and pepper. If the soup is too thick, add more water or stock until it reaches the preferred consistency.
6. In a small bowl, combine the basil leaves, sour cream, and lemon juice, and season with more salt and pepper to taste.
7. To serve, pour the soup into serving bowls, spoon a dollop of the sour cream mixture in the middle of each bowl, and sprinkle more coarsely ground black pepper on top.

SWEET POTATO VICHYSSOISE

CLASSIC VICHYSSOISE, the famous cold potato-leek soup, is delicate and velvety. But what if you're in the mood for sassy, not soothing? This approach keeps the texture but turns the vichyssoise wild. Sweet potatoes add gorgeous color and complexity and create a perfect base for an explosion of Latin spices, better served up in funky pottery than fancy china.

Serves 4 to 6

For the soup:

1½ pounds sweet potatoes, peeled and cut into 1-inch cubes
1 pound leeks, roots and dark green leaves removed, rinsed, chopped, and soaked for 10 minutes in cold water
4 cups Chicken Stock (page 118) *or* water
1 cup heavy cream
1 tablespoon whole coriander seeds, toasted and ground (*or* ½ tablespoon ground coriander)
½ teaspoon cumin seeds, toasted and ground (*or* ¼ teaspoon ground cumin)
½ cup fresh lime juice (about 4 limes)
Kosher salt and freshly cracked black pepper, to taste

For the garnish:

1 cup sour cream
⅓ cup fresh lime juice (about 3 limes)
2 tablespoons finely chopped fresh cilantro
1 tablespoon peeled and minced garlic, mashed to a paste
1 tablespoon kosher salt
½ tablespoon red pepper flakes
4 cups crumbled tortilla chips

1. In a large, heavy-bottomed saucepan, combine the sweet potatoes, leeks, chicken stock, cream, coriander, and cumin. Bring to a boil, then reduce heat to medium and simmer until the potatoes can easily be pierced with a fork, about 30 minutes.

2. Remove pan from heat, let cool slightly, and purée the soup in a food processor or blender, or with an immersion blender, until the consistency is that of a smooth applesauce. Transfer to a bowl or container and refrigerate until cold. Stir in the lime juice and season with salt and pepper.

3. While the soup is chilling, make the garnish: In a small bowl, combine the sour cream, lime juice, cilantro, garlic, salt, and red pepper flakes; mix well.

4. To serve, ladle the cold soup into bowls and top with a spoonful of the sour cream garnish (or drizzle it out of a squeeze bottle in a decorative pattern) and a sprinkle of tortilla chips. Use the garnish sparingly, about 1 tablespoon or less per serving.

Soup Starters

Every culinary student learns about the mirepoix, a combination of equal parts of diced carrot, celery, and onion that, when sautéed, provides a rich, aromatic base for almost any soup or stock and many braises. Deep in the South, traditional dishes start with what's called the trinity: celery, onion, and green pepper. The green pepper gives Southern dishes a characteristically earthy, vegetable flavor.

Black-Eyed Pea, Corn, and Sweet Potato Soup

Some Southerners swear that eating black-eyed peas on New Year's Day brings good luck the rest of the year. Joe, who was born in Georgia and raised in Texas, goes along with the tradition just so he can get some black-eyed peas. I don't blame him. Do what you want on New Year's, but for this soup, wait until summer, when you can get the corn for that all-important crunch of freshness.

Serves 4

6 slices bacon, cut into ½-inch strips
1 large yellow onion, peeled and cut into ½-inch dice
2 stalks celery, cut into ½-inch dice
6 garlic cloves, peeled and minced
1 tablespoon cumin seeds, toasted and ground
1 tablespoon chopped fresh sage leaves
1 small chipotle pepper in adobo sauce, minced (about 2 teaspoons), *or* 1 teaspoon red pepper flakes
1½ cups black-eyed peas, soaked overnight in 6 cups cold water, rinsed, and drained
5 cups water
1 large sweet potato, peeled and cut into ½-inch dice
2 cups fresh corn kernels (about 4 large ears corn)
2–4 splashes (to taste) Tabasco
Salt and freshly ground black pepper, to taste

1. In a heavy-bottomed, 4-quart stockpot over medium heat, cook the bacon, stirring frequently, until it begins to crisp and renders some fat, 8 to 10 minutes.

2. Raise the heat to medium-high and add the onions, stirring frequently and scraping up bacon drippings stuck to the pan, until the onions begin to brown, 8 to 10 minutes. Add the celery, garlic, cumin, sage, and chipotle; cook, stirring constantly, for 30 seconds.

3. Add the black-eyed peas and water, scraping up juices and any bits stuck to the bottom of the pan, and bring to a boil. Adjust heat to a simmer and cook just until the peas are tender, stirring occasionally, 30 minutes.

4. Add the sweet potatoes and simmer until tender, 20 to 30 minutes. Stir in the corn, return to a simmer for 5 minutes, and remove from heat. Season with Tabasco, salt, and pepper.

THIS SURPRISINGLY MELLOW soup gives you a hit of roasted chili flavor and an elegant khaki green color, perfect for when you want to rush the onset of summer. The crunch of pumpernickel croutons helps bring everything back down to earth.

Serves 4

For the soup:

4 fresh poblano peppers
2 tablespoons olive oil, divided
3 tablespoons butter
1 small white onion, peeled and roughly chopped
2 stalks celery, roughly chopped
1 carrot, peeled and roughly chopped
30 cloves garlic, peeled
1 bunch scallions, greens only, roughly chopped
2 teaspoons cumin seeds, toasted and ground
2 teaspoons coriander seeds, toasted and ground
3 cups water *or* Chicken Stock (page 118)
1 cup heavy cream
Salt and freshly ground black pepper, to taste
2 teaspoons chopped parsley leaves

For the pumpernickel croutons (makes about 2 cups):

4 slices pumpernickel bread, cut into ½-inch cubes
1 tablespoon olive oil
1 tablespoon paprika
2 cloves garlic, peeled and minced

ROASTED POBLANO AND GARLIC SOUP WITH PUMPERNICKEL CROUTONS

ROASTED POBLANO AND GARLIC SOUP WITH PUMPERNICKEL CROUTONS continued

1. Turn on broiler to high.
2. Rub the peppers with 1 tablespoon of the oil and place on a baking sheet. Broil for 10 to 15 minutes, turning, until the peppers start to blacken and blister.
3. Transfer the peppers to a large bowl and cover with plastic wrap. Let cool, and change the oven setting to bake, at 450°F.
4. In a 4-quart saucepan, heat the remaining tablespoon olive oil and the butter over medium-high heat. Add the onion, celery, carrot, garlic, and scallions. Cook, stirring, for 4 to 6 minutes, or until the vegetables begin to brown. Add the cumin and coriander, and cook for 1 minute more.
5. Add the water (or stock) and heavy cream, bring to a boil, and reduce heat to low. Simmer for 45 minutes.
6. Meanwhile, once the poblanos are cool enough to handle, use your hands to slip off the skins, then pull off the stem and remove the core and seeds. Roughly chop the peppers and add them to the soup while it simmers.
7. Toss the crouton ingredients in a mixing bowl. Place on a baking sheet. Bake for 7 to 8 minutes or until browned, watching carefully to avoid burning them. Remove immediately and let cool.
8. Purée the soup using an immersion blender or in batches in a food processor or blender. Season liberally with salt and pepper, garnish with pumpernickel croutons and parsley, and serve.

Sister Sorel's Sorrel Soup

WITH A RESTAURANT called SISTER SOREL (named, surprisingly, after my sister Sorel), I knew I had to have a sorrel soup on the menu, especially since I love the bright, lemony taste of this green almost as much as I love my sis. Look for it at farm stands starting in the early spring, or, if you're an addict like me, grow your own.

Serves 4 to 6

2 tablespoons butter
2 tablespoons, plus ¼ cup canola oil
2 large yellow onions, peeled and roughly chopped
8 cloves garlic, peeled and roughly chopped
2 teaspoons kosher salt, divided
1½ cups water or Vegetable Stock (page 120)
½ cup heavy cream
1¼ pounds sorrel, cleaned and trimmed of tough stems
1 tablespoon chili powder
1 teaspoon red pepper flakes
Additional salt and freshly ground black pepper, to taste

1. In 4- or 6-quart stockpot, heat the butter and 2 tablespoons of the canola oil over medium-low heat. Add the onions, garlic, and 1 teaspoon of the salt; cook, stirring frequently, until the onions are tender but not browned, about 15 minutes. Add the water (or stock), cream, and 1 pound of the sorrel. Raise heat to medium-high and bring to a boil, stirring to incorporate the sorrel. Adjust heat to simmer and cook, stirring occasionally, for 10 minutes.

2. While the soup cooks, finely julienne the remaining sorrel and set aside for garnish.

3. In a small sauté pan, heat the remaining ¼ cup canola oil over medium heat. Add the remaining 1 teaspoon salt, the chili powder, and red pepper flakes; cook, stirring frequently, for 4 minutes. Strain through a fine-mesh sieve, reserving the oil.

4. Purée the soup with an immersion blender or in batches in a food processor or blender (returning the puréed soup to a clean saucepan). Season to taste with salt and pepper, and keep hot.

5. Mound the julienned sorrel in the center of shallow soup bowls and ladle the hot soup around it. Drizzle with the chili oil and serve immediately.

CURRIED BUTTERNUT SQUASH SOUP WITH MINT OIL

IN FALL, when New England overflows with squashes and apples of all kinds, we always want to put them together. This could be the start of a fall harvest dinner, but it also makes for a wonderfully light vegetarian lunch when paired with fresh bread and a salad.

Serves 4 to 6

2 tablespoons butter, cut into 4 pieces
1 small yellow onion, peeled and roughly chopped
2 teaspoons peeled and chopped ginger (about ½-inch piece)
2 cloves garlic, peeled and chopped
2 tablespoons Tremont 647 Curry (page 8)
Salt and freshly ground black pepper
1 small *or* ½ large (about 1½ pounds) butternut squash, peeled, seeded, and cut into 1-inch cubes
2 McIntosh apples (about ½ pound), peeled, cored, and roughly chopped
2 cups water *or* Vegetable Stock (page 120)
½ cup apple cider *or* apple juice
¼ cup olive oil
¼ cup roughly chopped mint leaves
1 teaspoon kosher salt
1 teaspoon red pepper flakes
1 Granny Smith apple, peeled and cored
Juice of 1 lime (about 2 tablespoons)

1. In a 6- to 8-quart stockpot over low heat, melt the butter. Add the onion, ginger, garlic, curry, and a large pinch of salt; cook, stirring occasionally, until the onions are soft, 20 to 30 minutes.

2. Add the squash, apples, water (*or* stock), and apple cider (*or* juice); bring to a boil. Adjust heat to a simmer and cook, stirring occasionally, until the squash is very tender, about 20 minutes. Remove from heat.

3. While the vegetables are cooking, make the mint oil by combining the olive oil, mint, kosher salt, and red pepper flakes in a small, heavy-bottomed sauté pan over high heat. Let cook for 2 minutes and immediately remove from heat. Purée in a blender and strain through a fine-mesh sieve. Set aside.

4. When the squash is tender, purée the soup with an immersion blender or in batches in a food processor or blender (returning the purée to a clean saucepan). Season with salt and pepper, and keep hot.

5. To serve, coarsely grate the Granny Smith apple into a small bowl. Toss with the lime juice. Ladle the soup into wide, shallow soup bowls, place a small mound of apple in center of each serving, and drizzle the soup with the mint oil.

HOT-AND-SOUR SOUP

THIS SHARP SOUP will make you pucker up and dive in for more. Want to make it heartier without spoiling the clean flavors? Try adding ½ pound of peeled shrimp with the tofu.

Serves 4 to 6

2 tablespoons toasted sesame oil
2 tablespoons canola oil
2 tablespoons peeled and minced ginger
4 cloves garlic, peeled and minced
¼ pound fresh shiitake mushrooms, stems removed and caps sliced ⅛ inch thick
2 stalks celery, sliced diagonally ¼ inch thick
1 large carrot, peeled and julienned
3 cups water *or* Vegetable Stock (page 120)
½ cup soy sauce
¼ cup rice wine vinegar
¼ cup chili-garlic paste *or* 1 tablespoon red pepper flakes
3 tablespoons cornstarch
¾ cup water
½ pound tofu, drained and cut into ½-inch dice
2 eggs, beaten
¼ pound bean sprouts
½ cup toasted and coarsely ground unsalted peanuts
¼ cup cilantro leaves

1. In a 5-quart Dutch oven, heat the sesame and canola oils over medium heat. Add the ginger and garlic, and stir frequently for 2 to 3 minutes, until the ginger and garlic begin to turn golden and become fragrant. Add the shiitake, celery, and carrot, and continue cooking for 2 minutes more, stirring frequently.

2. Add the water (or stock), soy sauce, vinegar, and chili-garlic paste (*or* red pepper flakes). Increase heat to medium-high, bring to a boil, and simmer for 5 minutes.

3. In a separate bowl, mix together the cornstarch and ¾ cup water until fully combined; add to the soup, whisking vigorously. Return the soup to a boil, reduce heat, and simmer for 4 minutes. Add the tofu and return to a boil.

4. Holding the bowl of eggs next to the saucepan, use a fork to scoop up the eggs and drop them in a stream into the boiling soup. Repeat until all the egg is incorporated.

5. In each of 4 serving bowls, place some bean sprouts, peanuts, and cilantro leaves. Ladle in the soup, and serve immediately.

Storing Soups

Always store soups in an airtight container in the refrigerator. If uncovered, soups easily pick up flavors of nearby items, and if you're like either one of us, all it takes is one glance in your fridge to realize the potential disaster that could be.

Soups are also a breeze to freeze. Use gallon-sized heavy-duty sealable freezer bags, which makes defrosting as easy as dropping the bags into a pot of boiling water. Just be sure to label and date the bags, so you know when it's time to use it or lose it (expiration date: 4 months).

KIMCHI SOUP WITH SHRIMP

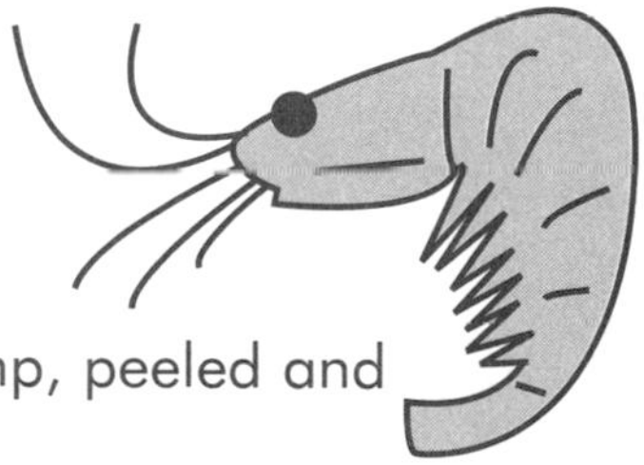

ONCE you've made our Four-Day Kimchi (page 169), one of the easiest uses for it is this soup. And don't despair if you haven't thought about this recipe 4 days in advance. If you've got an Asian supermarket nearby, look for kimchi in a jar. Warning: Depending on the kimchi, this soup is hot enough to clean out your sinuses.

Serves 4 to 6

3 cups water *or* Lobster Stock (page 107)
2 cups Four-Day Kimchi (page 169) *or* store-bought kimchi
24 cocktail-sized shrimp, peeled and deveined
Salt and freshly ground black pepper, to taste

In a 2-quart saucepan, heat the water (*or* stock) over high heat and bring to a boil. Add the kimchi and return to a boil. Add the shrimp. Remove from heat and let sit for 4 to 6 minutes or until the shrimp are firm and pink. Especially if using store-bought kimchi, taste first and then season with salt and pepper if necessary. Serve immediately.

TORTILLA SOUP

THIS RUDIMENTARY Mexican soup evokes chicken noodle, but with tortillas instead of noodles, and it's just as satisfying. It's usually on the menu at TREMONT 647'S annual Sauza Tequila dinners (reservations and taxis required) because like tequila, it seems to bring a flush to the skin and a smile to the lips. We take that back; nothing's really quite like tequila. But you probably knew that.

Serves 4 to 6

For the soup:

2 tablespoons, plus 2 teaspoons olive oil
2 plum tomatoes, cored and cut in half
½ teaspoon kosher salt
½ teaspoon freshly ground black pepper
1 large white onion, coarsely chopped
2 cloves garlic, peeled and minced
1 quart Chicken Stock (page 118)
1 cup shredded, cooked chicken
2 cups tortilla chips, crumbled into small pieces
¼ cup lime juice (about 2 limes)
Salt and freshly ground black pepper, to taste

For the garnish:

¼ cup cilantro leaves
1 tablespoon red pepper flakes
2 limes, cut into wedges

1. Set broiler to high.
2. Lightly oil the tomato halves and season with salt and pepper; place on a small baking sheet and broil until lightly charred.
3. In a food processor, combine the charred tomatoes, onions, and 1 clove garlic, and purée.
4. Heat the remaining oil in a 2-quart saucepan over medium-high heat. Add the garlic and cook for about 2 to 3 minutes, stirring often, until golden brown. Add the stock, tomato purée, and shredded chicken. Bring to a boil, reduce heat to medium, and simmer for 2 minutes. Skim off any foam that rises to the surface.
5. Add the tortilla chips and simmer for 2 minutes. Remove from heat.
6. Season with lime juice, salt, and pepper. Garnish with the cilantro, red pepper flakes, and lime wedges, and serve.

PORTUGUESE-STYLE STEW

THIS IS one of the quickest ways to get big flavors in a light stew. Don't despair if you don't have clams; this would also be great with shrimp.

Serves 4 to 6

3 tablespoons olive oil
2 links (about 8 ounces) linguiça, chorizo, or andouille sausage, cut into 1-inch chunks
1 pound red bliss *or* new potatoes, washed and quartered
½ bunch kale, washed and roughly chopped (about 6 cups)
1 large green bell pepper, seeded and cut into ½-inch dice
6 cloves garlic, peeled and minced
4 plum tomatoes, cored, halved lengthwise, and cut into ¼-inch-thick half-moons
1 tablespoon cumin seeds, toasted and ground
2 cups Fish Stock (page 118) *or* clam juice
20 small hard-shell clams (littlenecks, cockles, or manila), scrubbed to remove any sand
Salt and freshly ground black pepper, to taste
½ cup parsley leaves, minced
1 lemon, cut into 6 wedges

1. Heat the oil in a large, heavy-bottomed sauté pan over medium-high heat. Add the sausage and cook, stirring frequently, until the sausage starts to brown, about 2 minutes. Add the potatoes and cook, stirring frequently, until the potatoes start to brown, 4 to 6 minutes. Add the kale, green pepper, garlic, tomatoes, and cumin; cook for 1 minute, stirring constantly. Add the stock, scraping up the juices and any bits stuck to the bottom of the pan.

2. Bring to a boil, then reduce heat to medium and simmer, stirring occasionally, until the potatoes are just tender, about 8 to 10 minutes. Add the clams and cover the pot; simmer, stirring occasionally, until all the clams have opened, 6 to 8 minutes. Season with salt and pepper and garnish with parsley. Just before serving, squeeze a lemon wedge over each bowl.

TURNIP AND PUMPKIN SOUP WITH CANDIED SEEDS

IF YOU'RE A New Englander, look for the amazing Macomber turnip, which is available only here. Its sweet spiciness combines beautifully with onion and pumpkin. As for the candied seeds, make them only if you're using pumpkin; if it's not pumpkin season and you're settling for butternut squash instead, discard the seeds.

Serves 4 to 6

- 1 teaspoon cumin seeds, toasted and ground
- 1 teaspoon coriander seeds, toasted and ground
- 1 teaspoon chili powder
- 2 teaspoons salt
- 1 tablespoon coarse turbinado sugar (such as Sugar in the Raw)
- 1 small sugar pumpkin *or* butternut squash (about 3 pounds, to yield about 2 cups cubed)
- ¼ cup, plus 2 teaspoons (if using squash instead of pumpkin), canola oil

For the soup:

- 2 tablespoons canola oil
- 2 tablespoons butter
- 1 large yellow onion, peeled and roughly chopped
- 3 stalks celery, roughly chopped
- 1 tablespoon chopped fresh rosemary
- 2 tablespoons all-purpose flour
- 1 cup heavy cream
- 2 pounds turnips, peeled and roughly chopped
- 2½ cups water *or* Vegetable Stock (page 120)
- Salt and freshly ground pepper, to taste

1. Preheat oven to 350°F. In a small bowl, combine the cumin, coriander, chili powder, salt, and sugar. Set aside.

2. Cut the pumpkin in half and scoop out the strings and seeds. Rinse the pulp from the seeds, dry, and set aside.

3. Peel the pumpkin (*or* squash) and cut the meat into large chunks. Transfer to a baking sheet and drizzle with the ¼ cup canola oil, tossing to coat. Roast until fork-tender, about 20 to 30 minutes. Transfer to a large

bowl, leaving the oil behind. Pour the oil from the baking sheet into a small bowl; set aside. Mash the pumpkin and season with salt and pepper. If using squash instead of pumpkin, add the prepared spice mixture; if using pumpkin, follow the next step. Cover and keep warm until serving time.

4. If using pumpkin rather than squash, while roasting, put the pumpkin seeds in a heavy-bottomed sauté pan over medium heat, tossing gently for 3 to 5 minutes or until the seeds begin to brown. Add the 2 teaspoons canola oil, cook for 1 minute more, then add the prepared spice mixture and reduce heat to low. Stir with wooden spoon for 5 to 7 minutes or until the sugar begins to melt and the spices start to clump. Remove from pan and let cool.

5. To make the soup, heat the oil and butter over medium heat in a 3- or 4-quart saucepan. Add the onion, celery, and rosemary; cook, stirring occasionally, until the onions soften, about 15 minutes. Add the flour and cook, stirring frequently, until the mixture looks dry, about 4 minutes. Add the cream, stirring and scraping the bottom of the pan to incorporate the flour. Increase heat to medium-high, add the turnips and water (or stock), and mix well. Bring to a boil, reduce heat to medium, and simmer until the turnips are tender, 10 to 20 minutes.

6. Purée the soup with an immersion blender or in batches in a blender or food processor (returning the purée to a clean saucepan). Season with salt and pepper.

7. To serve, put a small spoonful of mashed pumpkin (or squash) in the center of each bowl. Ladle in the hot turnip soup, drizzle with the reserved pumpkin oil, and garnish with candied seeds.

Full Immersion

No soup lover should live without an immersion blender, also called a hand blender. Any cook who has ever wiped black beans off the ceiling knows the dangers of transferring hot soup to a regular blender. With an immersion blender, just stick it in, and whir away. You can even partially purée, stopping when the consistency is right, leaving it as chunky as you want it.

That said, there are some strategies you can use to make puréeing soup easier in a regular blender or food processor. First of all, don't be afraid to work in batches; never fill a blender jar more than half full of hot liquid. Hold the lid firmly in place with a dry, folded dishtowel. If the dishtowel slips, at least you'll have it to wipe up those beans.

CORN AND LOBSTER BISQUE

THIS IS the second-best way we know to combine corn and lobster. The first, of course, is to boil both and scarf them down in alternating mouthfuls with butter and beer. As a bisque, the same ingredients (save the beer) are refined to their very essence. *Refined* is the operative word: To make a really great bisque, you've got to get all the solid particles out of the soup, using a fine-mesh sieve such as the cone-shaped chinois and/or cheesecloth.

Serves 4

4½–5 cups corn kernels (reserved from stock, following)
½ cup peeled and roughly chopped garlic cloves
2 sticks cold butter, diced
¼ cup extra-virgin olive oil, divided
Lobster meat (reserved from stock, following)
¼ cup roughly chopped fresh chervil *or* tarragon
2 teaspoons peeled and minced fresh ginger
1 teaspoon red pepper flakes
Juice of 1 lemon (about ¼ cup)
Kosher salt and freshly cracked white *or* black pepper, to taste
4 cups Lobster Stock (following)
1 cup heavy cream

1. In a heavy-bottomed saucepan over low heat, combine the corn, garlic, butter, and 2 tablespoons of the oil. When the butter has melted, simmer the mixture gently for 30 minutes, stirring often to be sure the corn does not brown. Remove from heat and let cool for 5 minutes.

2. While the corn is cooking, make the garnish: Combine the remaining 2 tablespoons oil, the lobster meat, chervil (*or* tarragon), ginger, red pepper flakes, lemon juice, and salt and pepper in a medium-size bowl. Cover and set aside.

3. Transfer ¼ of the corn mixture to a food processor or blender and add 1 cup of the stock. Purée until smooth, and strain through a fine-mesh strainer or food mill into a large bowl.

Repeat with the remaining corn and stock in 3 batches. Strain the corn again, this time through a fine-mesh sieve such as the cone-shaped chinois and/or cheesecloth to remove any remaining corn pulp. Transfer to a clean pot and add the cream.

4. Place the soup over medium-low heat and heat through. Season with salt and pepper. To serve, ladle the soup into bowls and top each serving with a spoonful of the lobster garnish. (The soup and garnish may be covered and refrigerated separately for several hours before serving. Reheat the soup over low heat, and bring the garnish to room temperature.)

LOBSTER STOCK

Makes approximately 4 cups

2 live lobsters (about 1–1¼ pounds each)
10 ears shucked corn
½ head celery with leaves, washed well and roughly chopped
2 large carrots, peeled and roughly chopped
1 large white onion, peeled and roughly chopped
½ cup garlic cloves
2 cups roughly chopped fresh parsley leaves and stems
¼ cup fresh thyme sprigs
1 cup dry white wine

1. Fill a heavy-bottomed pot large enough to hold the lobsters about halfway with water. Bring to a boil, add the lobsters, and cover the pot. Cook just until the shell turns bright red, 6 to 8 minutes. Transfer the lobsters to a bowl and refrigerate until cool to the touch.

2. While the lobsters are cooling, cut the kernels from the corncobs. Reserve the kernels for the bisque, and place the cobs in a large stockpot. Add the celery, carrots, onion, garlic, parsley, thyme, and wine to the pot.

3. Remove the lobster tails and claws by grabbing firmly and twisting them away from the body. Rinse the body cavities to remove the green tomalley, and add the lobster bodies to the stockpot.

4. Using a sharp chef's knife, cut a lengthwise slit in the underside of the lobster tails. Use your hands to split open the shells and remove the meat. Place the meat in a bowl, and add the shells to the pot. Do the same with the claws, using a chef's knife or nutcracker to get inside. Coarsely chop the lobster meat, cover it, and refrigerate while making the stock.

5. Add enough water to the stockpot to cover the ingredients, and bring to a boil. Lower heat to a simmer and cook for 30 minutes. Strain and reserve the liquid; there should be about 4 cups. Discard the solids in the pan.

SEAFOOD STEW

MY COOKS AND I make this kind of stew in the restaurants, for staff or as a special, whenever we end up with a little more seafood than we need. For home cooks who buy just enough fish for each meal, that's not an issue. But that doesn't mean there's no need for a nice simple stew like this, which is perfect for an informal dinner anytime you want a taste of the sea.

Serves 4 to 6

4 slices bacon, cut crosswise into 1/4-inch strips
1 large white onion, peeled and cut into 1/4-inch dice
2 stalks celery, cut into 1/4-inch dice
1 large carrot, peeled and cut into 1/4-inch dice
2 cloves garlic, peeled and minced
1 pound skinless cod, cut into 1-inch chunks
1 tablespoon chopped fresh thyme leaves
1 tablespoon minced fresh oregano
2/3 cup dry white wine
2 cups water or Fish Stock (page 118)
1 (14.5-ounce) can crushed tomatoes
2 russet potatoes, peeled and cut into 1/2-inch dice
1/2 pound sea scallops, cut into 1/4-inch disks
1/2 pound fresh crabmeat
Salt and freshly ground black pepper, to taste
1/2 cup flat-leaf Italian parsley
1 lemon, cut into wedges

1. In a heavy-bottomed Dutch oven, cook the bacon over medium heat, stirring frequently, until it begins to brown and renders some fat, about 5 to 7 minutes. Raise heat to medium-high and add the onions, celery, garlic, and carrot. Cook until the onions start to soften, about 5 minutes, stirring frequently and scraping up any bacon bits stuck to the bottom of the pan.

2. Add the cod, thyme, and oregano; cook, stirring frequently, until the fish turns white, 3 to 5 minutes. Add the wine, water (or stock), tomatoes, and potatoes; mix well. Bring to a boil, then adjust heat to a simmer and cook until the potatoes are tender, 15 to 20 minutes.

3. Stir in the scallops and return to a simmer. Remove pan from heat. Add the crab and season with salt and pepper. Garnish each serving with parsley and a squeeze of lemon.

THIS SOUP manages to be both light and flavor-packed, thanks to all the aromatic ingredients. But it's also elegant, especially if you put the fresh ingredients in each serving bowl in front of each guest and then use a pretty ceramic teapot or gravy boat to pour the hot broth on top. The fragrant steam will win them over before they even take a bite.

SHRIMP WITH LEMONGRASS-GINGER BROTH

Serves 4 to 6

12 cocktail-size shrimp
2 tablespoons sesame oil
1 teaspoon red pepper flakes
1 stalk lemongrass, cut on an angle into 1-inch pieces
1 tablespoon peeled and roughly chopped garlic
1 tablespoon peeled and roughly chopped ginger (about a 1-inch piece)
3 cups water
1½ cups dry white wine
1 tablespoon canola oil
3 tablespoons fish sauce
2 jalapeños, cored, seeds removed, and minced
1 red bell pepper, cored, seeds removed, and cut into ¼-inch dice
1 tablespoon roughly chopped mint leaves
1 tablespoon roughly chopped cilantro
1 tablespoon roughly chopped basil leaves
½ cup toasted and roughly chopped peanuts
1 lime, cut into 6 wedges

1. Peel and devein the shrimp. Set aside, reserving the shells.

2. Heat the sesame oil in a heavy-bottomed saucepan over medium-high heat. Add the red pepper flakes and lemongrass; cook, stirring frequently, for 2 minutes. Add the shrimp shells and cook for 2 minutes more. Add the ginger and garlic, and cook for 2 minutes.

3. Add the water and wine. Bring to a boil and reduce heat to medium. Simmer for 45 minutes. (Note: You can make soup up to this point ahead of time, refrigerating the broth for up to 3 days before reheating and proceeding.)

4. While the stock is simmering, heat the canola oil over medium-high heat in a heavy-bottomed sauté pan. Add the shrimp and cook, tossing, for 2 to 3 minutes, until the shrimp are pink and no longer translucent. Remove from pan and set aside.

5. When the stock has simmered for 45 minutes, add the fish sauce and strain through a fine-mesh sieve, discarding the solids.

6. In serving bowls, evenly divide the shrimp, jalapeños, bell pepper, mint, cilantro, basil, and toasted peanuts. Ladle hot broth on top, then squeeze a lime wedge over each bowl and add the wedge to the bowl. Serve immediately.

AS ANY NEW ENGLANDER knows, you don't mess with clam chowder. Well, neither Joe nor I are Yankees, so this'll show 'em to lighten up, already. With tasso (a cured ham that is the pride of Louisiana), yams, okra, and corn added to the mix, this recipe takes chowder on a trip down South. From the taste of things, it may never come back home.

SOUTHERN CLAM CHOWDER

Serves 4 to 6

¼ cup canola oil
¼ pound tasso ham *or* 3 strips bacon, chopped
4 garlic cloves, peeled and chopped
1 large white onion, peeled and diced
1 large carrot, peeled and cut into ¼-inch dice
1 green bell pepper, stemmed, seeded, and cut into ¼-inch dice
1 tablespoon Creole Seasoning (page 4)
¼ cup all-purpose flour
1½ cups clam juice
1½ cups water
1 cup heavy cream
¾ pound yams *or* sweet potatoes, peeled and cut into ½-inch dice
½ pound okra, tops removed, and cut into ¼-inch slices
2 cups fresh corn kernels (about 4 large ears corn)
1½ cups chopped clams
Salt and freshly ground black pepper, to taste

1. In a heavy-bottomed 4-quart saucepan, heat the oil over medium heat. Add the tasso *or* bacon and cook for 4 to 6 minutes, stirring occasionally, until crisp and golden. Add the garlic, onion, carrot, green pepper, and Creole Seasoning; cook for 4 minutes, continuing to stir occasionally.

2. Sprinkle in the flour, evenly distributing it over the mixture in the saucepan. Stirring frequently, cook for 3 to 4 minutes, scraping the bottom of the pan and making sure not to burn the flour. Stir in the clam juice, water, and cream. Raise heat to medium-high. Add the yams or sweet potatoes and the okra. Simmer for 10 to 15 minutes or until the potatoes are easily pierced with a fork.

3. Add the corn and simmer for 1 minute. Add the chopped clams. Season with salt and freshly ground black pepper. Serve with Flaky Yankee Biscuits (page 244) or Fluffy Southern Biscuits (page 243).

CHICKEN SOUP
WITH GRIBENES TOAST

DURING the Depression, my grandparents, like many Jews, would smear schmaltz (rendered chicken fat) and gribenes (the cracklings that are a delicious by-product of the schmaltz) onto their toast. Nowadays, anybody too health-conscious might resist, but when used right—meaning sparingly—schmaltz and gribenes can add a rich element that is really no worse for you than eating chicken with the skin on. Make this soup on a rainy day, or when you feel the sniffles coming on, and you'll swear your grandmother, Jewish or not, is in the kitchen.

Serves 4 to 6

½ (3-pound) whole chicken, skin and extra fat removed, chopped, and reserved
1 large white onion, peeled and minced
¼ cup water
1 tablespoon salt
8 cloves garlic, peeled
2 bay leaves
1 large sprig fresh thyme
2 tablespoons canola oil
1 small carrot, peeled and cut into ¼-inch dice
1 stalk celery, cut into ¼-inch dice
1 medium-size yellow onion, peeled and cut into ¼-inch dice
1 small parsnip, peeled and cut into ¼-inch dice
1 small rutabaga, peeled and cut into ¼-inch dice (about ½ cup)
1 small turnip, peeled and cut into ¼-inch dice (about ½ cup)
Salt and freshly ground black pepper, to taste
1–2 tablespoons fresh dill
2 slices marble rye bread

1. To make gribenes, combine the chicken skin and fat, onion, water, and salt in a heavy-bottomed sauté pan over medium-low heat. Cook, stirring occasionally, until the onions collapse and the fat is rendered, about 1 hour. Reduce heat to low and continue cooking until the mixture turns golden brown and the skin starts to crisp, up to 1 hour more. Set aside. (Mixture can be made 1 day ahead; reheat before serving.)

2. Meanwhile, cut the chicken into 4 pieces and put it in a 2- to 3-quart saucepan. Add the garlic, bay leaves, thyme, and enough cold water to cover. Bring to a boil over medium-high heat, reduce heat to low, and simmer until the breast meat is done, about 15 minutes. Use tongs to remove the breast from the pot; set aside to cool. Continue cooking the rest of the chicken until it falls from the bones, about 45 minutes more. When the chicken is done, remove it and the garlic from the broth, reserving the broth, and set aside to cool. Pull the meat from the bones and shred it into bite-sized pieces; cover, and set aside.

3. In a wide saucepan or Dutch oven, heat the oil over medium-high heat. Add the carrots, celery, onion, parsnips, rutabaga, and turnip. Cook, stirring frequently, until the vegetables start to brown, 4 to 6 minutes. Strain the reserved chicken broth over the vegetables, and bring to a boil. Reduce heat and simmer until the vegetables are fork-tender, about 10 to 15 minutes. Season the soup with salt and pepper, and garnish with fresh dill.

4. When the soup is ready, toast the rye bread, and cut the slices in half. Spread hot gribenes on the toast, and serve along with the soup.

THIS SOUP is so quick to prepare and so intensely fragrant and flavorful, you'll think it can cure whatever ails you. Neither one of us are doctors, of course, but we can guarantee that you'll at least forget what ails you while you're eating it.

Serves 8

- 1 tablespoon canola oil
- 1 medium-size white onion, peeled and diced
- 1 tablespoon peeled and minced fresh ginger (about 1-inch piece)
- 1 garlic clove, peeled and minced
- 2 tablespoons Tremont 647 Curry (page 8)
- 3 kaffir lime leaves or 1 tablespoon lime zest
- 2 teaspoons red pepper flakes
- 4 cups Chicken Stock (page 118)
- 1 stalk lemongrass, trimmed of withered leaves, bruised, and cut in half crosswise
- ¾ pound boneless, skinless chicken breast, cut into ½-inch cubes
- 1 cup shiitake mushrooms, stems removed, caps cut into ¼-inch pieces
- 10 small button mushrooms, cleaned and quartered
- 1 portobello mushroom, stem removed, cap cut into ½-inch cubes
- 1 (14.5-ounce) can coconut milk
- Juice of 2 limes (about ¼ cup)
- 2 tablespoons fish sauce
- Freshly cracked black pepper, to taste
- 3 scallions, cut on the diagonal into thin slices
- ¼ cup minced cilantro leaves

1. Heat the oil in a 4-quart stockpot over medium-high heat. Add the onion and ginger. Cook, stirring frequently, until the onions start to soften, about 4 minutes. Add the garlic and cook for 1 minute. Add the curry, lime leaves, and red pepper flakes; cook, stirring constantly, for 1 minute. Stir in the stock and lemongrass, and bring to a boil. Adjust heat to simmer, and cook for 15 minutes.

2. Add the chicken, all the mushrooms, and coconut milk, and simmer until the chicken is cooked through, about 5 to 7 minutes. Discard the lemongrass.

3. Remove from heat and add the lime juice, fish sauce, and pepper. Garnish with scallions and cilantro just before serving.

CURRIED THAI CHICKEN AND MUSHROOM SOUP

PORK AND BLACK BEAN STEW

THIS HEARTY DISH is ideal for wintertime. On a particularly chilly night, put the finished stew in individual oven-safe crocks, top each with ¼ cup sharp Cheddar or Monterey jack, and broil until bubbly and browned. If that doesn't sufficiently warm up your guests, serve with generous portions of Salsa 101 (page 24).

Serves 6 to 8

5 slices thick-cut bacon, cut into ½-inch strips
1 pound pork shoulder *or* pork butt, cut into 1-inch cubes
1 large yellow onion, cut into ½-inch dice
10 garlic cloves, peeled and minced
2 tablespoons cumin seeds, toasted and ground
2 tablespoons freshly ground black pepper
2 bay leaves
½–1 teaspoon red pepper flakes
2 cups black beans, soaked overnight in 6 cups cold water, rinsed well and drained
7 cups cold water
¼ cup fresh lime juice (about 2 limes)
Salt and freshly ground black pepper, to taste
1 large red onion, peeled and cut into ½-inch dice
1 cup cilantro leaves, roughly chopped
½ cup Limed Sour Cream (page 22)

1. In an 8-quart, heavy-bottomed Dutch oven over medium heat, cook the bacon until the fat has rendered and the bacon starts to brown, 8 to 10 minutes. Using a slotted spoon, transfer the bacon to a large bowl, leaving the fat in the pan.

2. Raise the heat to medium-high. Season the pork with salt and pepper, and sear until well browned, working in batches as necessary to avoid crowding the pan. Transfer the pork to the bowl with the bacon.

3. Add the onion to the pan and cook, stirring frequently, until the onions soften and begin to brown, 8 to 10 minutes. Add the garlic, cumin, black pepper, bay leaves, and pepper flakes. Cook, stirring constantly, for 1 minute. Add the beans and 6 cups of the water, scraping up caramelized juices stuck to the bottom of the pan. Return the pork and bacon to the pan and mix well.

4. Bring to a boil, and adjust heat to a simmer. Cook, stirring occasionally from the bottom to prevent scorching, until the pork and beans are just tender, 1 to 2 hours. Add the lime juice and the remaining 1 cup water; return to a gentle simmer and cook for 20 minutes more, stirring frequently from the bottom. Season with salt and pepper.

5. Garnish each serving with the red onions, cilantro, and a spoonful of the Limed Sour Cream.

PORK SOUP WITH YELLOW PEPPER CURRY AND PECANS

IF YOU LIKE A SPICY, hearty soup, look no further. Here, tender pork is enlivened with the sweet-sour combination of red and yellow peppers, curry, and lime, along with some crunchy pecans for texture. Oh, yes, and the kick of chili flakes. If you want it hotter, unscrew the cap on the flakes, but be forewarned: There's no going back.

Serves 4 to 6

3 tablespoons canola oil
1 pound boneless country-style pork ribs *or* Boston butt, cut into ½-inch dice
Salt and freshly ground black pepper, to taste
6 cloves garlic, peeled and minced
1-inch piece fresh ginger, peeled and cut into ¼-inch dice (to yield 1 tablespoon)
2–3 teaspoons (or more, to taste) red pepper flakes
1 large yellow onion, peeled and roughly chopped
1 red bell pepper, cored, seeded, and cut into ¼-inch dice
2 kaffir lime leaves (optional)
5 cups water *or* Veal *or* Pork Stock (page 119)
Zest and juice of 2 limes
1 cup Spicy Roasted Yellow Pepper Curry (page 17)
½ cup toasted and roughly chopped pecans

1. In a 5- to 6-quart Dutch oven, heat the oil on high. Season the pork with salt and pepper, and sear until well browned, about 6 to 8 minutes, stirring frequently.

2. Add the garlic, ginger, red pepper flakes, onion, and red bell pepper; cook until the onions begin to soften, scraping the bottom of the pan occasionally, about 5 minutes. Add the lime leaves, if using, and 4 cups of the water *or* stock; bring to a boil. Adjust heat to a simmer, and cook until the pork is tender, 45 to 60 minutes.

3. Add the lime zest, juice, Yellow Pepper Curry, and up to 1 cup of the remaining water *or* stock as needed to thin the mixture to soup consistency. Season with salt and pepper, and garnish with the pecans.

LAMB TAGINE WITH SESAME-ALMOND GARNISH

THE WORD *tagine* means stew, and in Morocco the classic dish is cooked in a distinctively conical clay pot of the same name, over an open fire. Well, this *tagine* is made in a stockpot on the stovetop, but the spices, lamb, and dried fruit are true to the spirit, if not the traditional method, of a North African staple. The perfect accompaniment: couscous, of course.

Serves 6 to 8

3 tablespoons olive oil
2 pounds lamb stew meat *or* leg of lamb, cut into 1-inch cubes
Salt and freshly ground black pepper, to taste
1 red onion, peeled and roughly chopped
1 red bell pepper, seeded and cut into ½-inch dice
1 green bell pepper, seeded and cut into ½-inch dice
¼ cup peeled and roughly chopped ginger (about a 4-inch piece)
4 cloves garlic, peeled and minced
2 tablespoons North African Spice Mix (page 6)
4 cups water *or* Meat Stock (page 119)
2 small parsnips, peeled, sliced lengthwise, and cut into ¼-inch half-moons
2 small carrots, peeled, sliced lengthwise, and cut into ¼-inch half-moons
1 medium-size sweet potato, peeled and cut into ½-inch dice
1 cup golden raisins
½ cup other dried fruit (cherries and/or quartered apricots)
½ cup red wine vinegar

For the sesame-almond garnish:
½ cup toasted and coarsely chopped almonds
¼ cup roughly chopped parsley leaves
2 tablespoons sesame seeds, toasted
Zest of 1 lime
½ teaspoon caraway seeds, ground
1 tablespoon extra-virgin olive oil

1. In a heavy-bottomed 4-quart stockpot, heat the olive oil over high heat. Season the lamb with salt and pepper, and add it to the pan. Sear until well browned, stirring frequently, about 5 minutes; transfer to bowl and set aside.

2. Lower heat to medium-high and add the onion, peppers, ginger, and garlic. Cook, stirring frequently and scraping up juices and bits stuck to the bottom of the pan, until the vegetables soften, about 5 minutes. Add the North African Spice Mix and lamb, and cook for 1 minute, stirring frequently. Add the water and bring to a boil; adjust heat to a simmer. Cook until the lamb is barely tender, 25 to 30 minutes.

3. Add the parsnips, carrot, sweet potato, raisins, and dried fruit; simmer until the vegetables are tender, 10 to 15 minutes. Add the vinegar, and season with salt and pepper.

4. While the vegetables are cooking, combine the garnish ingredients in a medium-size bowl and mix well; sprinkle over the stew before serving.

WHEN JOE first told me that in Texas, real chili has neither beans nor tomatoes, I quipped, "Look it up." Wrong answer. "I don't need to look it up, Andy," he fired back. " 'Chile con carne' means *chili,* as in chili pepper, with meat." Well, tradition aside, we agreed to disagree—and to write a recipe for a chili we would both be proud to serve. This chili packs a smoky wallop, and even though I think it would be fine with beans and even a smidge of tomato paste, it's damn good without them, too.

SMOKY BOWL O'RED

Serves 4 to 6

4 tablespoons canola oil, divided
3 pounds lean beef stew meat, cut into ½-inch cubes
Salt and freshly ground black pepper, to taste
3 cloves garlic, peeled and minced
1 tablespoon cumin seeds, toasted, ground
1 tablespoon dried oregano
2 tablespoons cayenne pepper
1 tablespoon Tabasco
1 tablespoon minced chipotle in adobo
1 tablespoon kosher salt
½ cup tequila
1 (16-ounce) can Lone Star *or* other cheap beer
4 cups water *or* Beef Stock (page 119), low-sodium if using canned
2 tablespoons masa harina
½ cup water

1. Heat 2 tablespoons of the oil in a 5-quart Dutch oven over medium-high heat. Pat the beef dry with paper towels and season with salt and pepper. Add ⅓ of the beef and cook for 3 to 5 minutes or until evenly browned, stirring frequently. Remove the pieces from the pan as they are browned. Repeat with the next batch of beef, adding additional oil as needed, until all the beef is browned, taking care not to overcrowd the pan.

2. Return all the meat to the pan. Add the garlic, cumin, and oregano; cook for 2 minutes, continuing to stir. Add the cayenne, Tabasco, chipotle, salt, tequila, beer, and water *or* stock, and bring to a boil.

3. Reduce heat to low and simmer for 1 to 1½ hours, stirring occasionally to keep the mixture from burning, until the meat is tender. Add more water if needed.

4. When the meat is tender, mix together the masa harina and ½ cup water in a bowl; stir into the chili. Simmer for 30 more minutes, until the meat is melting into the sauce. Serve with soda crackers and grated Cheddar cheese, Limed Sour Cream (page 22), and onions or beans on the side.

FREEZING STOCKS

Stocks freeze beautifully. Our favorite way after cooling and defatting them is to pour them into ice-cube trays, freeze, then store in zipper bags. They keep for up to 4 months in the freezer, and the frozen cubes are easy to use. If space is tight, you can even take the extra time to reduce the stock before freezing; just make sure you mark on the bags how concentrated it is. When it's time to use, reconstitute in water (for stock reduced by 3/4, reconstitute by putting 1/4 cup of stock cubes in 3/4 cup water). Of course, you may not have to rehydrate; you can use the strong stuff in recipes that call for reduced stock, or otherwise adjust your recipe to compensate for the strength of the stock.

STOCKS

IN THE RESTAURANTS, of course, we always have stocks going, but smart home cooks keep a selection in their freezer at all times, too. Not only are flavorful stocks a crucial component in tasty soups, but they're a quick and easy way to make a pan sauce after pan-frying or roasting meat. (Note: We don't want you to cook your stocks with salt; that can create a seasoning problem later if they're reduced.)

CHICKEN STOCK

Some recipes call for roasting chicken bones before making stock. We prefer a lighter touch, which makes this stock more versatile—as appropriate for risotto as for good old-fashioned chicken soup.

Makes about 2 quarts

3 pounds chicken necks and backs (the meatier the better)
2 large yellow onions, peeled and roughly chopped
2 large carrots, scrubbed and roughly chopped
4 stalks celery, roughly chopped
Cold water
2 bay leaves
1 tablespoon dried thyme
1 tablespoon peppercorns
½ bunch parsley

1. Place the bones, onions, carrots, and celery in a large stockpot and cover with cold water by about 1 inch. Bring to a boil over high heat, then adjust heat to a simmer and skim the froth from the surface.

2. Add the remaining ingredients and simmer for 2 hours, continuing to skim off froth as it collects on the surface.

3. Strain through a fine-mesh sieve and chill until the fat rises to the top and solidifies; discard the fat. Refrigerate for up to 3 days, or freeze for up to 4 months.

FISH STOCK

Use the bodies of a medium-flavored white fish such as cod or fluke for this stock, and avoid strong-tasting fish such as salmon.

Makes about 2 quarts

3 tablespoons butter
2 pounds fish frames, rinsed
1 large yellow onion, peeled and roughly chopped
2 stalks celery, roughly chopped
¼ lightly packed cup roughly chopped parsley
4 shallots, peeled and roughly chopped
6 cloves garlic, peeled
2 bay leaves
1 teaspoon black peppercorns
1 teaspoon kosher salt
1½ cups dry white wine
About 2½ quarts cold water

1. Heat the butter in a large stockpot over medium heat. When the butter melts, add the fish bones and cook until the bones start to break up, 4 to 6 minutes. Add the onion, celery, parsley, shallots, and garlic; cook, stirring, for 4 minutes. Add the bay leaves, peppercorns, salt, wine, and cold water to cover by at least 1 inch.

2. Bring to a boil, adjust heat to a brisk simmer, and cook for 45 minutes, skimming off froth as it collects on the surface.

3. Strain through a fine-mesh sieve and chill until the fat rises to the top and solidifies; discard the fat. Refrigerate for up to 3 days, or freeze for up to 4 months.

MEAT STOCK (BEEF, VEAL, LAMB, OR PORK)

We're giving one recipe for four stocks here, and don't get us wrong: Whatever you do, don't mix different kinds of bones in the same stock. Depending on your choice, this rich, dark stock is the base for countless soups. For the most part, try to match the kind of bones used in the stock with the meat in the final dish. The only exception is veal stock, which is so versatile, you can use it for any soup except a seafood variety. If you're only going to have one meat stock in your freezer, make it veal.

Makes about 2 quarts

4 pounds beef, veal, lamb, or pork bones (the meatier the better)
2 large yellow onions
1 leek, cleaned well and roughly chopped
6 stalks celery, roughly chopped
6 cloves garlic, peeled
2 large carrots, scrubbed and roughly chopped
3 ½ quarts cold water
3 bay leaves
½ bunch parsley
1 tablespoon tomato paste
3 cups dry red wine
2 tablespoons dried thyme
2 tablespoons black peppercorns

1. Preheat oven to 400°F.
2. Spread out the bones in a large roasting pan and roast, turning occasionally, until the bones start to brown, about 1 hour. Add the onions, leek, celery, garlic, and carrots, and continue to roast until the bones and vegetables are browned, 20 to 30 minutes.
3. Transfer the bones and vegetables to a large stockpot and add the water, bay leaves, parsley, and tomato paste.
4. Place the roasting pan on the stovetop over medium heat. (If the roasting pan is large, use 2 burners.) Pour the wine into the roasting pan and bring to a simmer, scraping up caramelized bits, about 4 minutes; add to the stockpot. Bring to a boil, and skim off the froth as it collects on the surface. Adjust heat to a simmer, add the dried thyme and peppercorns, and cook for 4 ½ to 5 hours.
5. Strain the stock through a fine-mesh sieve, and chill until the fat rises to the top and solidifies; discard fat. Refrigerate for up to 3 days, or freeze for up to 4 months.

VEGETABLE STOCK

Just because you're vegetarian doesn't mean your soups have to be bland. This base is mild, to be sure, but it nonetheless complements the fresh flavors of any meat-free soup.

Makes about 2 quarts

1 large yellow onion, trimmed and roughly chopped
1 large carrot, washed well and roughly chopped
2 stalks celery, washed well and roughly chopped
1 large parsnip, washed well and roughly chopped
2 corncobs, with or without kernels
1 tablespoon dried thyme
2 bay leaves
½ bunch parsley
4 cloves garlic, smashed
1 tablespoon black peppercorns
2 ½ quarts water

Place all the ingredients in a 4-quart stockpot, and bring to a boil over high heat. Adjust heat to a simmer, and cook for 30 minutes. Strain and refrigerate for up to 3 days, or freeze for up to 4 months.

STOCK TO ORDER

We've given some basic stock recipes, but there is plenty of room for addition, especially when you're making a stock for a specific dish. Here are ways to tailor your stock to some of the flavors of the world:

1. **Latin:** Add 2 teaspoons chili pepper, ½ cup cilantro leaves, and 1 teaspoon each cumin seeds and coriander seeds, toasted.
2. **North African:** Add 2 teaspoons North African Spice Mix (page 6) and a 1-inch piece of ginger, cut in half and smashed.
3. **Chinese:** Add a 1-inch piece of ginger, cut in half and smashed; 2 teaspoons Szechuan pepper; ½ cup cilantro; and 2 tablespoons soy sauce.
4. **Southeast Asian:** Add 1 stalk lemongrass, cut into 1-inch pieces and smashed; a 1-inch piece ginger, cut in half and smashed; 2 tablespoons fish sauce; 2 whole staranise; and ¼ cup fresh mint leaves.

Made for Each Other

RICE AND BEANS

WHY ARE **RICE** AND **BEANS** SO OFTEN PAIRED? Their textures and flavors seem made for each other, and their nutritional offerings match up nicely, too. For vegetarians, the combination of beans and rice provides all nine essential amino acids that the body needs. That's why rice-and-bean dishes are a staple in so many cuisines. From Latin America's yellow rice and black beans with cumin, to India's basmati and curried lentils, to the American South's spicy red beans and rice, this is a culinary match made, if not in heaven, pretty much everywhere else.

Like any healthy couple, though, each partner has its own identity; they certainly don't always have to go everywhere together. Rice, for its part, takes on many disguises—creamy in risotti, fluffy in pilafs, crispy in rice cakes, sweet in rice puddings. Rice recipes fill many a cookbook on their own.

Beans of countless varieties, meanwhile, pair up with everything from pasta for pasta e fagioli in Italy to sesame tahini for hummus in the Middle East. And they make amazing soups; witness black bean "liquor," the liquid that results from cooking black beans in water with a hint of garlic and cumin.

I know what you're thinking. Those beans, they take too long. Soaking overnight, cooking for hours—who has the time? You do, once you learn that you don't have to soak unless you want to, and that a good pot of beans is worth the effort.

Under Pressure

If you think pressure cookers are still those rattling dangerous things your mother used and told you to stay away from when you were a kid, think again. Today's pressure cookers are much safer, yet they work with the same time-saving magic they have always had.

But lest you get the idea that anything could be better cooked this way, keep this in mind: It can take up to 30 minutes to bring the cooker up to pressure, and more time to cool it again before opening. That makes this method inappropriate for anything that would normally cook in under a half-hour anyway, such as plain white rice. Oh, and don't even think about putting beautiful green vegetables in there unless the point is to reduce them to mush.

Save the pressure cooker for when it counts: long-simmering dishes such as beans, brown rice, or other tough grains, and meat stews such as chili. Just make sure to read all the instructions; even with safety features, you should still be careful.

MASTER BEAN RECIPE

DRIED BEANS are all over the place when it comes to cooking times, depending on their age and storage conditions. The navy beans we have and the navy beans you have could easily have been harvested years apart. The older the bean, the longer the cooking time. Beans stored in cool, dry places cook more quickly than those stored in hotter, more humid places. Thus, this recipe is purposefully vague. If you love beans, buy them in large quantities, and when you cook from a batch the first time, take note of cooking time for the next round.

Yields about 2 to 2 1/4 cups beans

1 cup dried beans, washed and picked over to remove any rocks or debris
1/2 teaspoon kosher salt

1. Place the beans in a small saucepot or pressure cooker and cover with cold water by 1 inch. Bring to boil or up to pressure over high heat; lower heat to medium-low and simmer, stirring occasionally, until the beans are as tender as needed, anywhere from 45 minutes to 2 1/2 hours. (Make sure if you're using a pressure cooker to cool it properly before opening to check the beans.) Add more water if it has all been absorbed before the beans are tender.

2. When the beans are almost done, add the salt and continue cooking until tender. They will keep, refrigerated in an airtight container, for up to 3 days.

CHICKEN, BEANS, AND RICE

I WAS LIVING IN San Francisco, right above the stereo system of a bar, and was broker than broke. (Kitchen work will do that to you.) Anyway, I ate this at least two or three times a week, just as is or rolled up with tortillas and cheese, or even—in a particularly flush week—with some sour cream. Like the best stews, this gets better every time you reheat it.

Serves 2 as an entrée

2 tablespoons canola oil
1 pound boneless skinless chicken thighs, cut into ½-inch pieces
Salt and freshly ground black pepper, to taste
1 medium-size yellow onion, peeled and chopped
4 cloves garlic, peeled and minced
1 cup dried pinto beans
1½ teaspoons chili powder
1½ teaspoons cumin seeds, toasted and ground
1½ teaspoons coriander seeds, toasted and ground
½ teaspoon kosher salt
4½ cups water *or* Chicken Stock (page 118)
1 cup long-grain rice
Juice of 1 lime (about 2 tablespoons)

1. Heat the oil in a 3-quart saucepan over medium-high heat. Season the chicken with salt and pepper; cook, stirring frequently, until it begins to brown, 5 to 7 minutes. Add the onion and garlic, and cook, continuing to stir, for 3 minutes. Add the beans, chili powder, cumin, coriander, salt, and water *or* stock and bring to a boil.

2. Adjust heat to a simmer and cook until the beans are barely tender; this could take from 30 minutes to 2 hours, depending on the quality and freshness of the beans.

3. Add the rice and mix thoroughly. Simmer, stirring frequently, until the rice is tender, 15 to 20 minutes more. Remove from heat. Stir in the lime juice, and season with salt and pepper.

RED BEANS, SAUSAGE, AND RICE

IT'S SO HARD to find good versions of this dish outside New Orleans. After too many research and development trips to the Big Easy—all work and no play, of course—I had to come up with my own recipe just to get my fix.

Serves 4 to 6 as a side dish or 2 to 3 as an entrée

2 cups dried red beans, washed and picked over to remove any rocks or debris
1 tablespoon Creole Seasoning (page 4)
1 teaspoon kosher salt
Cold water
2 tablespoons canola or peanut oil
2 links andouille sausage, cut lengthwise and then into ½-inch half-moons
6 cloves garlic, peeled and cut into thin slivers
1 green bell pepper, seeded and cut into ½-inch dice
4 scallions, cut crosswise into ¼-inch pieces, dark greens kept separate for garnish
Tabasco sauce, to taste
Salt and freshly ground black pepper, to taste
4 cups just-cooked white rice

1. Combine the beans, Creole Seasoning, and salt in a saucepan; add cold water to cover by 1 inch. Bring to a boil over high heat, stirring occasionally. Adjust heat to a simmer and cook, stirring occasionally, until the beans are very tender and falling apart. (This can take anywhere from 45 minutes to 2½ hours, depending on the age, type, and quality of the beans. Add more cooking water if necessary.)

2. Remove from heat and allow the beans to cool in the cooking liquid. (Can be prepared to this point up to 3 days ahead. Cover and refrigerate when the beans are cool.)

3. While the beans are cooling, heat the oil in a large saucepan over medium-high heat. Add the sausage and cook, stirring frequently, until the sausage begins to brown, 5 to 7 minutes. Lower heat to medium and add the garlic, green pepper, and white and light green parts of the scallions. Cook, stirring, until the green pepper begins to soften, 5 to 7 minutes. Add the beans and cook, stirring occasionally, until piping hot and slightly thickened, 5 to 7 minutes. Season with Tabasco, salt, and pepper.

4. To serve, put the rice in a large serving bowl or individual bowls; make a well in the center, top with beans, and garnish with scallion greens.

MADE the classical way, *feijoada,* the national dish of Brazil, includes a multitude of fresh, salted, and smoked meats and involves a long sequence of soaking, stewing, combining, removing, and arranging. Well, TREMONT 647'S executive chef, Matt Audette (whose 6-foot-3 stature earned him the nickname "L'il Audette"), came up with this, a simpler interpretation that stays true to the tradition. In true Brazilian style, serve with a round of Caipirinha (page 282).

MATT'S FEIJOADA

Serves 4 to 6 as an entrée

1 cup dried black beans
1 cup dried red beans
1 rack baby back ribs, cut into sections of 2 ribs each
1 pound pork butt, cut into 1-inch chunks
4 slices bacon, cut into ½-inch strips
2 bay leaves
1 tablespoon paprika
1 teaspoon kosher salt
10 cups water
2 tablespoons canola oil
5 large cloves garlic, peeled and minced
1 large white onion, peeled and minced
Salt and freshly ground black pepper, to taste
4 cups cooked white rice
3 oranges, peeled and sliced ¼ inch thick

1. Combine the beans, ribs, pork, bacon, bay leaves, paprika, salt, and water in an 8-quart pot over medium-high heat. Bring to a boil and adjust heat to a simmer; cook, stirring occasionally, until the meat and beans are tender, 1½ to 2 hours.

2. Meanwhile, heat the oil in a heavy-bottomed sauté pan over medium heat. Add the garlic and onion; cook, stirring frequently, until golden brown, 20 to 25 minutes. Remove from heat and set aside.

3. When the meat and beans are done, use tongs to remove the ribs from the pot; set aside. Scoop 1 cup of beans into the onions. With a potato masher, mash the mixture until fairly smooth; stir the mixture into the stew. Season generously with salt and pepper.

4. To serve, pile the rice on a large serving platter and make a large well in the center. Ladle the *feijoada* into the well. Arrange the ribs on top, and place the orange slices around the edges.

BAKED BLACK BEANS WITH GOAT CHEESE

MY FAVORITE goat cheese is Nunsuch, owned by a former nun (and great cheese maker) in New Hampshire. Its mildness perfectly offsets these spicy black beans, making them perfect for a party.

Serves 6 to 8 as a side dish

1 small ancho chili
½ cup hot water
2 teaspoons canola oil
1 large yellow onion, peeled and diced
1 green pepper, seeded and diced
4 cloves garlic, peeled and minced
1 tablespoon chili powder
1 tablespoon cumin seeds, toasted and ground
1 tablespoon coriander seeds, toasted and ground
1 teaspoon kosher salt
2 cups dried black beans
4 cups water *or* Chicken Stock (page 118) *or* Pork Stock (page 119)
Salt and freshly ground black pepper, to taste
½ cup goat cheese
¼ cup finely diced red onion
¼ cup minced cilantro leaves
Tortilla chips, for serving

1. In a small, dry sauté pan, toast the ancho chili until fragrant. Transfer to a small bowl, cover with ½ cup hot water, and let stand until softened, about 15 minutes. Drain the chili, reserving the liquid. Remove and discard the stem and seeds; mince the chili and set aside.

2. Heat the oil in a 4-quart stockpot or Dutch oven over medium-high heat. Add the onion and green pepper; cook, stirring frequently, until the vegetables start to brown, 15 to 20 minutes. Add the ancho chili, garlic, chili powder, cumin, coriander, and salt; cook for 1 minute, stirring constantly. Add the beans and water *or* stock, mixing and scraping the bottom of the pan, and bring to a boil.

3. Adjust heat to a simmer and cook, stirring occasionally, until the beans are very tender and the water is absorbed, 1½ to 2 hours. Season liberally with salt and pepper.

4. To serve, preheat oven to 350°F. Transfer the beans to an 8- or 9-inch cast-iron pan or casserole dish that can be used for serving. Crumble the goat cheese evenly over the beans, and sprinkle red onions on top. Bake until the cheese starts to brown, about 20 minutes. Remove from the oven and let cool for 15 minutes before garnishing with cilantro and serving with tortilla chips.

CHEESY SPICY RED BEANS

THIS IS GOOEY, sticky, and spicy. You won't be able to get enough of it—as a dip, or wrapped in a tortilla with some grilled chicken for a quick soft taco.

Serves 4 to 6

½ cup shredded sharp Cheddar cheese
¼ cup sour cream
2 garlic cloves, peeled and minced
2 teaspoons chili powder
1 teaspoon hot (smoked) paprika
Juice of 1 lime (about 2 tablespoons)
1 jalapeño *or* serrano pepper, seeded and minced
1 tablespoon masa harina
2 cups cooked, drained red kidney beans (see Master Bean Recipe, page 123)
Salt and freshly ground black pepper, to taste
2 tablespoons canola oil

1. Combine the cheese, sour cream, garlic, chili powder, paprika, lime juice, hot pepper, and masa in a medium-size mixing bowl. Using a rubber spatula or wooden spoon, fold the beans into the cheese mixture and season with salt and pepper.

2. When ready to serve, heat the oil in a large nonstick skillet. Add the bean-cheese mixture and cook, stirring frequently, for 3 to 5 minutes, or until the beans are hot throughout.

SPICY, SWEET, AND SOUR LENTILS

CALL IT anything but mild; between the chili peppers, apricots, honey, and vinegar, this dish is having a ball with flavors. Holding it all together are the ever-accommodating lentils and some nice, creamy yogurt.

Serves 4 to 6

2 tablespoons olive oil
2 cloves garlic, peeled and minced
2 jalapeño or serrano peppers, cored, seeds removed, and minced
1 small red onion, peeled and diced
1 teaspoon red pepper flakes
1 cup dried apricots, cut into 1/4-inch slices
1 tablespoon honey
1 cup dried green lentils
1/2 teaspoon kosher salt
3 cups water
1/4 cup freshly squeezed lemon juice (about 1 lemon)
1/4 cup red wine vinegar
Salt and freshly ground black pepper, to taste
1/2 cup plain yogurt

1. Heat the oil in a 2-quart saucepan over medium-high heat. Add the garlic and chilies and cook, stirring frequently, for 3 to 5 minutes or until the garlic turns golden. Add the onion and cook, stirring, for 2 minutes. Add the red pepper flakes, apricots, honey, lentils, salt, and water.

2. Bring to a boil, reduce heat to medium, and simmer until the lentils are tender but not mushy, about 30 minutes. Add the lemon juice and vinegar, and season with salt and pepper. Dollop with yogurt before serving.

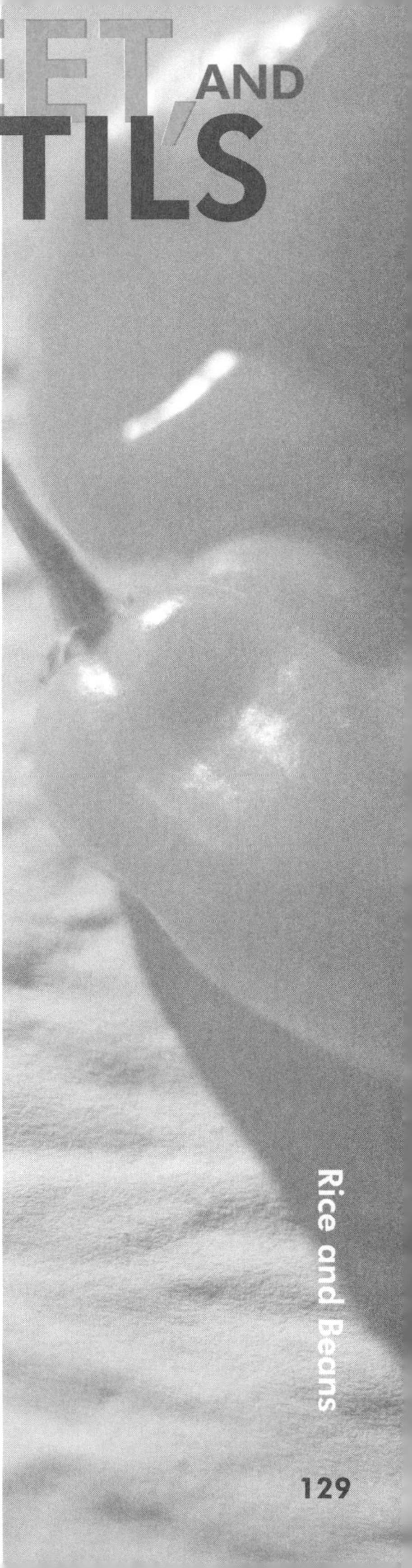

NORTH AFRICAN HUMMUS

ONE OF THE BEST THINGS about hummus is you don't have to bother cooking chickpeas, a.k.a. garbanzo beans. Unlike most beans, chickpeas retain their texture and flavor even when canned, so store-bought is fine. This hummus, which gets a boost of flavor from the North African Spice Mix, goes well with Za'tar Spiced Pita (page 131), Sesame Flatbread (page 237), lavash, or good old-fashioned toast.

Serves 4 as a side dish (makes about 2 cups)

1 (14-ounce) can chickpeas, drained
⅓ cup tahini paste, stirred well
¼ cup freshly squeezed lemon juice (about 1 lemon)
2 teaspoons North African Spice Mix (page 6)
2 cloves garlic, peeled
3 tablespoons extra-virgin olive oil
Salt and freshly ground black pepper, to taste

Place the chickpeas, tahini, lemon juice, North African Spice Mix, garlic, and olive oil in a food processor and purée until smooth. Season with salt and pepper.

ZA'TAR SPICED PITA

THESE JAZZED-UP PITA TRIANGLES just beg to be dipped into North African Hummus (page 130), but they're interesting enough to be eaten alone or as part of any crudité platter. They're spiced with za'tar, a powerful spice blend that you can find in Middle Eastern markets. Just in case you don't have any around, this recipe shows you how to make it from scratch.

Serves 4 to 6 as a side dish

1 tablespoon white sesame seeds
1 tablespoon sumac (found in Middle Eastern markets), or lemon zest
2 teaspoons cumin seeds, toasted and ground
1 teaspoon dried thyme
1 teaspoon dried marjoram *or* oregano
1 teaspoon kosher salt
3 tablespoons extra-virgin olive oil
4 (8-inch) loaves pita bread

1. Turn oven on broil with a rack set 4 to 6 inches from the top element.

2. Make the za'tar: In a small bowl, combine the sesame seeds, sumac, cumin, thyme, marjoram *or* oregano, and salt. Add the olive oil and blend well.

3. Arrange the pitas on a baking sheet and spread about 1 tablespoon za'tar evenly over each. Broil until puffed and deep golden brown, 2 to 4 minutes, watching carefully and rotating the pan halfway through to brown evenly. Cut into wedges, and serve.

BAKED BARBECUE WHITE BEANS

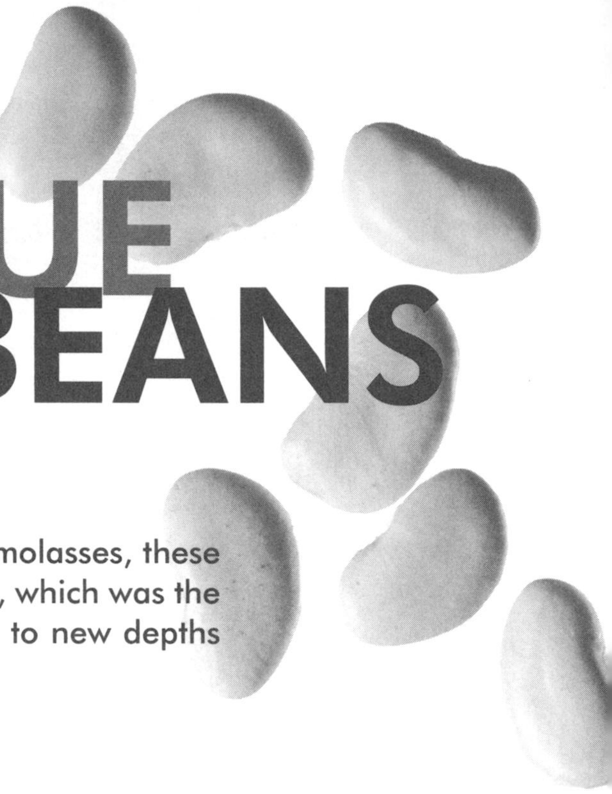

EVEN WITH the traditional bacon and molasses, these are a far cry from Boston baked beans, which was the point. Beer and barbecue sauce take these to new depths of flavor.

Serves 4 to 6 as a side dish

2 cups dried navy beans
About 4 cups water
1 medium-size yellow onion, peeled and cut into 1/4-inch dice
6 strips bacon, cut into 1/2-inch strips
1/3 cup dark molasses
1 tablespoon yellow mustard
1 cup Rolling Rock *or* other ale-style beer
1/2 cup UFO Social Club Barbecue Sauce (page 15) *or* commercial barbecue sauce
2 teaspoons kosher salt

1. Preheat oven to 350°F.
2. Place the beans in a 2-quart saucepan and add enough water (about 4 cups) to cover by 2 inches. Bring to a boil over medium-high heat, adjust heat to a simmer, and cook until the beans are tender, 20 to 45 minutes.
3. Strain the beans. Transfer to a 2-quart casserole dish and add the remaining ingredients; mix well. Bake, covered, until the beans are richly browned, 1 1/2 to 2 hours.

CABBAGE AND WHITE BEAN RAGOUT

A HEARTY, SOOTHING, slightly smoky soup that also makes a great base for pan-seared salmon, sautéed shrimp, or grilled and cut-up chicken breast. If you go the latter route, use about 2 pounds of meat.

Serves 4 to 6 as a soup or as an entrée with meat added

¼ pound bacon, sliced thin and cut into ¼-inch strips
1 medium-size yellow onion, peeled and cut into ¼-inch dice
4 cloves garlic, peeled and minced
2 stalks celery, cut into ¼-inch dice
1 bulb fennel, cored and cut into ½-inch dice, leafy top reserved for garnish
2 teaspoons cumin seeds, toasted and ground
2 teaspoons fennel seeds, toasted
1 tablespoon minced fresh rosemary
2 cups dried white beans
8 cups water *or* Veal *or* Pork Stock (page 119)
1 teaspoon kosher salt
½ head Savoy cabbage, cored and cut into ½-inch strips
Salt and freshly ground black pepper, to taste

1. Heat a 5-quart Dutch oven on low. Add the bacon and cook slowly until the fat is rendered. Add the onions and cook for 20 minutes, stirring occasionally, until the onions become soft.

2. Increase heat to medium-high. Add the garlic and cook for 1 minute, stirring frequently. Add the celery, fennel, cumin, fennel seeds, and rosemary; cook for 3 minutes, stirring frequently. Add the beans, water *or* stock, and kosher salt.

3. Bring to a boil and lower heat to medium. Simmer for 2 hours, stirring occasionally. Add the cabbage and simmer for 30 minutes or until the beans are tender. Season with salt and pepper.

4. Garnish ragout with feathery fronds from fennel top and serve immediately.

SIMPLIFIED CASSOULET WITH LAMB, CHICKEN, AND SAUSAGE

TRADITIONAL CASSOULET, as you Francophiles know, usually includes duck confit—that delectable meat cured in its own fat—and requires several hours of baking, then cooling, then more baking. That's all well and good for a cook who has a free day or so handy, but what about the rest of us? This stripped-down version suffices nicely, with hearty flavors that require a fraction of the time. (For extra richness, you could certainly add a few pieces of store-bought duck confit.)

Serves 4 to 6 as an entrée

2 tablespoons olive oil
½ pound lamb stew meat, or leg, cut into 1-inch cubes
¾ pound skinless and boneless chicken thighs, quartered
Salt and freshly ground black pepper, to taste
5 strips bacon, cut into ½-inch pieces
2 links (about 8 ounces) garlic pork sausage, cut into 3 pieces each
1 large carrot, peeled and cut into ¼-inch dice
1 medium-size yellow onion, peeled and cut into ¼-inch dice
2 stalks celery, cut into ¼-inch dice
4 large garlic cloves, peeled and minced
1 pound (about 2 cups) dried flageolet or navy beans
2 teaspoons dried thyme
½ teaspoon ground allspice
6 cups Chicken Stock (page 118)
2 cups dry white wine
1 bay leaf
1 teaspoon kosher salt
2 tablespoons tomato paste

1. Heat the oil in a heavy-bottomed, 6-quart saucepan over medium-high heat. Season the lamb and chicken with salt and pepper; sear the meat, stirring frequently, until it is lightly browned, about 5 to 7 minutes.

2. Transfer the meat to a bowl and lower heat to medium. Add the bacon and sausage; cook, stirring occasionally, until the meat is lightly browned, 5 to 7 minutes. Add the carrot, onion, celery, and garlic; cook until the onions soften, about 5 minutes, stirring and scraping up caramelized bits stuck to the bottom of the pan.

3. Return the lamb and chicken to the pan, along with beans, thyme, allspice, stock, wine, bay leaf, and salt. Bring to a boil, then adjust heat to a simmer; cook, stirring occasionally, for about 2 hours.

4. When the beans are firm but close to done, gently stir in the tomato paste. Continue cooking until the beans are soft enough to mash between your fingers, about 30 to 45 minutes more. Remove and discard the bay leaf, season with salt and pepper, and serve.

WHITE BEAN SPREAD WITH GARLIC CONFIT

THIS SIMPLE PURÉE can play one of two roles: Spread it on a plate as a bed for grilled steak or pork chops, or use it as a dip for pita chips, your favorite cracker, or a crusty baguette.

Serves 6 to 8 as an appetizer or side dish

6 tablespoons olive oil
4 large cloves garlic, peeled
2 1/4 cups cooked white beans, drained (see Master Bean Recipe, page 123)
2 teaspoons minced fresh summer savory *or* rosemary
Juice of 1 lemon (about 1/4 cup)
Salt and freshly ground black pepper, to taste

1. Put the oil and garlic in a small saucepan over low heat. Simmer, stirring occasionally, until the garlic turns golden brown and is easily pierced with a fork, about 45 minutes. Set aside.

2. In a food processor, purée the beans, garlic and oil, savory *or* rosemary, and lemon juice until smooth. Season with salt and pepper, and serve. (This spread can be made ahead and refrigerated for up to 5 days, but let it come to room temperature before serving.)

SAFFRON RISOTTO WITH CRAB AND GREEN OLIVES

YOU'VE HEARD the saying, or something like it: The only way to make risotto is to hire an old Italian cook to stand at the stove all day stirring. Now we know what an exaggeration that was. Sure, you have to be careful, stirring occasionally and adding the liquid in batches, but risotto isn't nearly as laborious as we were taught. Now that the burden's been lifted, we have time to play with the ingredients and flavors; this one gets a nice zip with lemon crab, brown butter, and olives.

Serves 4 as a side dish

3 cups Chicken Stock (page 118)
2 teaspoons saffron threads
8 tablespoons butter, divided
1 fennel bulb, cored and julienned
1 small yellow onion, peeled and chopped
2 cloves garlic, peeled and minced
1 teaspoon kosher salt
1 cup arborio rice
1 cup dry white wine
12 large green olives, pitted and chopped (about 1/2 cup)
1/4 cup grated Parmesan cheese
Salt and freshly ground black pepper, to taste
6 sage leaves, roughly chopped
Juice of 1 lemon (about 1/4 cup)
8 ounces fresh lump crabmeat

1. Bring the stock to a boil in a saucepan over medium-high heat. Turn heat to very low and add the saffron, stirring to dissolve. Keep mixture hot.

2. Meanwhile, heat 2 tablespoons of the butter in a heavy-bottomed, 3-quart saucepan over medium-high heat. Add the fennel, onion, garlic, and salt; cook, stirring occasionally, until the fennel and onions are translucent, 8 to 10 minutes. Add the rice, stirring to coat the grains with butter.

3. Stir in the wine and adjust heat to a simmer. Cook, stirring occasionally, until almost all the liquid is absorbed. Add enough hot stock to cover the surface of the rice and stir it in; simmer, stirring occasionally, until almost all the liquid is absorbed. Add more stock to cover the surface of the rice and stir it in; simmer, adjusting heat as necessary so that the liquid absorbs into the rice (rather than evaporates away). Repeat until the rice is al dente and almost all the stock has been added, 15 to 18 minutes.

4. When the rice is al dente, remove from heat. Stir in the olives and cheese, and season with salt and pepper. Keep warm while you prepare the topping.

5. To make the crab topping, heat the remaining 6 tablespoons butter in a small sauté pan over medium-high heat. Add the sage and cook until the butter begins to brown, 3 to 5 minutes. Remove from heat and stir in the lemon juice and crabmeat. Season with salt and pepper.

6. If the risotto has thickened while standing, stir in any remaining hot stock to loosen it. Divide the risotto among serving bowls, and top each with the crab mixture.

HAM AND ENGLISH PEA RISOTTO

OF THE MANY CLASSIC combinations we've grown up with, ham and peas are a favorite. Here, wonderfully flavorful Smithfield ham from Virginia combines with a fresh pea purée to produce a hearty take on an elegant risotto. And don't fret if risotto intimidates you; it's not as hard as you've heard.

Serves 4 to 6 as a side dish

2 cups water
1 teaspoon kosher salt
1 cup English peas, removed from pod, or frozen peas
2 1/2 cups Chicken Stock (page 118), unsalted or low-sodium if canned
1 tablespoon olive oil
1 tablespoon butter
1/2 pound Smithfield or other country-cured ham, cut into 1/4-inch by 1-inch julienne
1 small yellow onion, peeled and cut into 1/2-inch dice
1 cup arborio rice
1/4 cup finely grated Parmigiano-Reggiano cheese
1 teaspoon fresh thyme leaves
Salt and freshly ground black pepper, to taste

1. Bring the water and salt to a boil in a saucepan over high heat. Add the peas and cook for 2 minutes; strain and rinse with cold water until completely cool. Drain well, transfer to food processor, and purée. (Note: If using frozen peas, do not blanch; just thaw and purée.)

2. In the same saucepan, bring the stock to a boil over medium-high heat; turn heat to very low and keep hot.

3. Heat the olive oil and butter in a heavy-bottomed 2-quart saucepan over low heat. When the butter is melted and hot, add the ham and onion; cook, stirring occasionally, until the onion softens, about 15 minutes.

4. Raise heat to medium-high and add the rice, stirring to coat with oil. Add enough hot stock to cover the surface of the rice and stir it in; simmer, stirring occasionally, until most of the liquid is absorbed. Add more stock to cover the surface of the rice and stir it in; simmer, adjusting heat as necessary so that the liquid absorbs into the rice (rather than evaporates away). Repeat until all the stock has been used and the rice is al dente (not mushy, but with a slight bite in the very center), 15 to 18 minutes. Add the pea purée, stirring until well blended.

5. Remove pan from heat and stir in the cheese and thyme. Season with salt and pepper.

THE LONG AND THE SHORT OF RICE

Rice feeds the world, and there are thousands of varieties cultivated in more than 100 countries. Here's a broad look at the 3 major categories of white rice, based on grain size:

Short grain: Arborio, sushi rice, Valencia. High starch content, moist and viscous, grains stick together. Used for sushi and risotto, short-grain rice becomes creamy when liquid is added gradually.

Medium grain: Carolina Gold, and some other American varieties. Fluffy after cooking, grains remain more separate than short grain but stickier than long grain, with more starch.

Long grain: Basmati, jasmine. Firmer, less sticky, fluffier, and drier than other types. When cooked, grains are separate and denser than medium grain. Basmati, an Indian variety now grown domestically, is more expensive. Jasmine is the fragrant rice from Thailand.

ROSEMARY ARANCINI

WHAT COULD BE BETTER than a fried risotto ball filled with cheese? We start here with a recipe for rosemary risotto, but these are also perfect for leftover risotto, and both the Ham and English Pea Risotto (page 137) and Saffron Risotto (page 136) work well here, too. *Arancini,* whose name means "little oranges," are also known as *supplì al telefono* because they look like telephone wires when you pull them apart and the cheese strings between the two halves. Whatever the name, they give us yet another reason to thank the Italians—as if we needed another.

Serves 4 to 6 as a side dish or appetizer (makes 10 to 15 balls)

2 1/4 cups Chicken Stock (page 118) *or* water
1 tablespoon olive oil
1 tablespoon butter
2 garlic cloves, peeled and minced
2 teaspoons minced fresh rosemary
1 cup arborio rice
1 cup dry white wine
1 teaspoon kosher salt
Salt and freshly ground black pepper, to taste
1/4 cup grated Parmesan cheese
Canola oil, for deep-frying
2 cups yellow cornmeal
6 ounces mozzarella *or* fontina cheese, cut into 1/2-inch cubes
1 cup marinara sauce

ROSEMARY ARANCINI continued

1. Bring the stock *or* water to a boil over medium-high heat. Turn heat to very low and keep hot.

2. Heat the olive oil and butter in a heavy-bottomed 2-quart saucepan over medium-low heat. When the butter is melted and hot, add the garlic and rosemary; cook, stirring occasionally, for 3 minutes.

3. Raise heat to medium and add the rice, stirring to coat. Cook for 2 minutes, stirring often.

4. Stir in the wine and salt and adjust heat to a simmer. Cook, stirring occasionally, until almost all the liquid is absorbed. Add enough hot stock *or* water to cover the surface of the rice and stir it in; simmer, stirring occasionally, until almost all the liquid is absorbed. Add more stock to cover the surface of the rice and stir it in; simmer, adjusting heat as necessary so that the liquid absorbs into the rice (rather than evaporates away). Repeat until the risotto is just beyond al dente (slightly mushy and overcooked) and all the stock has been used, about 20 minutes.

5. Stir in Parmesan cheese, season with salt and pepper to taste, and refrigerate until cold. (To speed cooling, spread the risotto on a baking sheet or platter. Risotto may be made up to 3 days ahead.)

6. When the risotto is completely cold, pour the canola oil into a saucepan to a depth of 2 inches. Place over medium-high heat, and bring the oil to 350°F on a deep-fry thermometer, or until a grain of rice sizzles vigorously on the oil's surface. (If the rice sinks or bubbles slowly, the oil is not hot enough.)

7. While the oil is heating, put the cornmeal in a shallow bowl. Scoop up about ¼ cup of risotto and flatten it in your palm to form a ¼-inch-thick disk. Place a cube of cheese in the center of the disk, and mold the risotto around it to enclose the cheese, forming a 1- to 1½-inch ball. Repeat with the remaining risotto and cheese cubes.

8. When all the risotto is formed into balls, roll the balls in the cornmeal until thoroughly coated. Place the coated *arancini* on a plate beside the pan of hot oil, along with a long-handled, slotted spoon and a paper towel-lined baking sheet or platter.

9. Using the slotted spoon, lower a few *arancini* into the hot oil, stirring occasionally to keep them apart. Fry until golden brown, 6 to 8 minutes, then transfer to paper towels to drain. Season the hot *arancini* with coarse salt and allow to cool slightly. Serve with hot marinara on the side for dipping.

LEMONGRASS RICE WITH LAMB

JUST TRY to stop eating this fragrant, tangy, and downright addictive dish, which combines vegetables, starch, and protein all in one. If it's spring, definitely try using pea tendrils for their unique crunch; spinach fills in admirably the rest of the year.

Serves 2 to 3 as an entrée or 4 to 6 as an appetizer

2 cups water
1 stalk lemongrass, cut into 1-inch pieces and smashed
2 tablespoons canola oil
1 pound boneless leg of lamb, cut into ½-inch cubes
Salt and freshly ground black pepper, to taste
3 cloves garlic, peeled and minced
1 tablespoon peeled and minced ginger (about 1-inch piece)
1 small red onion, peeled and cut into ¼-inch dice
1 cup jasmine rice
¼ pound pea tendrils *or* baby spinach leaves, roughly chopped
½ cup Vietnamese Cilantro Dipping Sauce (page 16)
1 tablespoon black sesame seeds *or* toasted white sesame seeds

1. Combine the water and lemongrass in a saucepan over medium-high heat and bring to a slow simmer.

2. Heat the oil in a 3-quart saucepan over high heat. Season the lamb with salt and pepper and add it to the pan; sear, stirring occasionally, until the meat begins to brown, 5 to 7 minutes. Turn heat to medium and add the garlic and ginger; cook for 2 minutes, stirring frequently. Add the onion and rice; cook, stirring from the bottom of the pan, for 2 minutes.

3. Strain the simmering lemongrass water over the lamb mixture and mix well, scraping up juices and bits stuck to the pan. Bring to a boil, stir again, adjust heat to a simmer, and cover the pan. Cook gently until the liquid is absorbed and the rice is fluffy and tender, 15 to 18 minutes.

4. Put the pea tendrils in a large mixing bowl, and spoon the lamb mixture on top. Pour the dipping sauce over the top, and toss to combine. Garnish with sesame seeds.

BASMATI RICE
WITH SPICY APPLE RELISH

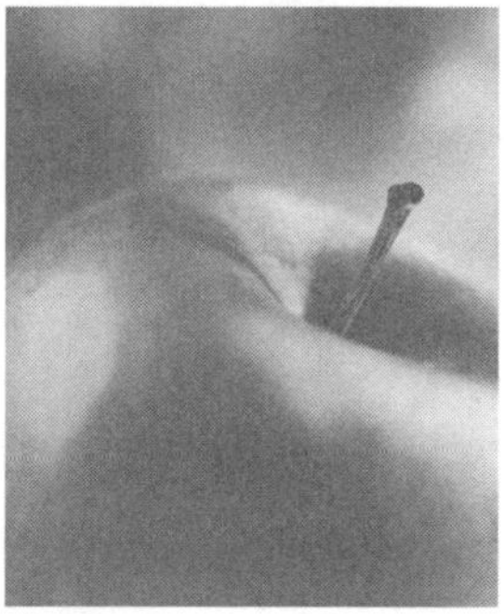

SOME of our favorite heady flavors liven up already spectacular basmati rice, creating a sensational dish, perfect with grilled lamb. The only downside is that when you taste this for seasoning, you might not be able to stop, and there goes your dinner party. Come to think of it, you might double this recipe for just that reason.

Serves 4 to 6 as a side dish

1 cup dried apples, cut into ½-inch-wide strips
½ cup orange juice
½ cup dry red wine
2 teaspoons peeled and minced ginger (about ½-inch piece)
6 mint leaves, chopped
1 teaspoon minced fresh rosemary
1 teaspoon cumin seeds, toasted and ground
1 red bell pepper, seeded and cut into ¼-inch dice
½ cup toasted and roughly chopped pecans
¼ cup roughly chopped cilantro leaves
2 tablespoons red wine vinegar
1 tablespoon extra-virgin olive oil
½ teaspoon red pepper flakes
Salt and freshly ground black pepper, to taste
2 cups hot, cooked basmati rice

1. In a heavy-bottomed, 1½-quart saucepan, combine the apples, orange juice, wine, ginger, mint, rosemary, and cumin. Bring to a boil, adjust heat to a simmer, and cook for 10 minutes. Strain the mixture, discarding the liquid. Allow the apples to cool for 5 minutes.

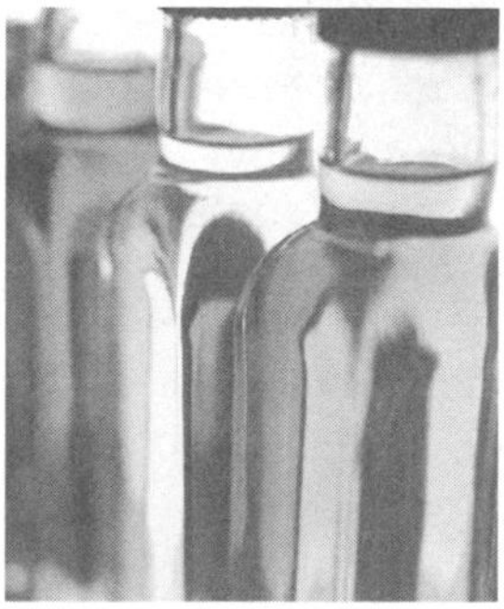

2. While the apples are cooking, combine the bell pepper, pecans, cilantro, vinegar, oil, and red pepper flakes in a medium-size bowl. Add the apples, and mix well. Season with salt and pepper.

3. To serve, spoon the hot rice into bowls and spoon the relish on top.

THIS IS BASED on one of my favorite Indian foods, which is chicken biryani. This recipe is great with chicken or lamb and hot peppers, or simply served by itself as a vegetarian entrée.

CURRIED BASMATI RICE WITH ALMONDS AND GOLDEN RAISINS

Serves 4 as a side dish

2 tablespoons olive oil
1 cup chopped yellow onion
1 red pepper, stemmed, cored, and cut into ¼-inch dice
1 tablespoon peeled and minced garlic
1 tablespoon minced fresh ginger
1 cup basmati rice
2 tablespoons Tremont 647 Curry (page 8)
½ teaspoon kosher salt
1 cup unsweetened coconut milk
1 cup water
½ cup golden raisins
½ cup slivered almonds, toasted to golden brown
¼ cup red wine vinegar
¼ cup chopped cilantro leaves
Salt and freshly ground black pepper, to taste

1. In a heavy-bottomed saucepan over medium-high heat, heat the oil until hot but not smoking. Add the onions and peppers; sauté, stirring occasionally, until the onions are transparent, 7 to 9 minutes. Add the garlic and ginger, and cook for 1 minute. Stir in the rice, curry, and salt; continue to cook, stirring constantly, until the rice looks dry and separate, about 2 minutes.

2. Add the coconut milk, water, and raisins, and mix well. Reduce heat to low, cover, and simmer for 18 to 20 minutes or until all the liquid has been absorbed, stirring only once halfway through.

3. Remove from heat, and add the almonds, vinegar, cilantro, and salt and pepper. Serve hot.

GREEN RICE

HERE'S a simple way to take rice to new heights: by adding color and garlicky flavor from Parsley Purée (page 23), cilantro, and peppery arugula leaves—oh, yeah, and some chili peppers. This green-flecked rice makes the perfect accompaniment to Roasted Chicken Breasts with Cranberry-Orange Sauce (page 227) or Easy Grilled Pork Chops with Sweet Peas and Corn (page 225).

Serves 6 to 8 as a side dish

2 poblano or Anaheim chili peppers, seeded and roughly chopped
1 small yellow onion, peeled and roughly chopped
¼ lightly packed cup arugula, washed well
1 teaspoon kosher salt
3 ½ cups water, divided
1 tablespoon olive oil
2 cups white rice
½ cup Parsley Purée (page 23)
¼ cup minced cilantro leaves
Salt and freshly ground black pepper, to taste

1. Combine the peppers, onion, arugula, salt, and 1 cup of the water in a food processor or blender; process until smooth.

2. Heat the oil in a heavy-bottomed 3-quart saucepan over medium-high heat. Add the rice, stirring to coat with the oil. Continue to cook, stirring frequently, until the rice starts to look dry again, about 2 minutes. Add the remaining water and the chili pepper purée, and mix well. Bring to a boil, cover the pan, and adjust heat to a simmer. Cook until the rice is tender but not mushy, 15 to 18 minutes.

3. Make the Parsley Purée while the rice is cooking. When the rice is done, gently fold in the Parsley Purée and minced cilantro. Season with salt and pepper, and serve.

A PERFECT USE for leftover rice, and easy (and fast) enough for a kid's meal. Of course, just about anything goes nicely with a good fried rice, so we've listed an optional way to turn this into an entrée by adding leftover meat. Serve with Coriander-Lime-Glazed Swordfish Kebabs (page 205).

Serves 4 as a side dish or 2 as an entrée with meat

2 tablespoons canola oil, divided
1 egg, beaten
2 cloves garlic, peeled and minced
2 tablespoons peeled and minced ginger
1 small carrot, peeled and cut into ¼-inch dice
2 cups cubed leftover chicken, pork, *or* shrimp (optional)
4 cups cooked white *or* brown rice, cooled
2 scallions, cut diagonally into 1-inch pieces
½ cup bean sprouts
¼ cup soy sauce
Freshly ground black pepper, to taste

1. Heat 1 tablespoon of the oil in a heavy-bottomed sauté pan over medium-high heat. Add the egg and cook, stirring, until scrambled and starting to brown but still moist. Transfer to a cutting board and chop. Set aside.

2. Add the remaining oil to the pan over medium-high heat. Add the garlic, ginger, carrots, and leftover meat if using. Cook, stirring frequently, until the carrots start to brown, 3 minutes. Add the rice and cook, stirring, until heated through, 3 minutes. Stir in the scallions, bean sprouts, soy sauce, and chopped egg. Season with pepper. Serve hot or cold.

GINGER FRIED RICE

IF YOU DIDN'T KNOW that dirty rice is a good thing, then you're obviously not from the South, where this is a classic, named for the dark flecks in it. In Louisiana, the meat is often ground, but we like it in bigger chunks for variety. What should you serve it with? More pork, of course, such as Basil-Crusted Pork Tenderloin with Bacon Corn Relish (page 215), or with Blackened Salmon with Lemon-Scallion Butter (page 188).

DIRTY RICE WITH PORK

Serves 4 to 6 as a side dish

3 tablespoons peanut *or* canola oil
1 pound pork picnic shoulder *or* Boston butt, cut into ½-inch cubes
Salt and freshly ground black pepper, to taste
1 red bell pepper, seeded and cut into ¼-inch dice
1 green bell pepper, seeded and cut into ¼-inch dice
1 stalk celery, minced
1 medium-size yellow onion, peeled and cut into ¼-inch dice
8 cloves garlic, peeled and thinly sliced
2 tablespoons Creole Seasoning (page 4)
½ teaspoon kosher salt
2 teaspoons cumin seeds, toasted and ground
¼ pound chicken livers, minced
2 tablespoons balsamic vinegar
3 cups cold water *or* Pork Stock (page 119)
1½ cups white rice

1. Heat the oil in a heavy-bottomed 4-quart stockpot or Dutch oven over high heat. Season the pork with salt and pepper. Working in batches to avoid overcrowding the pan, sear the meat, stirring frequently, until the meat is browned, 12 to 15 minutes.

2. Add the peppers, celery, and onion; cook, stirring, until softened and the moisture evaporates, 8 to 10 minutes. Add the garlic, Creole Seasoning, salt, and cumin; cook for 1 minute more, stirring constantly. Add the chicken livers and balsamic vinegar, and cook, stirring and scraping the bottom of the pan, for 2 minutes. Add the water *or* stock and mix well. Bring to a boil.

3. Stir in the rice, return to a boil, and turn heat to low. Cover and simmer gently until the rice is tender and the liquid is absorbed, 18 to 20 minutes. Fluff with a fork and season with salt and pepper.

FALL RICE PILAF WITH BUTTERNUT SQUASH

SQUASH, an uncommon ingredient in rice, gives this pilaf a creamy richness. When combined with the so-called baker's spices (cinnamon, allspice, and nutmeg), the result is a dish that so convincingly brings to mind that breezy golden heartiness of autumn, you may feel compelled to plan a leaf-peeping drive after lunch.

Serves 4 to 6 as a side dish

3 tablespoons olive oil, divided
2 stalks celery, cut into ¼-inch dice
1 small yellow onion, peeled and cut into ¼-inch dice
1 small carrot, peeled and cut into ¼-inch dice
2 garlic cloves, peeled and minced
1 cup butternut squash, peeled and cut into ¼-inch dice
½ cup toasted and minced pecans
2 tablespoons minced fresh sage
1 teaspoon ground cinnamon
¼ teaspoon ground allspice
¼ teaspoon grated nutmeg
1 teaspoon kosher salt
1½ teaspoons ground ginger
1½ cups white rice
3 cups water
½ cup dried cranberries
Salt and freshly ground black pepper, to taste

1. Preheat oven to 350°F.

2. Heat 2 tablespoons of the oil in a heavy-bottomed sauté pan over medium-high heat. Add the celery, onion, garlic, and carrot; cook, stirring frequently, until the vegetables begin to brown, 8 to 10 minutes. Add the squash, pecans, sage, cinnamon, allspice, nutmeg, salt, and ginger; cook, stirring constantly, for 1 minute. Transfer the vegetables to a 2-quart baking dish.

3. Return pan to heat and add the remaining oil. Add the rice, stirring to coat with oil; cook, stirring frequently, until the rice starts to turn golden, 3 to 5 minutes. Transfer the rice to the baking dish with the vegetables.

4. Return pan to heat and add the water and dried cranberries. Bring to a boil and pour over the rice mixture, stirring well. Cover tightly with a lid or foil, and bake undisturbed until the rice is tender and the water is absorbed, 30 to 40 minutes. Fluff the rice with a fork and season generously with salt and pepper.

SWEET POTATO RICE CAKE

THIS MAKES a beautiful centerpiece dish, especially since its layered colors make it so pretty to cut into. The beauty goes beyond mere looks, though. One bite of the creamy sweet potatoes and rice, combined with the crunchy almonds and sweet raisins, and your guests will understand that all too easily.

Serves 6 as a side dish

- 2 tablespoons olive oil, divided
- 1 red bell pepper, seeded and minced
- 2 garlic cloves, peeled and minced
- 1 tablespoon peeled and minced ginger (about 1-inch piece)
- 2 cups white rice
- ½ cup slivered almonds, toasted
- 2 teaspoons turmeric
- 2 teaspoons North African Spice Mix (page 6) *or* 2 teaspoons cumin seeds, toasted and ground
- 1 teaspoon kosher salt
- 2 teaspoons freshly ground black pepper
- 1 cup raisins
- 4 scallions, cut into ¼-inch slices
- 1 large sweet potato (about 1 pound), peeled and cut into ¼-inch-thick slices
- 4 ½ cups boiling water

1. Preheat oven to 350°F.

2. Heat 1 tablespoon of the oil in a well-seasoned 12-inch cast-iron skillet (or heavy nonstick skillet) over medium-high heat. Add the bell pepper, garlic, and ginger; cook, stirring frequently, for 2 minutes. Add the rice, almonds, turmeric, and North African Spice Mix *or* cumin, salt, and pepper; cook for 1 minute, stirring to coat the rice with oil. Transfer the rice mixture to a mixing bowl. Add the raisins and scallions, and stir to combine.

3. Return the empty pan to medium-high heat and add the remaining olive oil. Carefully and quickly arrange the sweet potatoes in the pan, starting in the center and forming slightly overlapping, concentric circles. Spoon the rice mixture evenly on top.

4. Pull out the oven rack and place the skillet on the rack. Gently pour the boiling water over the rice, and carefully push in the oven rack. Bake for 20 minutes, covered, then uncover and bake another 10 minutes. Remove the skillet from the oven and allow to sit 15 minutes.

5. Place a large serving platter face down over the skillet and quickly invert the pan onto the plate. Serve hot or cold.

SOMETIMES the best dishes are the simplest. In that vein, few combinations beat coconut milk and jasmine rice, especially when ginger and sesame oil are in the mix, too. Serve this with any good roasted pork or chicken, Kung Pao Shrimp with Cashews and Mangoes (page 195), or with our version of **TREMONT 647'S** signature dish, Atlantic Cod in Banana Leaves (page 182).

Serves 4 as a side dish

2 teaspoons canola oil
2 teaspoons sesame oil
2 tablespoons peeled and minced fresh ginger (about 2-inch piece)
1 (14-ounce) can unsweetened coconut milk, mixed well
1¼ cups cold water
1 teaspoon kosher salt
1½ cups uncooked jasmine rice
Salt and freshly ground black pepper, to taste

1. Heat the canola and sesame oils in a 2-quart saucepan over medium heat. Add the ginger and cook, stirring frequently, for 3 to 4 minutes, or until the ginger becomes fragrant and golden. Add the coconut milk and water, and bring to a boil.

2. Add the rice and salt, and stir well; reduce heat to low, and cover. After 5 minutes, stir again, replace cover, and continue to cook for 13 to 15 minutes or until the rice is tender but not mushy. Adjust seasoning with salt and pepper. Fluff with a fork and serve.

COCONUT JASMINE RICE

ASIAN CHICKEN AND RICE SALAD

AS WONDERFULLY light as this is fresh, it's even better the next day, when the flavors have melded and it becomes a prime lunch-box candidate. Substitution possibilities abound: Use beef, pork, or shrimp instead of the chicken, pound for pound, or use broccoli or fresh corn kernels instead of the snow peas.

Serves 2 to 3 as an entrée or 4 to 6 as a side dish

1 tablespoon olive oil
1 tablespoon toasted sesame oil
1 pound boneless, skinless chicken breasts, cut into bite-size pieces
Salt and freshly ground black pepper, to taste
2 tablespoons peeled and minced fresh ginger (about 2 inches)
1 cup sugar snap peas, strings removed and cut in half diagonally
2 cups cooked white rice
1 small red bell pepper, cored and cut into ½-inch dice
1 small red onion, peeled and cut into ¼-inch dice
½ cup Sweet-and-Spicy Soy Glaze (page 28)
2 tablespoons soy sauce
1 tablespoon sesame seeds
¼ cup cashews, toasted and chopped
¼ cup minced chives

1. Heat the olive and sesame oils in a heavy-bottomed sauté pan over medium-high heat. Season the chicken with salt and pepper and add to the pan. Cook, stirring occasionally, for 3 minutes. Add the ginger and snap peas; cook, stirring frequently, until the chicken is done, 3 to 5 minutes more. Transfer the chicken to a large mixing bowl, and let cool to room temperature.

2. When the chicken is cool, add the rice, red pepper, red onion, glaze, and soy sauce, and toss to mix well. Garnish with sesame seeds, cashews, and chives, and adjust seasoning with salt and pepper. Will keep for up to 3 days in the refrigerator.

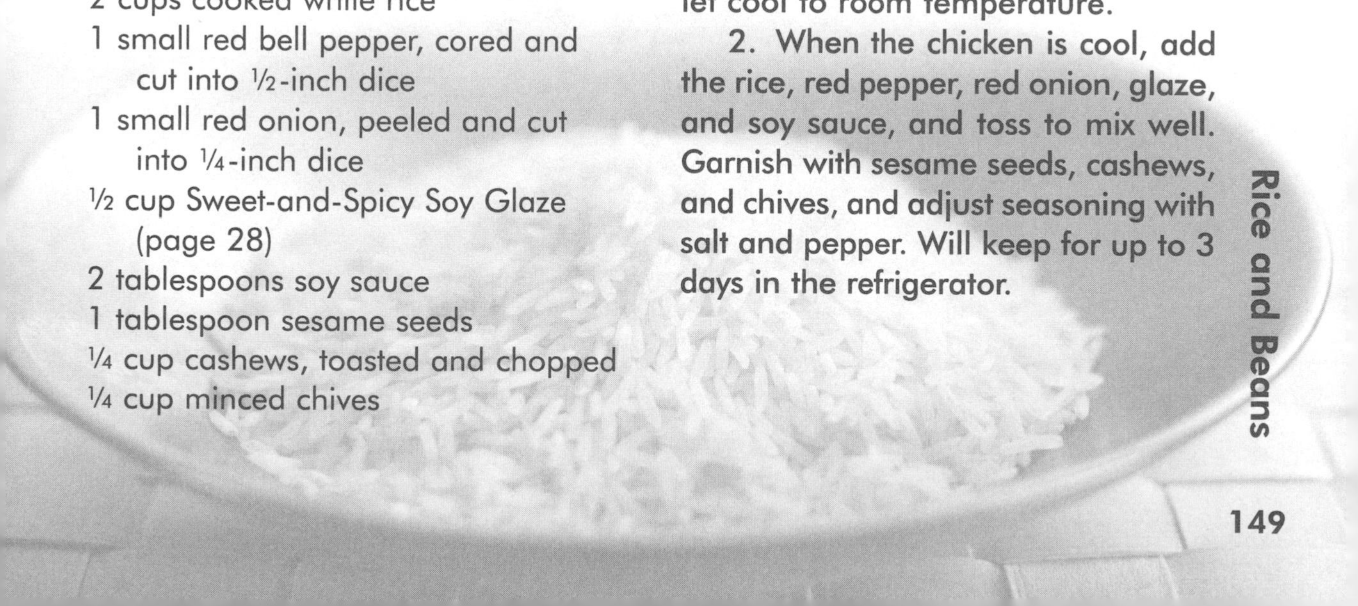

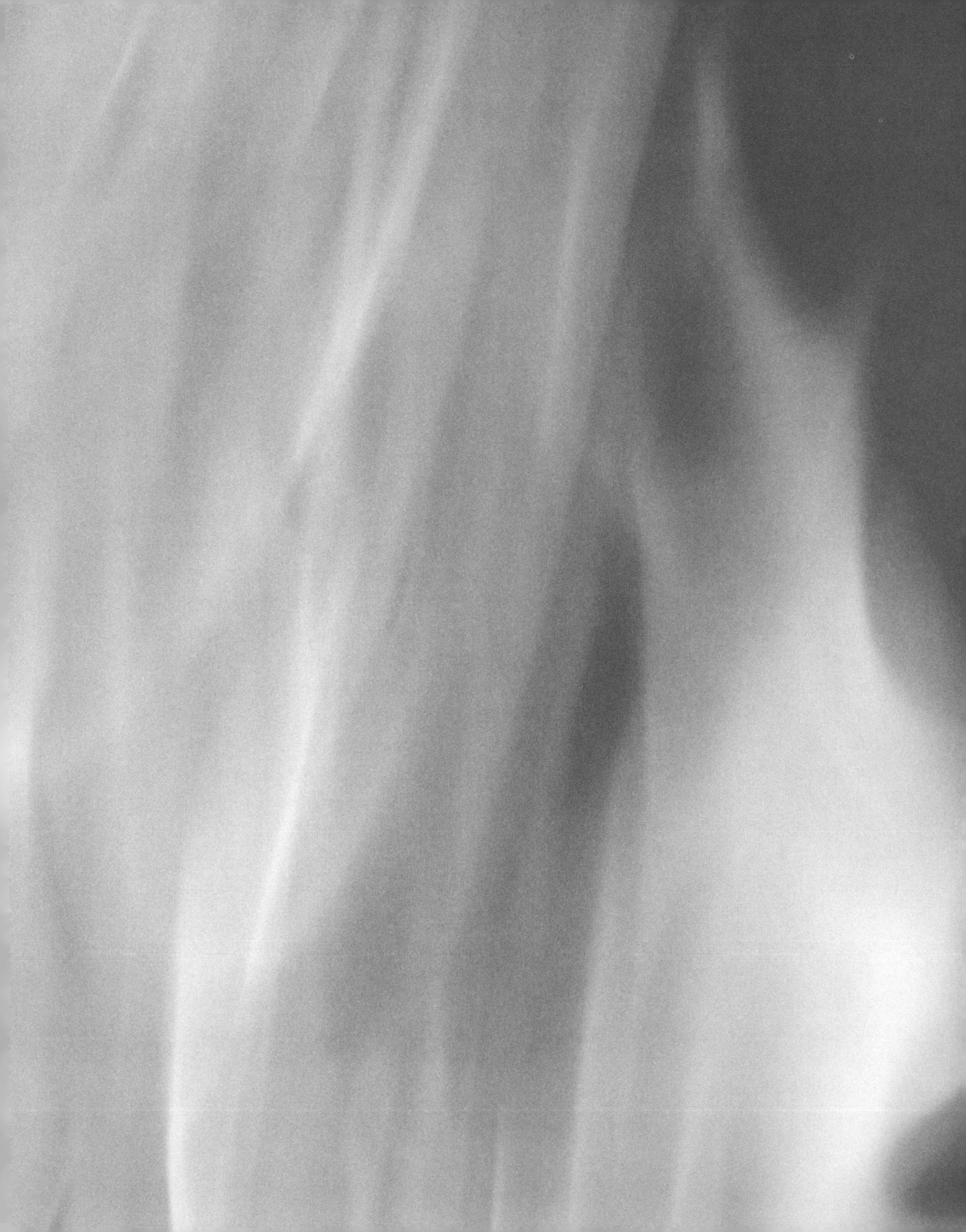

Going Green

VEGETABLES

DID YOUR MOTHER BOIL **BROCCOLI** WITHIN AN INCH OF ITS LIFE? Too many did. No wonder so many kids of the '60s and '70s grew up hating broccoli!

Thank God, we Americans have finally learned how to cook vegetables. We lightly steam, blanch, or grill tender broccoli, asparagus, and peppers and reserve braising, stewing, and boiling for tougher products like collard greens and chard, techniques Europeans used long before we finally got a clue. We have access to many more varieties of fresh vegetables from around the world than ever before, and we're cooking them with respect.

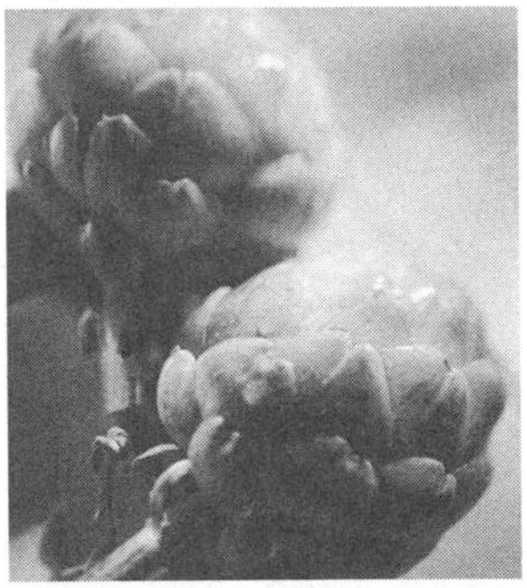

Vegetables are crucial, of course, because they are one of the most important pieces of our diet, providing the fiber we need for digestion and the nutrients and carbohydrates that we need for energy. Vegetables are our fuel.

In writing menus, I'm always trying to come up with vegetarian (or at least vegetable-centered) dishes that a meat lover like myself would love to eat, a meal that is both rich and satisfying.

None of the following recipes are entrées, but in true tapas style, all you have to do is throw a few of them together and you can have a wholly vegetarian meal, or with touches of meat here and there. And fear not: Except for potatoes, you'll find very little boiling.

going green

COLLARD GREENS WITH SMOKED TURKEY BUTT

INSTEAD of the fatty ham hock, we like to use the much leaner smoked turkey butt (also called turkey tail), which still gives collards a hearty flavor and becomes tender much more quickly. Smoked turkey legs work well, too, as do yesterday's grilled pork chops or roast chicken. Be sure to save the "pot likker," which tastes every bit as good as the greens; it's perfect for sopping up with Stacy's Spicy Corn Bread (page 239) or Fluffy Southern Biscuits (page 243).

Serves 4 to 6 as a side dish

2 medium-size yellow onions, peeled and diced large
6 cloves garlic, peeled and minced
2 (about 6 ounces each) smoked turkey butts (tails)
2 bunches collard greens, washed and cut into
  1- to 1½-inch strips
2 quarts cold water
½ cup cider vinegar
10 dashes, or to taste, Tabasco sauce
Salt and freshly ground black pepper, to taste

1. In a large, heavy-bottomed saucepan over medium-high heat, combine the onions, garlic, turkey butts, collard greens, and water. Bring to a boil, then lower heat to medium; simmer, stirring occasionally, until the collards are tender and the meat has fallen off the bone, about 45 minutes.

2. Remove pan from heat. Add the vinegar, and season to taste with Tabasco and salt and pepper.

BLUE-CHEESE-STUFFED AND BAKED ARTICHOKES

WHEN I WAS A KID and my father would boil artichokes, I'd dip the leaves in mayo but wouldn't touch the heart because I thought it sounded "gross." Later, thankfully, I discovered not only the joys of artichoke hearts, but the advantages of steaming over boiling. Here, the dip is built right in, and it's a tangy, rich, cheesy delight.

Serves 2 (generously) as an appetizer or side dish

2 large artichokes
2 sprigs fresh thyme or 1 teaspoon dried thyme
2 teaspoons peppercorns
1 tablespoon capers
½ cup blue cheese (about ¼ pound)
½ cup goat cheese (about ¼ pound)
¼ cup finely minced red onion
3 tablespoons dried bread crumbs, divided
Salt and freshly ground black pepper, to taste
1 lemon, quartered
Kosher salt

1. Preheat oven to 425°F.
2. Cut off the stem of each artichoke to create a flat base and then cut off the top ¼ inch. With kitchen scissors, cut off all the pointed tips of the leaves. Use a knife to trim off the bottom outer leaves.
3. Set the artichokes upright in a steamer over water. Add the thyme and peppercorns to the steamer, cover, and steam for 25 to 40 minutes or until an outer leaf pulls off easily and its meat is tender.
4. Meanwhile, combine the capers, blue cheese, goat cheese, red onion, and 1 tablespoon of the bread crumbs in a small mixing bowl; mix well. Season with salt and pepper.
5. When the artichokes are tender, remove them from the steamer and let cool upside down to drain excess water. When cool to the touch, scoop out the hairy interior choke with a melon baller and discard.
6. Place the artichokes on a baking sheet, hollowed side up. Fill with the cheese mixture, then sprinkle the remaining 2 tablespoons bread crumbs on top, and bake for 15 minutes.
7. To serve, place each artichoke in a shallow soup bowl. Squeeze the lemon wedge over exposed edges of the artichokes and sprinkle with kosher salt.

HONEY-GLAZED CARROTS WITH ALMONDS AND YOGURT

ZING! The combination of tangy yogurt, sweet honey, and crunchy almonds make these Greek-style carrots pretty irresistible, either as a cold salad or warm side dish. They're a perfect accompaniment to grilled lamb chops.

Serves 4 to 6 as a side dish

- 2 quarts salted water
- 1½ pounds carrots, peeled and cut into 2-inch-by-¼-inch sticks (about 6 cups)
- 2 tablespoons olive oil
- 2 cloves garlic, peeled and minced
- ¼ cup toasted and ground almonds
- 3 tablespoons honey
- 3 tablespoons butter
- 1 teaspoon minced fresh oregano
- ¼ cup plain yogurt
- 2 tablespoons fresh-squeezed lemon juice (about ½ lemon)
- Salt and freshly ground black pepper, to taste
- 8–10 mint leaves, julienned

1. Bring 2 quarts salted water to a boil. Add the carrots, return to a boil, and blanch for 1 minute. Drain, cool quickly in ice water or under cold running water, and drain again very well.

2. Heat the oil in a large, heavy-bottomed sauté pan over high heat. Add the carrots and cook, stirring frequently, until they start to brown, 6 to 8 minutes. Reduce heat to medium and add the garlic; cook, stirring constantly, for 1 minute. Reduce heat to low and add the almonds, honey, butter, and oregano. Cook, stirring gently, until the butter melts and the carrots look glazed.

3. In a small bowl, combine the yogurt and lemon juice; mix well and set aside.

4. Season the carrots generously with salt and pepper, and garnish with mint and drizzles of the yogurt mixture.

SWEET-AND-SOUR CIPOLLINI

IF YOU'VE never tried cipollini, those saucer-shaped pearl onions from Italy, this introduction will have you hooked. They're already on the sweet side, and they hold together beautifully when roasted, qualities that make them well-suited for our treatment, which results in a rich, deep glaze and an almost candied texture. Serve with such roasted dishes as Apple-Stuffed Game Hens (page 223).

Servers 4 to 6 as a side dish

1½ pounds cipollini or pearl onions, peeled
2 tablespoons extra-virgin olive oil
¼ cup balsamic vinegar
2 tablespoons brown sugar
½ teaspoon fennel seeds, coarsely ground
½ cup oil-cured black olives, pitted and roughly chopped
Salt and freshly ground black pepper, to taste
6–8 large basil leaves, julienned
2 tablespoons minced fresh parsley

1. Set oven rack in the top position. Preheat oven to 450°F.

2. In a heavy roasting pan just large enough to hold the onions in a single layer, toss the onions with the oil and spread them out. Roast on the top rack until the onions start to brown on the bottom, about 15 minutes; then turn over the onions and roast until the second side is golden brown, about 10 minutes.

3. While the onions are roasting, in a small bowl combine the vinegar, brown sugar, and fennel, and mix well to dissolve the sugar. When the onions are browned, scatter the olives around them and pour the vinegar mixture on top. Stir gently to coat.

4. Return pan to oven and roast, stirring every few minutes, until the onions are glazed and very tender, 5 to 10 minutes. Season with salt and pepper. Serve warm or chilled, garnished with basil and parsley just before serving.

When made right, onion rings are unbeatable. Forget potato chips; who can eat just 1 of these? Alongside barbecued meat or grilled or broiled steak, and served with ketchup, buttermilk dressing, or Blue Cheese Vinaigrette (page 20), these crispy little devils will be gone in a flash.

PEPPERY ONION RINGS

Serves 4 to 6 as a side dish

1 large yellow onion, sliced into rings as thin as possible
2 cups buttermilk
2 tablespoons paprika, divided
2 teaspoons cayenne pepper, divided
1½ cups yellow cornmeal
1½ cups all-purpose flour
1 tablespoon ground black pepper
2 teaspoons dried thyme
1 tablespoon chili powder
4–6 cups canola *or* peanut oil
Salt, to taste

1. In a medium-size mixing bowl, separate the onion slices into rings. Add the buttermilk, 1 tablespoon of the paprika, and 1 teaspoon of the cayenne. Toss to combine, cover, and refrigerate for at least 1 hour, or up to 12 hours.

2. In another large bowl, combine the remaining paprika and cayenne with the cornmeal, flour, pepper, thyme, and chili powder; mix well.

3. In a medium-size saucepan, pour the oil to a depth of at least 2 inches (leaving at least ½ inch of room at the top). Turn heat to medium-high and heat the oil to 350°F.

4. While the oil is heating, drain the onions well, discarding the liquid. Place the onions, flour mixture, and a plate covered with several layers of paper towels beside the stove.

5. Test the oil by dropping a piece of onion into it; it should sizzle vigorously and immediately on the surface without sinking or burning. When it is hot, add about ¼ of the onions to the flour mixture, tossing to coat. Lift out, lightly shaking off excess flour, and carefully add to the oil.

6. As the onions fry, use tongs to separate and move them around in the oil. Fry until the onions are golden brown, 4 to 6 minutes. Transfer to a towel-lined plate, allowing excess oil to drip back into the pan. Season generously with salt, and repeat until all the onions have been fried. Serve immediately.

WINE-BRAISED CABBAGE

THIS is more than the mere sum of its parts. The wine and vinegar infuse the cabbage with tang, while the bacon perfumes it with smoke. Alongside pork roast or grilled pork chops, it's just the thing for a wind-whipped night when you need something warm.

Serves 4 as a side dish

8 strips top-quality bacon, cut into ¼-inch strips
1 large head Savoy cabbage (about 1½ pounds), cored and cut into 1-inch strips
4 cups Gewurztraminer *or* fruity chardonnay
2 tablespoons cider vinegar
1 teaspoon fresh thyme leaves
4 tablespoons cold butter, cut into 8 pieces
Salt and freshly ground black pepper, to taste

1. In a heavy-bottomed sauté pan large enough to hold the cabbage, cook the bacon over medium heat, stirring occasionally, until browned, about 10 minutes.

2. Add the cabbage, wine, vinegar, and thyme. Raise temperature to medium-high, stirring occasionally. When the wine boils, lower heat to medium and simmer, stirring occasionally, until the wine has reduced by ⅔, about 20 minutes. Continue to simmer, stirring frequently to avoid burning, until most of the wine evaporates, about 10 minutes more.

3. When the cabbage looks almost dry, remove pan from heat and add the cold butter, stirring briskly but gently until the butter has melted. Season with salt and pepper, and serve immediately. (Note: Reheat leftovers gently. To make ahead, stop after the wine has evaporated and refrigerate until use; then slowly warm up the cabbage until hot, add the butter, stir until melted, season, and serve.)

SWEET AND SPICY MASHED SQUASH

WHO SAYS Thanksgiving dishes have to be either bland on the one hand or syrupy sweet on the other? Put this on your holiday table, and your guests will forget they ever ate anything that had tiny little marshmallows on top.

Serves 4 to 6 as a side dish

1 pound butternut squash, peeled, seeded, and cut into 1-inch chunks
1 large russet potato, peeled and cut into 1-inch chunks
2 tablespoons butter
4 sage leaves, minced
1 jalapeño or serrano chili, seeded and minced (optional)
2 cloves garlic, peeled and minced
½ cup half-and-half
1 teaspoon ground cinnamon
2 tablespoons brown sugar
Salt and freshly ground black pepper, to taste

1. Put the squash and potatoes in a large saucepan and cover by 1 inch with salted cold water. Bring to a boil and cook until the squash and potatoes are tender but not mushy, about 20 minutes.
2. While the potatoes and squash are cooking, melt the butter in a small saucepan over medium-high heat. Add the sage and chili pepper, and cook, stirring frequently until the butter begins to brown and smell nutty, 4 to 6 minutes. Add the garlic and cook, stirring, for another 2 minutes.
3. When the squash and potatoes are tender, drain very well and return to the hot, empty pan. Add the browned butter mixture along with the half-and-half, cinnamon, and brown sugar, and mash thoroughly by hand. Season with salt and pepper.

FENNEL'S intoxicating anise flavor makes it one of our favorite vegetables, shaved very thin when raw as a crunchy salad ingredient or left thicker and roasted or braised until tender. This dish goes the latter route, combining it with salty anchovies and delicate pine nuts to create a perfect accompaniment to Italian-Style Meat Loaf (page 211) or any other roasted meat or Italian entrée.

1. Preheat oven to 350°F.

2. Cut each fennel bulb into 8 wedges, so that each wedge is held together by a piece of the core. Arrange the wedges on a baking sheet or in a roasting pan, and drizzle with 1 tablespoon olive oil. Roast for 15 minutes, turn over the wedges, and roast until the fennel starts to brown, about 10 minutes more. Remove the fennel from the oven and raise the temperature to 425°F.

ROASTED FENNEL WITH ANCHOVIES AND PINE NUTS

Serves 4 as a side dish

- 2 bulbs fennel, tops removed
- 1/4 cup olive oil, divided
- 1/2 cup pine nuts, toasted
- 8 anchovy fillets
- 8 large leaves fresh basil
- 2 cloves garlic, peeled
- 1/2 teaspoon freshly ground black pepper
- 1/4 teaspoon red pepper flakes

3. While the fennel is roasting, combine the remaining oil, the pine nuts, anchovies, basil, garlic, black pepper, and red pepper flakes in a food processor or blender. Pulse to form a coarse paste.

4. Transfer the roasted fennel to a large mixing bowl and add the anchovy mixture, tossing gently to coat and using a spoon if necessary to scoop the mixture from the bottom of the bowl and spread onto the wedges. Return the wedges, cut-side up, to the roasting pan, spooning any remaining purée on top. Bake until the fennel is tender and the topping is browned, 15 to 20 minutes.

WASH OR WIPE?

Since mushrooms are so spongy, resist the urge to soak them, no matter how dirty they seem, or they'll wind up soggy. But that doesn't mean you can't give them a quick rinse if they really need it—just don't let them sit in water, and dry them off as quickly as possible. For the most part, however, slightly dirty mushrooms should be gently wiped clean. You can use a mushroom brush, but we find a damp paper towel is just as effective.

ROASTED PORTOBELLO MUSHROOM AND WILTED SPINACH

WE WANTED a substitute for the classic steak side of creamed spinach. Rather than cooking the spinach until tender and creaming it, this recipe merely wilts it and combines it with meaty roasted mushrooms. Alongside a porterhouse or T-bone (medium-rare, please), it's heavenly.

Serves 4 to 6

3 large portobello mushrooms, wiped clean
Salt and freshly ground black pepper, to taste
2 tablespoons olive oil
4 sage leaves, julienned
2 cloves garlic, peeled and minced
1/4 pound flat-leaf spinach, washed, tough stems removed, and leaves roughly chopped
1/4 cup coarse bread crumbs or croutons
1/4 cup oil-cured black olives, pitted and chopped
2 tablespoons balsamic vinegar

1. Preheat oven to 425°F.

2. Separate the mushroom caps from the stems, discarding the bottom half of each stem. Cut each cap into 6 wedges, and julienne the remaining stems. Sprinkle with salt and pepper. Transfer to a shallow roasting pan, drizzle with the oil, sprinkle with the sage leaves and garlic, and roast for 15 minutes. Use a spatula to turn over the mushrooms, and roast 7 minutes more.

3. Remove pan from oven, add the spinach, and toss to combine.

4. Transfer the mixture to a serving bowl. Add the bread crumbs, olives, and vinegar; toss with the mushrooms to combine. Season with salt and pepper.

A Cut Above

Of the many knife cuts we know, one of our favorites is the chiffonade, which results in curly strands. Feel free to try this anytime we call for a green leafy vegetable or large herb to be julienned, shredded, or chopped, especially for raw garnish.

Here's how to do it: Stack the washed and dried leaves on top of one another, and roll tightly lengthwise as if you were making a cigarette. Holding the roll on one end, cut thin slices from the other end, working your way down.

GRILLED ASPARAGUS WITH BACON

WHEN IT'S THE SEASON, look no further than your grill for an easy side dish. Vegetarians, take heart: Substitute shaved Parmigiano-Reggiano cheese for the bacon bits, and you're in business.

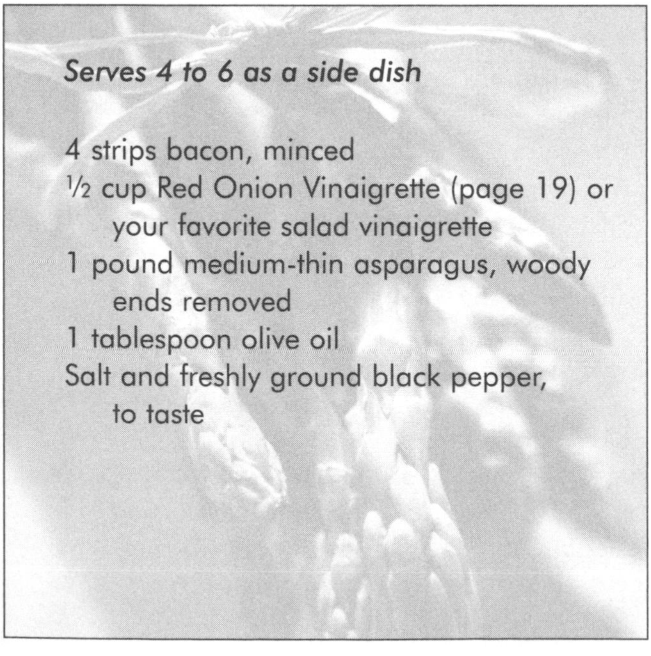

Serves 4 to 6 as a side dish

4 strips bacon, minced
½ cup Red Onion Vinaigrette (page 19) or your favorite salad vinaigrette
1 pound medium-thin asparagus, woody ends removed
1 tablespoon olive oil
Salt and freshly ground black pepper, to taste

1. Prepare a medium-hot fire in a grill.
2. While the grill is heating, put a heavy-bottomed sauté pan over medium heat. Add the bacon and cook, stirring occasionally, until brown and crunchy, 7 to 10 minutes. Drain on paper towels and transfer the bacon to a small bowl.
3. On the stove or in the microwave, warm the vinaigrette slightly and set aside.
4. In a mixing bowl, combine the asparagus with the oil, and the salt and pepper, and toss to combine. When the grill is medium-hot (you cannot keep your hand 5 inches above the grates for more than 3 or 4 seconds), use tongs to arrange the asparagus on the grill, perpendicular to the grates. Grill until lightly charred, rolling frequently for even browning, for 5 to 7 minutes. Transfer to a serving plate.
5. Spoon the warmed vinaigrette on top, sprinkle with the bacon bits, and serve.

THESE AREN'T dried so much as concentrated. The tomatoes shrivel up but still retain some moisture and seem to pack even more flavor than they started with. They're great for snacking, but also for adding to sauces, using on top of salads, mixing with cured olives, or tossing with pasta and Parmigiano-Reggiano cheese.

SLOW-ROASTED TOMATOES

Makes about 2 cups

10 tomatoes of any variety, cut in half lengthwise
2 tablespoons extra-virgin olive oil
2 teaspoons cumin seeds, toasted and ground
2 teaspoons fresh rosemary, minced
2 teaspoons kosher salt
2 teaspoons freshly ground black pepper

1. Preheat oven to 225°F.
2. Toss together all the ingredients in a mixing bowl.
3. Put the tomatoes cut-side up on a rack set on a baking sheet; bake for 6 to 8 hours or until they are shriveled and about ¼ inch thick. (If you want them drier, remove the skins halfway through.)
4. Remove and let cool to room temperature. The tomatoes can be stored in an airtight container for up to 1 week in the refrigerator.

CREOLE CARAMELIZED CORN AND SWEET PEPPERS

FEW MARRIAGES are as perfectly secure as that of corn and butter, but every relationship needs spicing up now and then. Brown both the corn and butter, add the Creole Seasoning and sweet bell pepper, and you've got yourself a full-flavored side dish for grilled pork or chicken or a great topping for a grilled steak.

Serves 4 as a side dish

2 tablespoons olive or canola oil
Kernels from 6 ears of corn (about 3 cups)
2 cloves garlic, peeled and minced
1 tablespoon butter
1 red bell pepper, seeded and cut into ¼-inch dice
2 teaspoons Creole Seasoning (page 4)
Salt and freshly ground black pepper, to taste
Tabasco sauce, to taste (optional)

1. Heat the oil in a heavy, preferably cast-iron, skillet over high heat. Add the corn and garlic; cook, stirring frequently, until the corn starts to brown, about 4 to 6 minutes. (Kernels may pop; be careful of splatters.)

2. Add the butter, red pepper, and Creole Seasoning; cook for 2 minutes, continuing to stir. Season with salt and pepper, and a few splashes of Tabasco if you dare.

OFF THE COB

Fresh corn is a wonder, and as much as we love grilling it on the cob slathered with butter, sometimes you want those kernels. Here's the easiest, safest way to do it:

After husking and desilking the cobs, make sure they and your hands are dry. Cut off the end of each cob. Hold a cob in the palm of your non-dominant hand, cut-end up, keeping your fingers less than halfway wrapped around the cob, and resting one end of the cob on the cutting board. Using a sharp cook's knife, swipe off the kernels of the exposed side of the cob, keeping the knife pressed as tightly to the cob as possible to avoid waste. Repeat, turning the cob, until all the kernels are removed.

Braised Pumpkin with Curry

THIS FALL DISH has big enough flavors to stand alone as a vegetarian entrée, or to hold up its end of the bargain as a side dish to grilled lamb or Curried Chicken Skewers (page 41).

Serves 4 to 6 as a side dish

½ cup dry red wine
¼ cup raisins
¼ cup dried apricots, cut into ¼-inch strips
3 tablespoons olive oil
1 tablespoon peeled and minced fresh ginger (about ½-inch piece)
2 cloves garlic, peeled and minced
1 large yellow onion, peeled and cut into ¼-inch dice
1 red bell pepper, seeded and cut into ¼-inch dice
1 serrano (hotter) *or* jalapeño (milder) chili, seeded and minced
2 pounds pumpkin (about ½ medium-size sugar pumpkin) *or* butternut squash, peeled, seeded, and cut into 1-inch chunks
1 tablespoon Tremont 647 Curry (page 8)
2 tablespoons butter
½ cup hot Chicken Stock (page 118) *or* water
Salt and freshly ground black pepper, to taste
½ cup chopped fresh cilantro leaves

1. Preheat oven to 400°F.

2. Combine the wine, raisins, and apricots in a medium-size bowl. Set aside.

3. Heat the oil in an oven-safe, heavy-bottomed sauté pan over medium heat. Add the ginger and garlic; cook, stirring frequently, until fragrant but not brown, about 2 minutes. Raise heat to medium-high and add the onions, bell pepper, chili, and pumpkin *or* squash; cook, stirring frequently, until the pumpkin starts to brown, 3 to 5 minutes.

4. Add the wine and dried fruit mixture, Tremont 647 Curry, and butter; cook, stirring, for 1 minute. Add the hot stock *or* water, cover the pan, and bake until the pumpkin can easily be pierced with a fork, 10 to 12 minutes. Season with salt and pepper and sprinkle with cilantro.

CRISPY PLANTAIN CAKES

PLANTAINS, a starchier, less sweet variety of banana, are used in savory dishes throughout Latin America, Africa, and the West Indies. We like them mashed, sometimes made into chips, but best of all, allowed to ripen (and therefore to get a bit sweeter) and formed into these cakes, which you can fry up for a hearty side dish with roasted meats such as Yucatan Roasted Pork (page 210).

Serves 8 as a side dish (makes about 2 dozen 2-inch cakes)

2 pounds (about 3 large) very ripe plantains, peeled and mashed
1 small red onion, peeled and minced
3/4 cup fresh corn kernels (about 1–2 large ears) or canned or frozen corn, drained well
1/4 cup chopped fresh cilantro leaves
3 garlic cloves, peeled and minced
1 tablespoon red wine vinegar
1 1/2 teaspoons cumin seeds, toasted and ground
1 teaspoon kosher salt
1/4 teaspoon freshly ground black pepper
1 cup instant masa harina
1/2 cup canola oil
1 cup sour cream

1. In the bowl of an electric mixer, combine the plantains, onion, corn, cilantro, garlic, vinegar, cumin, salt, and pepper. Beat on high speed for 30 seconds until well blended, then gradually add the masa (about 1/2 cup) until the mixture forms a stiff batter. Spread the remaining masa on a plate.

2. With slightly wet hands, form the batter into 1 1/2-inch balls. Roll the balls in the masa and flatten each ball into a 2-inch circle.

3. Meanwhile, heat the canola oil in a large cast-iron or heavy-bottomed sauté pan over medium-high heat. When the oil is sizzling hot, add cakes, working in batches as necessary to avoid crowding the pan. Fry until deep golden brown on both sides, 1 to 2 minutes per side, and transfer to paper towels to drain. Sprinkle with additional salt, and allow the cakes to stand for at least 5 minutes before serving. Serve with sour cream.

EGGPLANT CHUTNEY

CHUTNEY is usually limited to condiment status; like ketchup or salsa, it's meant to be spooned on grilled meat or used as a dip. This chutney, though, is so hearty that it can stand on its own—well, on the side, anyway—with roasted chicken or pork.

Serves 4 to 6 as a side dish (makes about 3 cups)

1 tablespoon olive oil
1 small yellow onion, peeled and cut into ½-inch dice
1 teaspoon peeled and minced fresh ginger (about ½ inch)
1 teaspoon kosher salt, divided
1 medium-size eggplant (about 1 pound), peeled and cut into ½-inch chunks
1 clove garlic, peeled and minced
1 cup tomato juice
1 teaspoon Ethiopian Spice Mix (page 5)
Juice of 1 lime (about 2 tablespoons)
1 packed teaspoon light brown sugar
¼ cup roughly chopped fresh mint leaves
¼ cup roughly chopped fresh parsley
Salt and freshly ground black pepper, to taste

1. Heat the oil in a heavy-bottomed sauté pan over medium-high heat. Add the onion, ginger, and ½ teaspoon of the salt. Cook, stirring occasionally, until the onions are brown, 15 to 20 minutes.

2. While the onions are cooking, set a colander over a large plate. Toss the eggplant and remaining salt together in a colander, and cover with another plate and a heavy jar or other weight. Let sit until the onions are ready, then rinse with cold water and gently squeeze out extra liquid. (This helps remove extra bitterness from the eggplant.)

3. When the onions are brown, reduce heat to medium-low and add the eggplant, garlic, tomato juice, and Ethiopian Spice Mix. Cook, stirring occasionally, until the eggplant is very tender, even mushy, about 15 to 20 minutes. Add the lime juice and brown sugar, and cook, stirring, for 5 minutes more.

4. Remove from heat and stir in the mint and parsley. Season with salt and pepper.

MASHED SWEET POTATOES WITH SAUSAGE

MEAT AND MASHED POTATOES are such a classic pairing; why not let them get even more intimately acquainted? This dish's hint of Latin flavors means it goes nicely with roasted or barbecued pork.

Serves 6 to 8 as a side dish

1 large sweet potato (1½ pounds), peeled and cut into 1-inch chunks
4–6 small Yukon gold potatoes (1 pound), peeled and cut into 1-inch chunks
1 tablespoon canola oil
2 links spicy Italian sausage or chorizo, casings removed
6 cloves garlic, peeled and minced
2 teaspoons cumin seeds, toasted and ground
1 teaspoon chili powder
½ cup half-and-half
2 tablespoons butter
Salt and freshly ground black pepper, to taste

1. Put all the potatoes in a large saucepan and cover by 1 inch with cold, salted water. Bring to a boil and cook until the potatoes are tender and easily pierced with a fork, 20 to 25 minutes. Drain well.

2. Meanwhile, heat the oil in a large, heavy-bottomed sauté pan over medium-high heat. Add the sausage and cook, stirring frequently to crumble the meat, until the sausage is cooked through and lightly browned, 7 to 10 minutes. Add the garlic and spices, and cook, stirring, for 1 minute. Add the half-and-half and butter, quickly scraping up any juices stuck to the pan, and remove from heat.

3. Strain the potatoes and transfer to the sauté pan with the sausage. With a large fork or potato masher, mash thoroughly. Season generously with salt and pepper.

IF YOU'RE A FAN of Korean food, you're most likely also a fan of kimchi, that pungent, fermented vegetable dish that gives its flavor so generously to whatever you serve it with. We use it for Kimchi Soup with Shrimp (page 101), but it's wonderful on its own with a side of white rice, or stirred into any Asian-style dish that you think could use an extra punch. Be forewarned: This is powerful stuff, and not for delicate palates.

FOUR-DAY KIMCHI

Makes about 4 cups

1 head Napa cabbage, cut into 1-inch strips
1 large carrot, peeled and julienned
1 red pepper, cored, seeded, and julienned
1 green pepper, cored, seeded, and julienned
1 stalk lemongrass, cut crosswise into thirds
1 red onion, peeled and julienned
2 scallions, white and light green parts only, cut into 1-inch pieces
½ cup chili garlic paste
½ cup salt

1. Combine all ingredients in very large bowl, 10 quarts or more, or work in batches if you're using a smaller bowl. Mix well. Transfer to a large stockpot and cover with a plate that will fit into the pot and sit on top of the vegetables. Top with weight, such as a jug of water, to press, then cover with a garbage bag and seal as tightly as possible. Store in a cool, dark, dry place such as a lower cabinet or basement, and leave undisturbed for 4 days.

2. Remove lemongrass, and transfer kimchi and liquid to a clean glass container and refrigerate for up to 2 weeks, stirring every 2 days or so until vegetables have pickled and softened.

DEEP-FRIED GREEN BEANS

WE WERE SKEPTICAL when we first heard of it, but indeed, frying gives green beans a unique, wrinkly texture and dark green color, and even seems to seal in and concentrate the flavor. One taste, and you'll be a convert.

Serves 4 to 6 as a side dish

Vegetable oil, for frying
1 pound green beans, washed, ends snipped, and dried well
½ cup Soy-Curry Glaze (page 27)
½ pound bean sprouts
1 carrot, peeled and julienned
3 scallions, stems removed, chopped
¼ cup toasted and ground peanuts
6 cilantro sprigs

1. In a deep skillet, add 1½ to 2 inches of oil and heat over medium-high heat until it reaches 375°F.

2. Add the green beans (in batches to avoid overcrowding) and fry, stirring occasionally, for 5 to 7 minutes or until they begin to brown and become wrinkled. Remove with a slotted spoon and drain on paper towels.

3. If the glaze is cold, reheat in microwave. Combine the bean sprouts, carrot, and scallions in a large mixing bowl. Add the green beans and toss with the Soy-Curry Glaze. Garnish with the toasted nuts and cilantro sprigs, and serve.

SCALLION AND CORN CAKES

EAT these tasty little cakes with sour cream and caviar, or make them a little bigger and use instead of tortillas to wrap around pulled pork and barbecue sauce. As a side, serve them hot and drizzled with honey, dolloped with sour cream, or use to accompany your favorite chili, such as our Smoky Bowl O'Red (page 116).

Serves 4 to 6 as a side dish or appetizer (makes about 30 silver-dollar-sized pancakes)

2 eggs, beaten well
1 cup buttermilk
3 tablespoons vegetable oil
1 1/2 cups all-purpose flour
1 tablespoon baking powder
1 1/2 teaspoons salt
1/4 teaspoon baking soda
1 teaspoon cumin seeds, toasted and ground
1 teaspoon paprika
1/2 teaspoon cayenne
1 cup hot water
3/4 cup cornmeal
1 tablespoon dark molasses
Kernels from 3 large ears corn (1 1/2 cups)
2 scallions, sliced
Freshly ground black pepper, to taste

1. In a small mixing bowl, whisk together the eggs, buttermilk, and oil.

2. In another bowl, combine the flour, baking powder, baking soda, salt, and spices; mix well.

3. In a large mixing bowl, whisk together the hot water, cornmeal, and molasses until smooth and slightly thickened, about 1 minute. Add the flour and egg mixtures alternately, in 3 additions each, blending well after each addition. Stir in the corn and scallions, and season with pepper.

4. Heat a heavy nonstick skillet or griddle over medium heat. When the pan is hot, spoon the batter into the pan, using 2 to 3 tablespoons batter to form each cake. Cook until the bottom is golden brown and the edges look dry, 2 to 3 minutes. Flip and cook until the second side is golden brown, about 1 minute more.

POTATOES

Pity the poor potato. With the popularity of low-carb diets, we think it's been getting a bad rap. No offense to Dr. Atkins, may he rest in peace, but there are certainly schools of thought that disagree with his casting of the potato and other starchy foods as the bad guys of the American diet. We're such fans of them, in fact, that we couldn't write this cookbook without devoting at least a subchapter to what is arguably the most comforting food in the world. Potatoes, after all, are more than just a vegetable; they're an institution.

FONTINA-STUFFED CRISPY TATERS

THESE HAVE BEEN on our menu at Tremont 647 from the very beginning, for good reason. They're crispy, rich, and gooey. We don't sell them as a separate side, but only with our grilled steak, because we're worried they would be so popular we wouldn't be able to keep up. Of course, we have been known to make exceptions for VIPs; Joe, for instance, talks us into sliding him some just about every time he comes in. Serve with Grilled Giant Party Steak (page 219).

Serves 4 as a side dish

1 large baking potato
1 ounce fontina or sharp Cheddar cheese, cut into ½-inch cubes
4 ½ teaspoons black truffle oil, divided
1 tablespoon all-purpose flour
Salt and freshly ground black pepper, to taste
Vegetable oil, for frying

FONTINA-STUFFED CRISPY TATERS continued

1. Place the potato in a pot of cold salted water to cover. Bring to a boil and cook for 25 to 30 minutes, or until the potato is just cooked through (it can be pierced with a fork without breaking apart). Drain well and let cool to room temperature.

2. Meanwhile, combine the cheese and 3 teaspoons (1 tablespoon) of the truffle oil in a small bowl and toss lightly.

3. Peel and grate the cooled potato on the large holes of a box grater, and spread onto a large plate. Sprinkle with the flour, remaining 1½ teaspoons truffle oil, and a generous amount of salt and pepper. Mix well, tasting to adjust seasoning, and divide the mixture into 8 mounds.

4. Form each mound into a flattened ball. Place 1 piece of truffled cheese in the center and wrap the potato around the cheese to form a tater-tot-shaped cylinder, making sure the cheese is fully enclosed.

5. In a saucepan, heat 3 inches vegetable oil to 350°F. (Test the oil by dropping a piece of potato in; it should sizzle vigorously and immediately on the surface of the oil without sinking or burning.) Fry the taters until golden brown, about 2 minutes, working in batches if necessary to avoid crowding the pan.

6. Drain on paper towels and season with salt and pepper.

WHICH POTATO?

We always specify which kind of potato to use in which recipe, but why is the variety important? It's because some, like the starchy potatoes, are better for baking and mashing, thanks to higher starch levels that leave them light and fluffy, while the so-called waxy potatoes are better for salads, thanks to a lower starch content that gives them firmer flesh.

Starchy potatoes (a.k.a., baking potatoes): Long white, purple, Idaho (a.k.a., Russet).

Waxy potatoes: new, round red, round white, yellow (Yukon gold among others).

MAKING THE PERFECT FRENCH FRY—crunchy outside, fluffy within—requires double duty with the oil. It's true that the potatoes absorb more oil this way, but trust us: It's worth it. Who treats fries as diet food, anyway? Serve these with the Soft-Shell Crab BLT with Basil Aioli (page 190), or remove the barbecue spice and serve with Brasserie-Style Steak and Mussels (page 218).

Serves 4 to 6 as a side dish

4 large Idaho potatoes
Canola or peanut oil, for frying
2 tablespoons Basic Barbecue Rub (page 7)
2 tablespoons kosher salt

1. Fill a large saucepan (at least 4 inches deep) two-thirds full with oil and heat over medium-low to 175°F.

2. Meanwhile, cut the potatoes into sticks 1/4 inch by 1/4 inch by 3 inches long and place in a gallon container. Rinse under cold running water until the water in the container is clear.

3. Remove the potatoes from the water and drain on paper towels. Pat them dry.

4. When the oil is at 175°F, add the fries in batches and let blanch for 10 to 12 minutes, or until 1 fry removed from the oil can be broken with your fingers but not so tender that it mashes. Remove with a slotted spoon or basket and set on a rack placed over a baking sheet. Repeat until all the fries are blanched.

5. Let the fries cool to room temperature. (Note: Fries can be made up until this point and refrigerated up to 2 days before proceeding with the final cooking steps.)

6. Raise heat to medium-high.

7. Meanwhile, combine the barbecue spice and salt and set aside. Place several layers of paper towels on a large plate or baking sheet.

8. When the oil has reached 375°F, fry the potatoes in batches, leaving plenty of room for them to move around without touching, about 3 to 5 minutes or until golden brown.

9. Remove with a slotted spoon or basket and drain on paper towels. Liberally season with the barbecue spice and serve.

BARBECUED FRENCH FRIES

CRISPY HERBED HASH BROWNS

EVERYBODY loves hash browns, and they're not just for breakfast anymore. At ROUGE, we serve them with pan-seared steak. Of course, they're also great with fried eggs, over easy—any time of the day.

Serves 4 to 6 as a side dish

3 large baking potatoes, peeled
Salt and freshly ground black pepper, to taste
¼ cup vegetable oil, divided
1 teaspoon minced fresh rosemary
1 teaspoon minced fresh thyme
1 teaspoon minced fresh sage

1. In a medium-size saucepan, cover the potato with cold, salted water and bring to a boil; cook for about 30 to 35 minutes or until the potato can be pierced with a fork but does not fall apart.

2. Drain the potatoes well and let cool to room temperature.

3. Grate the potatoes on the coarse side of a grater, season to taste with salt and pepper (you will probably need more salt than you think), and set aside.

4. Heat 2 tablespoons of the oil in a cast-iron or heavy-bottomed sauté pan over high heat. When the oil starts to smoke, swirl it around the pan to coat. Add the potatoes, spreading them in an even layer in the pan, and lower heat to medium. Sprinkle the herbs on top. Cook, undisturbed, for 3 to 5 minutes. Check for browning on the bottom, and when the potatoes are brown on one side, slide them onto a plate; cover with another plate, flip, and slide back into the pan.

5. Pour the remaining oil into the pan around the edges of the hash browns and cook for 3 to 5 minutes or until browned. Adjust seasoning if necessary and serve.

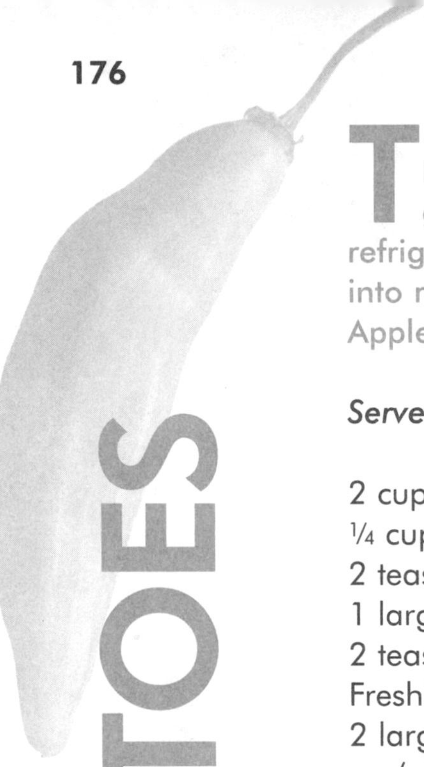

SCALLOPED SWEET POTATOES WITH CHIPOTLE

THIS RICH, SPICY DISH is a decadent companion to grilled or roasted meat. For an elegant presentation, refrigerate the potatoes until cool, use a biscuit cutter to cut into rounds, then gently reheat in the microwave. Serve with Apple-Stuffed Game Hens (page 223).

Serves 4 to 6 as a side dish

2 cups heavy cream
¼ cup minced chives
2 teaspoons fresh rosemary leaves
1 large chipotle pepper in adobo, minced (about 2 teaspoons)
2 teaspoons kosher salt
Freshly ground black pepper, to taste
2 large sweet potatoes, peeled and cut in ⅛-inch-thick slices (about 2 pounds)
2 tablespoons all-purpose flour, divided

1. Preheat oven to 400°F. Grease a 9" × 9" baking pan, and place it on a foil-lined baking sheet.
2. Combine the cream, chives, rosemary, chipotle, salt, and black pepper to taste in a medium-size bowl, and mix thoroughly.
3. Spread ⅓ of the potato slices in the bottom of the prepared baking pan. Sprinkle with 1 tablespoon flour. Repeat with another ⅓ of the potatoes and flour, and top with the remaining potatoes. Stir the cream mixture well, and pour evenly over the potatoes.
4. Bake in the center of the oven for about 20 minutes, then use the back of a wooden spoon to lightly press on the potatoes and submerge the top layer. Continue baking until the potatoes are easily pierced by a knife and the cream is golden brown on top, a total of 45 minutes to 1 hour. Halfway through cooking, use the back of a large spoon to lightly press down on the potatoes to submerge the top layer.

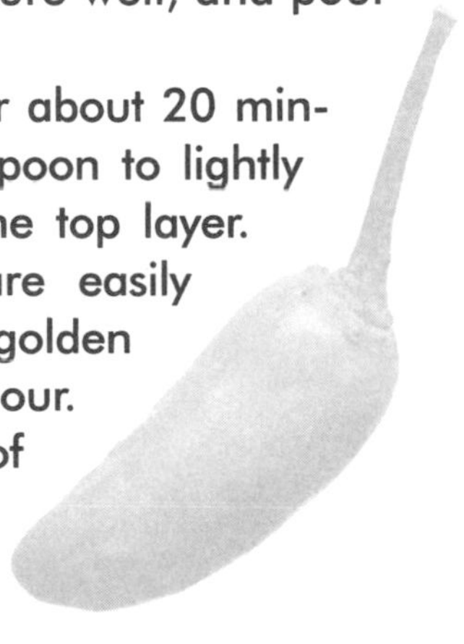

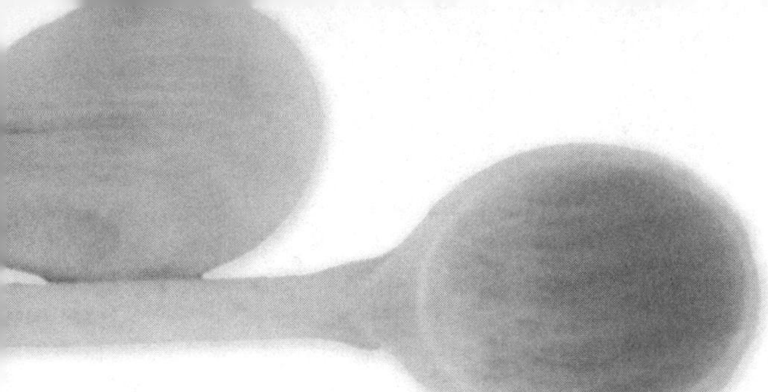

STICKY HERBED NEW POTATOES

WHEN STOCK is reduced, the natural sugars and gelatin make it nice and sticky, not to mention concentrated in flavor, giving these potatoes a heartiness appropriate for a fall or winter table, alongside roasted fish or meat.

Serves 4 to 6 as a side dish

2 pounds new potatoes, washed and cut in half
1 cup minced shallots (6 to 8)
2 garlic cloves, peeled and minced
2 teaspoons minced fresh rosemary
2 teaspoons minced fresh sage
2 teaspoons minced fresh thyme
6 cups Beef, Veal, *or* Chicken Stock (page 119 and 118), *or* store-bought low-sodium stock, reduced to 1½ cups and cooled to room temperature
Salt and freshly ground black pepper, to taste

1. Preheat oven to 400°F.

2. Put the potatoes, shallots, garlic, and herbs in a 9" × 13" baking dish. Add the stock to come ¼ inch up the sides of the potatoes (about ¾ cup). Mix well, and roast for 15 minutes. Remove pan from oven, stir potatoes, and roast for another 15 minutes. Repeat every 15 minutes, stirring and adding ¼ cup stock at a time if necessary to keep the mixture from scorching, and scraping up caramelized bits from the bottom of the pan into the sauce. Roast until the potatoes can easily be pierced with a fork and the stock has become a sticky glaze, 40 to 60 minutes total cooking time. Season with salt and pepper, and serve.

Potato Cakes

Sometimes, despite your best effort, you end up with mashed potato leftovers. Of course, you can scarf them down with the next day's lunch as is, or microwave them, or you can turn them into fabulously crispy potato pancakes—they're terrific topped with a poached egg or alongside a fried egg. Here's how to do it:

Heat 1/4 inch peanut oil in a heavy-bottomed sauté pan (preferably nonstick) until hot. Form spoonfuls of cold potatoes into small patties. Dip in beaten egg and then dry bread crumbs, and fry until crispy and golden.

MASHED POTATOES WITH SALT COD

FOR A WHILE, it seemed as if good old mashed potatoes had disappeared from restaurant menus. Instead, you'd see potato purées, piped onto plates in fussy patterns. We prefer them chunkier and funkier, we must confess. This recipe leaves the peels on, and combines the spuds with salt cod (called *bacalao* in Spain) for an earthy punch that does almost all the seasoning for you. Serve with Braised Lamb Shanks with Eggplant and Chickpeas (page 217), Zinfandel-Braised Beef Brisket (page 232), or use atop 647 Pizza (page 240).

Serves 4 to 6 as a side dish

1/2 pound salt cod
2 cups heavy cream
4 large cloves garlic, peeled and minced
1 1/4 pounds Yukon gold potatoes, skins on, washed and quartered
1 tablespoon chopped fresh thyme leaves
Salt and freshly ground black pepper, to taste

1. Two days in advance: Place the cod in a container with cold water to cover. Cover tightly and refrigerate until the fish is completely softened, 24 to 48 hours, changing the water twice a day.

2. In a small, heavy-bottomed saucepan over medium-high heat, combine the salt cod, cream, and garlic. Bring to a boil and cook, stirring and scraping from the bottom of the pan to prevent scorching, until the mixture is thickened and the cod is broken into small pieces, 10 to 15 minutes. Set aside until the potatoes are done.

3. Meanwhile, place the potatoes in a medium-size saucepan with cold water to cover by at least 1 inch. Bring to a boil over medium-high heat and cook until the potatoes can easily be pierced with a knife, 20 to 25 minutes. Drain and return the potatoes to the pot. Add the salt cod mixture and thyme, and mash with a fork or potato masher to desired consistency. Season with salt and pepper, and serve.

Deep Thoughts

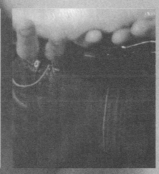

SEAFOOD

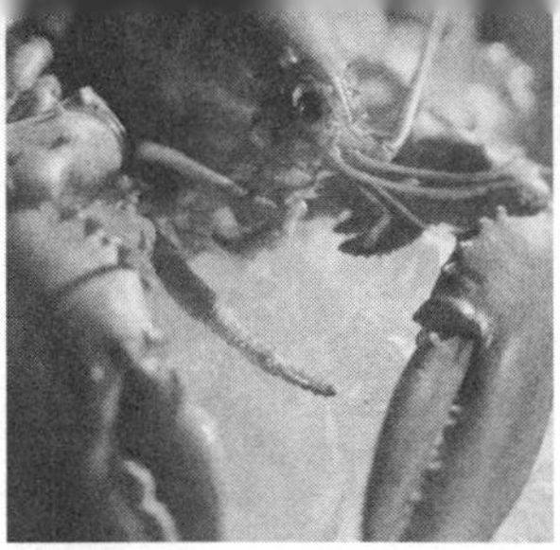

IT'S HARD TO **IMAGINE** NOW, since we're such seafood fans, but both of us grew up with disdain for most fish, in my case a more severe disdain than Joe's. I remember shopping in Seattle with my dad, who would pick out some mysterious tasteless whitefish, slap some lemon on it, and broil it too long. For Joe, it was a function of being landlocked in a cow town in West Texas, where he developed a taste for the catfish caught in a local lake and for Gulf shrimp when he visited Galveston, but otherwise had to brave the frozen seafood of chain restaurants.

The East Coast, frankly, was a godsend. As an avid diner, Joe traded the horrors of chain restaurants for the glories of seaside clam shacks. And as a budding chef, I worked on Block Island, where I had a seafood revelation, trying and loving things I never thought I would.

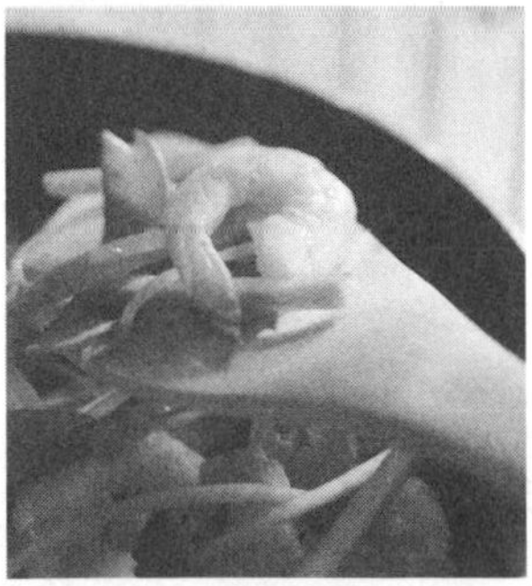

Now, I teach for a program called Kids up Front, part of the antihunger agency Share Our Strength, where I help children learn good eating habits, explaining that fish is brain food, because it's one of the best sources of protein available. Plus, the omega-3 fatty acids in oily fish can help lower cholesterol.

The best thing about fish, though, is its versatility. Grilled, roasted, fried, or eaten raw, it presents an ocean of possibilities. Of course, it must be purchased and eaten fresh. Find a good fishmonger, ask him lots of questions, and reward him with your loyalty. It will pay off.

You always hear that fish shouldn't smell fishy; but how could that be? Shouldn't fish smell like fish? Let us put it this way: There's a big difference between the crisp, salty smell of the sea that all fresh fish has, and the putrid stench of fish that is getting old. Trust us; you'll know. And if after reading these recipes you still have a hankering for mysterious tasteless whitefish broiled with lemon, we may have to start calling you "Dad."

deep thoughts

SEAFOOD

ATLANTIC COD IN BANANA LEAVES

THIS HAS BEEN on **TREMONT 647'S** menu since the beginning, and for good reason. When the just-opened little package is placed before diners, the puff of fragrant steam and the undulating bonito flakes—an Asian staple made from dried fish—always delight. And that's before the first bite. Don't fret if you can't find bonito flakes, though; the taste is fantastic even without them.

Serves 4 as an entrée

1 red bell pepper, seeded and julienned
1 green bell pepper, seeded and julienned
½ pound snow peas, threads removed
1 large carrot, peeled and julienned
1 package frozen banana leaves, thawed overnight in the refrigerator or microwaved for 20 seconds
2 cups Coconut Jasmine Rice (page 148)
¾ cup Soy-Curry Glaze (page 27), cooled
4 (6-ounce) Atlantic cod fillets
4 (3-foot) pieces twine, for tying
1 lime, cut into quarters
½ cup bonito flakes (optional)

Bonito Flakes

Where do those fluttering, flavorful bonito flakes come from? From bonito tuna, a species that usually weighs about 25 pounds and is generally dried and shaved into superfine flakes. Called katsuobushi in Japan, bonito flakes are a main ingredient in dashi, the stock used in Japanese soups. Look for them in good Asian markets.

ATLANTIC COD IN BANANA LEAVES continued

1. Combine the bell peppers, snow peas, and carrot in a small bowl. Toss well, and divide the mixture into 4 portions. Set aside.

2. Remove the banana leaves from the package and carefully unfold the leaves. Cut 8 pieces, each about 18 inches long. Stack 2 pieces perpendicular to each other on the work surface, to form a cross.

3. Spread ½ cup cooled rice in the center of the cross. Top with a portion of mixed vegetables and 2 tablespoons Soy-Curry Glaze. Arrange 1 cod fillet on top, and spread 1 tablespoon Soy-Curry Glaze on the fish. Carefully fold the leaves over the filling to enclose completely and form a snug package. Repeat with the remaining ingredients to form 3 more packages.

4. Tie a piece of twine around each package, twisting underneath and bringing around and tying tightly in the center (as you would a ribbon around a present). Snip off any excess twine.

5. To steam the fish, add water to a large sauté pan to a depth of 1 inch. Bring to a boil over medium-high heat. Place the packages in the water knot-side down, and cover the pan. Cook for 6 minutes, checking halfway through to be sure the water is still at least ½ inch deep. (Add more water as needed.) Turn the packages, cover the pan, and cook until an instant-read thermometer poked into the fish reads 150°F, about 4 to 6 minutes more.

6. Place each package knot-side up in a shallow bowl or rimmed plate. Snip the string and cut a slit down the center of each package and pull the leaves apart to expose the fish. Squeeze lime wedge on top of each, and sprinkle bonito flakes over the top. Serve immediately.

THESE LITTLE BABIES, a play on New England's ubiquitous crab cakes, are unbeatable party food. They freeze beautifully, and the recipe is so flexible as to be a mere starting point. For a twist, try adding a whole-grain or exotically flavored mustard of your choice; dark rye or whole wheat bread crumbs; another vegetable, such as carrots or corn, with or without the peas; or minced chipotles instead of the red pepper flakes. Just remember to keep the proportions the same, or it may change the texture of the cakes.

Makes four 4-inch or eight 2-inch cakes

- 3 slices light rye bread, toasted
- ½ pound salmon, skinned, boned, and cut into large chunks
- 2 shallots, peeled and roughly chopped
- 1 tablespoon fresh thyme leaves
- 1 teaspoon red pepper flakes
- 1 teaspoon cumin seeds, toasted and ground, *or* ½ teaspoon ground cumin
- 1 tablespoon Dijon mustard
- Salt and freshly ground black pepper, to taste
- ¾ cup shelled fresh English peas, blanched, *or* ¾ cup frozen peas
- 1 bunch fresh chives, minced
- ½ cup canola oil, for frying
- 1 lemon, sliced into thin wedges, for garnish
- ½ cup sour cream *or* ½ cup Achiote Caesar Dressing (page 66), for dipping

1. Break up the toast into a food processor bowl, and pulse until the bread forms coarse crumbs.

2. In the same processor bowl, add the salmon, shallots, thyme, red pepper flakes, cumin, mustard, and salt and pepper; process until the mixture is smooth. Transfer the salmon mixture to a large bowl and add the peas and chives. Toss the mixture with your hands until the peas and chives are well incorporated, and shape into 4 or 8½-inch-thick patties. (Salmon cakes can be covered and refrigerated or frozen until cooking time.)

3. In a heavy-bottomed frying pan over high heat, heat the oil until it shimmers. Reduce heat to medium-high, and carefully place the patties in the oil. Fry the patties until a golden brown crust forms on the bottom, 2 to 4 minutes; flip and brown the other side. Drain the patties on a paper towel, and season with salt and pepper. Transfer to a serving dish, and garnish with lemon wedges and sour cream.

SALMON CAKES

TREMONT ALE STEAMERS

BEER AND STEAMERS are a perfect match. The hoppy flavor works its way into the clams, and a single whiff will bring your neighbors knocking. Seasoned with that dependable Old Bay, these steamers disappear in a flash. For an entrée-sized mini-clambake, add potatoes, onions, lobster, and sausage (see following recipe).

Serves 4 as an appetizer

2 pounds steamer clams, soaked in cold water to remove the sand
4 cups of your favorite ale or beer (Tremont Ale is my favorite)
2 tablespoons Old Bay Seasoning
10 tablespoons unsalted butter, divided
2 garlic cloves, peeled
1 lemon, cut into 8 wedges
1 cup roughly chopped fresh parsley

1. In a large, heavy-bottomed saucepan, combine the steamers, ale, Old Bay, and 2 tablespoons butter over medium-high heat. Cover the pan and steam until all the clams open, 6 to 10 minutes.

2. Meanwhile, in a small saucepan over low heat, combine the remaining butter and the garlic cloves, swirling the pan until the butter melts. Remove from heat, remove the garlic, and pour the butter into a small bowl.

3. When the steamers have all opened, transfer them to a large bowl, leaving the liquid behind. Pour the liquid into a bowl, leaving any sediment in the bottom of the pot. Squeeze the lemon wedges over the clams, sprinkle with parsley, and serve the clam liquid and butter on the side for dipping. Provide a big bowl for the empty shells.

MINI-CLAMBAKE

IF YOU'VE EVER BEEN FOOLISH—er, brave—enough to try a traditional clambake on the beach, you know how infuriatingly unpredictable it can be. Save this recipe for when you want the same free-for-all, communal, hands-on feeling you get from a clambake, but without the hungry, annoyed guests. Pile this onto a big platter, wear a grass skirt when you serve it, and nobody will be the wiser that you're not at the beach.

Serves 4 to 6 as an entrée

1 pound potatoes, washed, peeled, and cut into 1-inch chunks
2 medium-size onions, peeled and sliced into rounds
8 cups of your favorite ale or beer (Tremont Ale is my favorite)
4 tablespoons Old Bay Seasoning
2 sticks unsalted butter, divided
1 pound sausage, cut into 1-inch slices
2 pounds steamer clams, soaked in cold water to remove the sand
2 (1-pound) lobsters
4 garlic cloves, peeled
1 lemon, cut into 8 wedges
1 cup roughly chopped fresh parsley

1. In a large, heavy-bottomed saucepan, combine the potatoes, onions, ale, Old Bay, and 2 tablespoons of the butter over medium-high heat. Cover the pan and cook until the potatoes and onions are tender. Add the sausage, clams, and lobsters, and cover again. Steam until all the clams open and the lobsters are bright red, 6 to 10 minutes.

2. Meanwhile, in a small saucepan over low heat, combine the remaining butter and the garlic cloves, swirling the pan until the butter melts. Remove from heat, remove the garlic, and pour the butter into a small bowl.

3. When all the steamers have opened and the lobsters are bright red, transfer seafood, vegetables, and sausage to a large bowl, leaving the liquid behind. Pour the liquid into a bowl, leaving any sediment in the bottom of the pot. Squeeze the lemon wedges over the clams, sprinkle with parsley, and serve the seafood liquid and butter on the side for dipping. Provide a big bowl for the empty shells.

BEER BATTER COD
WITH CHUNKY TARTAR SAUCE

WHEN I WAS A KID, I did one of those aw-shucks-isn't-his-voice-cute radio commercials for Ivar's, a fish-and-chip palace in Seattle. I wasn't acting; that combination of fried fish and fried potatoes was one of the few ways I liked fish. I'm all grown up now, and so are these fish and chips; nowadays I use a strong ale to give the batter a hoppy flavor. You can use a milder brew if you want to tone it down, but whatever you choose, these are guaranteed to make you feel like a kid again.

Serves 6

For the Chunky Tartar Sauce:

1¼ cups Aioli (page 11)
1 medium-size kosher dill pickle, minced, plus 2 tablespoons pickle juice
1 small red onion, peeled and minced
1 small red bell pepper, seeded and minced
1 tablespoon granulated sugar
¼ cup chopped parsley leaves
Salt and freshly ground black pepper, to taste

For the Beer Batter Cod:

2 pounds cod fillet, cut into ½-inch strips
5 cups all-purpose flour, divided
2 cups cornmeal
2 teaspoons dried thyme
1 tablespoon chili powder
2 teaspoons cayenne pepper
2 teaspoons baking powder
2 teaspoons salt
2 bottles (24 ounces) of your favorite ale, such as Harpoon IPA
½ cup water
Canola or peanut oil, for frying
Salt and freshly ground black pepper, to taste

1. In a small bowl, combine all the tartar sauce ingredients, stir to mix thoroughly, and set aside.
2. In a medium-size bowl, combine the cod and 2 cups of the flour, and toss to coat.
3. In a large bowl, combine the remaining 3 cups flour, the cornmeal, thyme, chili powder, cayenne, baking powder, and salt. Add the ale and water; mix well.
4. Add the oil to a stockpot or Dutch oven to a depth of 4 inches, and heat to 350°F. Test by dropping a piece of fish into the oil; it should sizzle vigorously and immediately on the surface without sinking or burning.
5. When the oil is hot, lift a single cod piece out of the flour, lightly shaking off excess, and drop into the batter. Use tongs to transfer the coated pieces, one at a time, into the oil, frying in batches so as not to crowd the pan.
6. As the fish fries, use the tongs to separate and move the pieces around. Fry until dark golden brown underneath, about 2 minutes; turn and cook the second side, 1 to 2 minutes more. Remove fish, allowing excess oil to drip back into the pan, then transfer to a plate lined with paper towels. Season with salt and pepper, and serve hot with tartar sauce.

EVER SINCE Paul Prudhomme in New Orleans made blackened redfish famous, home cooks have been smoking up their kitchens, setting off their smoke alarms, and causing coughing fits among their guests—all so they could serve up a combination of spicy, charred exterior and mild, creamy interior. Here, we turn down the spiciness a bit, change the fish to rich salmon, and combine with a tangy butter sauce. Just make sure you have a powerful vent hood—or, at the very least, lots of open windows and a few good fans. Serve with Dirty Rice (page 145).

BLACKENED SALMON WITH LEMON-SCALLION BUTTER

Serves 4 as an entrée

4 (6-ounce) skinless salmon fillets
1 tablespoon peanut *or* canola oil
2 tablespoons Creole Seasoning (page 4)
1 tablespoon kosher salt
1 tablespoon freshly ground black pepper
3 tablespoons cold butter, cut into ½-inch pieces
4 scallions, cut into ¼-inch pieces
2 teaspoons granulated sugar
Juice of 1 lemon (about ¼ cup)
Salt, to taste

1. Turn on the vent hood to high. Put a large, heavy-bottomed sauté pan (preferably cast iron) over medium-high heat, and allow it to become smoking hot, 3 to 5 minutes.

2. While the pan is heating, put the salmon on a large plate and coat both sides generously with oil. Combine the Creole Seasoning, salt, and pepper in a small bowl, and mix well. Coat the fish on top and bottom with the seasoning, leaving the sides clean.

3. Lay the fish in the pan without crowding, and sear until you can see that the cooked part reaches ⅓ of the way up the sides of the fillets, 3 to 4 minutes. Turn and repeat on the other side, cooking for another 2 to 3 minutes or until you can cut into the fish and see almost all pale pink flesh but darker red in the very center. If you like salmon cooked more, leave it on for another minute or until pink throughout.

4. Transfer the fillets to a serving platter, and remove the pan from heat. Immediately add the butter and scallions, stirring constantly until the butter melts. Add the sugar and lemon juice, mix well, and season with salt to taste. Spoon the sauce over the fillets and serve immediately.

Better Now Than Later

Seafood is quick to spoil, and just as quick to pick up flavors from other foods. That's why it's best used immediately. It can be refrigerated for a day or 2, but you must make sure that you keep it at 34° to 36°F (most refrigerators range from 36° to 40°F). One easy way to accomplish that is to lay your seafood on a bed of ice in a colander placed over another bowl to catch the water. Be sure to cover it with plastic wrap, and change the ice if it melts too quickly.

If using within several hours, you can skip the ice, but make sure to wrap the fish in plastic before sealing in an airtight container. And if you need to keep it any longer than a day or 2, pop it in the freezer, again sealed tightly in plastic wrap and another container, such as a sealable freezer bag. While it's okay to freeze fish for up to 3 months, it needs to be in a freezer that gets below 0°F; anything warmer, and the fish can spoil.

SOFT-SHELL CRAB BLT WITH BASIL AIOLI

TWO OF OUR FAVORITE sandwiches are the good old BLT when we're up in Boston, and the fried soft-shell po' boy when we're down in New Orleans. So when we've had a cold New England winter, and are trying to rush spring, why not combine them? We like making these oversized, with thick slabs of tomato and bacon combined with the crunchy-on-the-outside, gooey-on-the-inside crab. Serve with the Barbecued French Fries (page 174).

Serves 4 as an entrée

4 large soft-shell crabs, cleaned by a fishmonger
1½ cups buttermilk
1 cup all-purpose flour
1 cup cornmeal
1 tablespoon paprika
1 teaspoon dried thyme
½ cup Aioli (page 11) or store-bought mayonnaise
10 large basil leaves, chopped
1 cup canola or peanut oil
Salt and freshly ground black pepper, to taste
8 slices crusty bread
8 strips bacon, fried until crisp
1 large beefsteak tomato, cut into 8 slices and chilled
¼ head iceberg lettuce, cut into thin strips and chilled

1. Put the crabs in a bowl or dish and cover with buttermilk. Set aside.

2. In a shallow bowl or pan, combine the flour, cornmeal, paprika, and thyme; mix well. Set aside.

3. Combine the aioli and basil in a food processor or blender and blend until incorporated. (If using store-bought mayonnaise, add 2 cloves garlic, peeled and chopped, with the basil.)

4. Heat the oil in a large, heavy-bottomed sauté pan over high heat until sizzling hot. One at a time, lift the crabs from the buttermilk, allowing excess to drip back into the bowl. Gently dredge the crab in the flour mixture to coat well, and fry for about 3 to 4 minutes per side, until crisp and golden. Transfer to a plate lined with paper towels to drain, and season with salt and pepper.

5. To make the sandwiches, toast the bread, and spread generously with aioli. Stack with bacon, tomato, iceberg, and crab, and serve immediately.

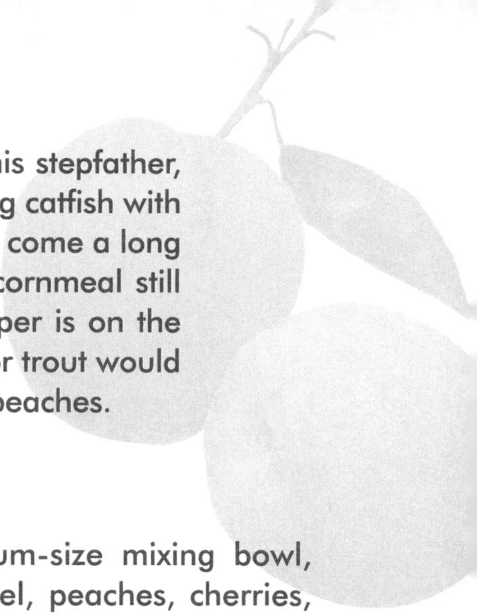

FRIED GROUPER WITH PEACH-CHERRY RELISH

ONE OF Joe's fondest childhood food memories is of his stepfather, Vernon Lee Jones, a Texan through and through, coating catfish with cornmeal and frying it up in a cast-iron skillet. Our palates have come a long way since then, but with the right kind of fish, the crunch of cornmeal still strikes us as just the thing to offset a mild-flavored fish. Grouper is on the sweeter side, so it goes well with a tart fruit relish, but snapper or trout would work well, too—as would apricots or nectarines instead of the peaches.

Serves 4 as an entrée

- 1 fennel bulb, stems removed, cored, and thinly sliced
- 4 small or 2 large barely ripe peaches, halved, pitted, and cut into thin wedges
- 1 cup cherries, pitted and halved
- ½ cup chopped flat-leaf Italian parsley
- 1 large shallot, peeled and minced
- 1 green pepper, cored, seeded, and julienned
- 2 tablespoons red wine vinegar
- 1 tablespoon olive oil
- Salt and freshly ground black pepper, to taste
- 2 cups cornmeal
- 1 cup all-purpose flour
- 2 teaspoons cumin seeds, toasted and ground
- 2 pounds skinless grouper fillets
- Canola oil, for frying

1. In a medium-size mixing bowl, combine the fennel, peaches, cherries, parsley, shallot, green pepper, vinegar, and olive oil; mix thoroughly. Season with salt and pepper and set aside.

2. In a shallow pan, combine the flour, cornmeal, and cumin; mix well. Season the fillets generously with salt and pepper, then lay them flat in the cornmeal mixture, pat down, flip, and pat down again.

3. Add the canola oil to a depth of ½ inch in a shallow frying pan over high heat. When the oil is sizzling hot, remove the grouper from the cornmeal, shaking gently to remove excess, and fry for 2 to 4 minutes per side, or until golden brown. Transfer to a plate lined with paper towels to drain. Season with salt and pepper. Spoon the peach relish onto a serving platter, place the fried fish on top, and serve.

THIS DISH is for those who like their squid simple. Toss it with some garlic and peppers, add some fire and tart vinegar, and combine it with greens for a light, single-dish lunch alongside some good crusty bread, or as an appetizer that beats little crustless sandwiches any day.

Serves 2 as an entrée or 4 as an appetizer

3 tablespoons extra-virgin olive oil
7 cloves garlic, peeled and thinly sliced
1 small red bell pepper, seeded and julienned
1 small green bell pepper, seeded and julienned
2 teaspoons fennel seed
1 pound cleaned squid, tubes cut into ¼-inch rings and drained well, tentacles left whole
½ teaspoon (or to taste) red pepper flakes
2 tablespoons balsamic vinegar
½ pound baby spinach leaves *or* arugula, washed well and dried
Salt and freshly ground black pepper, to taste

1. Put the oil and garlic in a large, heavy-bottomed sauté pan, and place the pan over very low heat. Cook slowly, stirring occasionally until the garlic sizzles and just starts to color, about 20 minutes. Remove the garlic with a slotted spoon and set aside.

2. Raise heat to high, and allow the oil to become sizzling hot before adding the bell peppers and fennel seed. Cook, stirring frequently, until the peppers just start to brown, 4 to 5 minutes. Add the squid tentacles and cook for 1 minute, stirring constantly. Add the squid rings and red pepper flakes; cook, tossing and stirring, until the squid is no longer translucent, about 1 minute more. Add the balsamic and reserved garlic, and cook for 30 seconds more, tossing to coat.

3. Remove pan from heat and add the greens, stirring and tossing until wilted, 1 to 2 minutes. Season with salt and pepper, and serve.

GARLICKY SQUID WITH WILTED GREENS

HALIBUT AND PROSCIUTTO WITH WHITE BEANS

FORGET THE PYRAMIDS, the Sphinx, the Great Wall of China—we think prosciutto, Italy's glorious dry-cured ham, belongs among the seven wonders of the world, right alongside foie gras and Mission figs. When combined with a mild fish such as halibut, salty prosciutto bastes it, adding moisture to the inside and crunchiness to the outside. What could be more wonderful?

Serves 4 as an entrée

4 (6-ounce) skinless halibut fillets
8 paper-thin slices prosciutto
2 tablespoons olive oil
2 cups cooked white beans (see Master Bean Recipe, page 123)
4 plum tomatoes, core removed, sliced in half lengthwise, and cut into ¼-inch half-moons
1 teaspoon hot red pepper flakes
2 teaspoons fennel seeds, toasted and ground
20 large fresh basil leaves, chopped
2 tablespoons balsamic vinegar
Salt and freshly ground black pepper, to taste
½ cup chopped fresh parsley
1 lemon, cut into 6 wedges

1. Preheat oven to 350°F.
2. Wrap each fillet with 2 slices prosciutto, leaving ½ inch of the fish exposed at each end.
3. Heat the oil in a large, heavy nonstick sauté pan over high heat. Add the wrapped fish fillets without crowding the pan, and sear on one side until the prosciutto is crispy, 2 to 3 minutes. Turn the fillets and sear the second side; transfer to a baking sheet and roast until the fish flakes easily with a fork, about 4 minutes.
4. While the fish is roasting, return sauté pan to medium-high heat. Add the beans, tomatoes, red pepper flakes, and fennel seeds; cook, stirring, for 2 minutes. Add the basil and vinegar, remove from heat, and season with salt and pepper.
5. To serve, spoon the bean mixture onto a serving platter, top with the fish fillets, and garnish with parsley and lemon.

JERK TROUT WITH ROASTED PINEAPPLE SALSA

I WAS IN JAMAICA for a conference a few years ago, and after a long, hot, and sticky trip, I ended up at Boston Bay, which I was told was birthplace of the jerk rub. In front of all these little shacks were smoldering fires on which pigs, chickens, and striped bass were being barbecued and grilled. The flavors—and the big plastic jug of jerk rub that I brought back home—inspired me to combine the spicy rub with trout, and to offset the heat with some sweet roasted pineapple salsa.

Serves 4 as an entrée

1 ripe pineapple, peeled, cored, and cut into ½-inch dice
3 tablespoons molasses, divided
¼ cup spiced rum
2 tablespoons butter
1 habanero or jalapeño pepper, stem and seeds removed, chopped
1 tablespoon brown sugar
1 tablespoon white vinegar
2 teaspoons kosher salt
1 teaspoon ground cinnamon
½ teaspoon cumin seeds, toasted and ground
½ teaspoon dried thyme
½ teaspoon dried oregano
½ teaspoon ground allspice
¼ teaspoon ground nutmeg
¾ cup fresh lime juice (from about 6 limes), divided
4 tablespoons canola oil, divided
4 (10-ounce) whole boneless trout, head removed but tail left on
¼ cup chopped cilantro leaves
Salt and freshly ground black pepper, to taste

1. Preheat oven to 350°F.

2. In a roasting pan or baking dish, combine the pineapple, 2 tablespoons molasses, rum, and butter, and mix well. Bake for 20 minutes, stirring halfway through. Set aside, but keep oven on.

3. Meanwhile, combine the remaining 1 tablespoon molasses, habanero or jalapeño, brown sugar, vinegar, salt, cinnamon, cumin, thyme, oregano, allspice, nutmeg, and ¼ cup of the lime juice in a food processor or blender; process until smooth. Rub the mixture over the trout's exposed flesh, but not the skin.

4. Heat 1 tablespoon of the canola oil in a large nonstick pan over high heat. Add 1 trout, skin-side down, and sear just until the skin is crispy and golden, 3 to 5 minutes. Use a large spatula to transfer the trout to a large baking sheet, and repeat with the remaining trout. When all the fish have been seared, transfer to the oven and bake until the trout are just cooked through and the interior has turned white, 3 to 5 minutes.

5. Add the remaining ½ cup lime juice, the cilantro, and salt and pepper to the pineapple and mix well.

6. Remove trout from the oven and carefully transfer each to individual plates, and top with pineapple salsa.

KUNG PAO SHRIMP WITH CASHEWS AND MANGOES

WHEN I GO on late-night trips to Chinatown with my chef friends, we always make a point to ask for dishes we've never heard of—what better opportunity to learn something, right?—but I always make sure to get a Kung Pao something. In this version of the classic, the heat combines with crunchy cashews and sweet mangoes, and calls for Coconut Jasmine Rice (page 148) to cool the palate. Of course, as with take-out Chinese food, it's even better the next day, eaten with your fingers while standing at the fridge.

Serves 4 as an entrée

24 cocktail-size shrimp, peeled and deveined
½ cup, plus 1 tablespoon cornstarch
3 tablespoons soy sauce
1 tablespoon dry white wine
1 tablespoon brown sugar
½ teaspoon kosher salt
1 tablespoon sesame oil
2 tablespoons canola oil
1 tablespoon peeled and minced fresh ginger
3–4 serrano chilies, stemmed and minced with seeds
1 red bell pepper, seeded and cut into ½-inch dice
2 celery stalks, cut diagonally into ¼-inch slices
1 carrot, peeled and julienned
1 firm but ripe mango, peeled and cut into ½-inch dice
2 scallions, cut crosswise into 1-inch pieces
½ cup unsalted cashews, toasted and roughly chopped

1. In a small bowl, toss the shrimp with the ½ cup cornstarch until the shrimp is thoroughly coated; refrigerate until needed. In another small bowl, combine the remaining 1 tablespoon of cornstarch, the soy sauce, wine, brown sugar, and salt; whisk well to combine and set aside.

2. Heat the sesame and canola oils in a heavy-bottomed 12-inch sauté pan over high heat until smoking. Remove the shrimp from the cornstarch, lightly shaking off excess, and sear for 2 minutes on each side, or until golden brown. Remove and set aside. Add the ginger and chilies to the pan and cook, stirring constantly, for 1 minute. Add the bell pepper, celery, and carrot; cook, stirring frequently, until crisp-tender, about 3 minutes. Adjust heat to medium.

3. Return the shrimp to the pan along with the mango, scallions, and cashews. Whisk the reserved sauce again and add to the pan, stirring constantly. Simmer for 3 minutes, stirring occasionally, and serve.

YOU KNOW you've done it; we all have. You buy a frozen potpie at the grocery store because something about that little foil tin, doughy crust, and scalding filling takes you right back to your burned-tongue childhood. If you'd rather not make that trip, try this combination of rich lobster (or the same amount of shrimp or scallops), puff pastry (your own or store-bought), and crunchy corn. You still need to blow on each spoonful, though, or it will burn just the same.

LOBSTER POTPIE

Serves 6 as an entrée

¼ cup kosher salt
2 medium-size Yukon Gold potatoes, cut into ½-inch dice
1 large carrot, peeled and cut into ½-inch dice
Kernels from 2 large corncobs (about 1 cup)
½ cup fresh English peas (or frozen peas, thawed)
2 cups roughly chopped fresh lobster meat
4 tablespoons butter
1 large yellow onion, peeled and cut into ¼-inch dice
4 cloves garlic, peeled and minced
3 tablespoons all-purpose flour
1½ cups Fish Stock (page 118) *or* canned clam juice
1½ cups half-and-half
1 teaspoon minced fresh thyme leaves
2 teaspoons minced fresh chervil *or* tarragon
Salt and freshly ground black pepper, to taste
1 piece Savory Herbed Pie Dough (page 257), kept cold
1 egg, whisked with 2 tablespoons water

THAT ROUX YOU DO

Roux, a cooked mixture of flour and fat used for thickening, is a staple of Southern cooking, particularly Creole and Cajun dishes. It's usually half flour and half fat (traditionally oil, although we use butter for all but the darkest roux). For most uses, we melt the butter over low heat, remove the pan from the heat, whisk in the flour, return to heat, and cook for 3 to 5 minutes, stirring constantly, until it smells nutty and is the color of a pecan.

But that's for what we call a brown roux. For a white roux, stop before it colors much at all, and for a blond roux, just let it turn golden. We most often make blond or brown roux, using butter for blond and oil or even meat drippings for the brown. In any case, be sure to constantly stir to avoid burning, and use a long spoon. In the Rouge kitchen, the chefs tape down their sleeves to protect against splatters from a dangerously hot and sticky roux. No wonder Louisiana chef extraordinaire Paul Prudhomme, who would take roux to a nearly black color for his gumbos, once called it "Cajun napalm."

1. Preheat oven to 350°F.

2. Bring a 4-quart pot half full of water to a boil. Add the salt, potatoes, and carrots, and cook until the potatoes and carrots are fork-tender, about 5 minutes. Drain well and transfer to a bowl of ice water or run cold water over to stop the cooking process; drain again and transfer to a large bowl. Add the corn, peas, and lobster meat; set aside.

3. Return pot to stove over low heat and add the butter. When it is melted and hot, add the onion and garlic; cook, stirring occasionally, until the onions are soft and translucent, 10 to 15 minutes. Raise heat to medium and add the flour, stirring until the roux is lightly browned, 3 to 4 minutes.

4. Whisk the stock into the roux until smooth, and raise heat to medium-high. Stir in the half-and-half and bring to a boil; reduce heat, and simmer for 10 minutes, stirring occasionally. Add the herbs, and salt and pepper, and remove from heat. Add the lobster mixture to the sauce, stirring to mix well. Transfer to a shallow 2-quart casserole dish or soufflé dish and set aside.

5. Roll the chilled pastry just enough to erase seams and form a circle 1 inch larger than the casserole dish. Lay the pastry over the filling, crimping edges decoratively if desired. Brush with the beaten egg and place on a baking sheet. Bake immediately until puffed and golden brown, 40 to 50 minutes. Let cool for 10 to 15 minutes, then serve.

MOROCCAN-STYLE ROASTED MONKFISH WITH PITA

MONKFISH goes by many names: angler fish, lotte, and even "poor man's lobster," a nickname it got for its crustacean-like texture, which we love. Its heartiness helps it stand up to such treatments as this Moroccan stew, an easy way to build complex flavors on a plate. Just be sure to strip off the outer membrane before cooking (or have your fishmonger do it), or the fish will become rubbery. And nobody loves that.

Serves 4 as an entrée

½ cup all-purpose flour
2 pounds monkfish fillet, membrane removed, cut into 8-ounce pieces
6 tablespoons olive oil, plus extra for brushing
1 tablespoon peeled and minced ginger (about 1-inch piece)
2 cloves garlic, peeled and minced
1 yellow onion, peeled and chopped
1 small eggplant, peeled and cut into ½-inch dice
1 red bell pepper, cored, seeded, and chopped
1 cup Fish Stock (page 118) *or* water
1 (14.5-ounce) can crushed tomatoes
¼ cup red wine vinegar
2 tablespoons North African Spice Mix (page 6)
1 pinch (about ½ teaspoon) high-quality saffron
1 cup dried cherries *or* cranberries
2 pitas
Salt and freshly ground black pepper, to taste
1 cup toasted and roughly chopped almonds
½ cup chopped fresh cilantro leaves
1 lime, quartered

1. Preheat oven to 425°F.

2. Place the flour in a baking pan or large mixing bowl, and lightly dredge the monkfish; set aside.

3. Heat 2 tablespoons of the olive oil in a large ovenproof sauté pan or Dutch oven over medium-high heat. Sear the monkfish fillets for 2 minutes on each side and remove.

4. Add the remaining 4 tablespoons oil, the ginger, garlic, onions, red pepper, and eggplant; cook for 4 to 6 minutes, stirring occasionally, until the vegetables begin to brown. Add the stock or water, tomatoes, vinegar, spice mix, saffron, and dried cherries or cranberries. Bring to a boil, stirring frequently, then reduce heat to medium and simmer for 10 minutes. Season to taste with salt and pepper.

5. Place the monkfish fillets on top of the tomato stew and spoon about 2 tablespoons of stew over each of them. Bake uncovered for 7 minutes. With tongs or a slotted metal spoon, turn the monkfish and bake for 7 to 10 minutes more or until the fish is white and flaky, not translucent or rubbery. Remove from oven.

6. Meanwhile, brush the pitas with olive oil, season with salt and pepper, and toast in heated oven until golden, about 7 minutes. Cut into wedges.

7. Serve the stew on a platter or in individual shallow bowls, garnished with the toasted almonds, cilantro, and lime wedges; serve the toasted pitas on the side.

PEANUT-CRUSTED GRILLED SCALLOPS

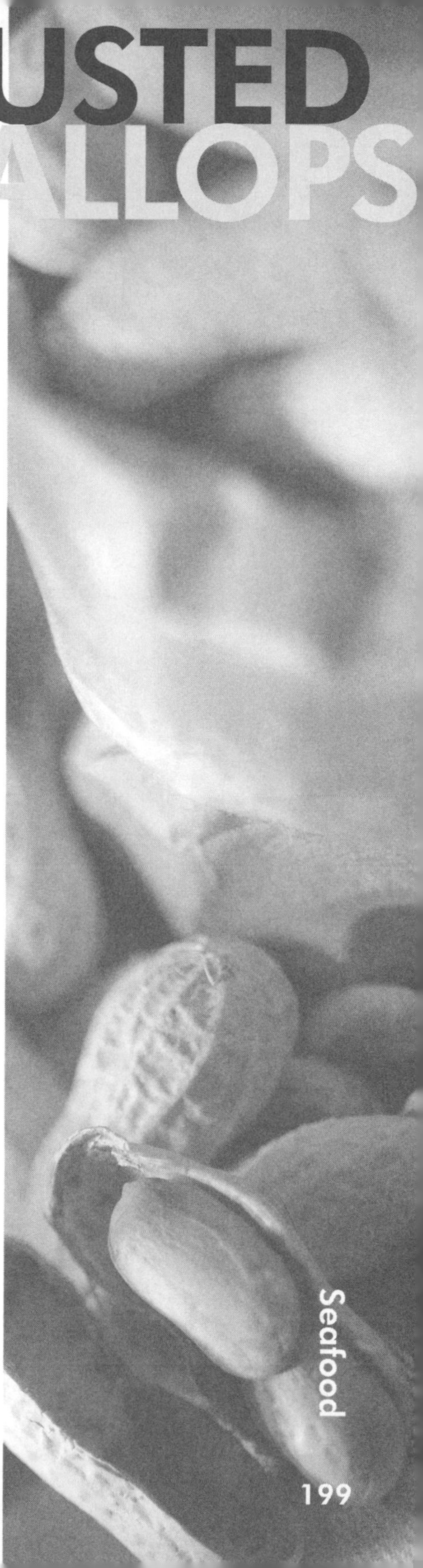

WHEN YOU HAVE high-quality seafood, less can be more. Highlight the flavors of your fish, and do it simply, rather than engaging in the kind of muss and fuss that serves only to confuse the palate. You could hardly get simpler than this, especially if you have some of that delectable Apricot Thai Glaze (page 26) in your refrigerator.

Serves 4 as an entrée

2 pounds large sea scallops, cleaned and patted dry
2 tablespoons canola oil
Salt and freshly ground black pepper, to taste
1 cup Apricot Thai Glaze (page 26), warmed
1 cup toasted and coarsely ground unsalted peanuts

1. Prepare medium-hot fire in grill.
2. While the grill is heating, toss the sea scallops with the oil in a medium-size bowl and lightly season with salt and pepper.
3. When grill temperature is medium (you cannot keep your hand 5 inches above the grates for more than 3 to 4 seconds), grill the scallops for 2 to 4 minutes per side, or until dark golden brown and firm but not rubbery.
4. Put the warmed glaze in a small bowl next to a platter. Using tongs or a fork, swirl the scallops 1 at a time in the glaze to coat, allowing excess to drip back into the bowl. Transfer to the platter and sprinkle the peanuts on top, turning and sprinkling again to coat. Repeat with the remaining scallops and serve, or chill and serve cold.

Sesame-Crusted Grilled Salmon

LIKE the Peanut-Crusted Grilled Scallops (page 199), these are an easy way to let the salmon shine without covering up its flavor. The glaze caramelizes, and along with the crunchy sesame seeds, makes this dish seem almost like *unagi,* the broiled eel dish that is one of our favorite sushi-restaurant staples. Come to think of it, if it's not grilling season, this also works just fine by putting the salmon under the broiler—just watch it closely so it doesn't burn.

Serves 4 as an entrée

4 (8-ounce) skinless salmon fillets, pin bones removed
2 tablespoons canola oil
Salt and freshly ground black pepper, to taste
½ cup Soy-Curry Glaze (page 27)
¼ cup sesame seeds, toasted
½ lime, cut into thin slices

1. Prepare a hot fire in the grill.
2. Lightly coat the salmon with oil, and season with salt and pepper. When the grill is hot (you cannot keep your hand 5 inches above the grates for more than 1 to 2 seconds), add the salmon fillets. Grill until you can see that it has cooked ⅓ of the way up the side of the fish, 3 to 5 minutes. Turn the fillets, brush generously with the glaze, and grill for 3 to 5 minutes more, until soft pink.
3. Sprinkle on the sesame seeds until coated, garnish with lime, and serve.

Handle with Care

We've all done it. The fish goes on the grill, and within mere seconds, we feel the uncontrollable urge to move it. We know what's going to happen—the fish is going to stick—and we do it anyway. Be strong. It's time to resist. When grilling fish, make sure the grates are clean and well-oiled, and once you put it on the grill, leave it there until it has a nice golden-brown sear on the bottom, 1 to 3 minutes depending on grill temperature. Then—and only then—use tongs or two spatulas to carefully flip it. If you've followed our orders, it shouldn't break.

RED SNAPPER AU POIVRE

YOU'VE PROBABLY had steak au poivre, that classic French bistro dish that calls for coating the beef in coarsely cracked peppercorns and combining with a simple butter sauce—or perhaps flambéed and flavored with brandy. Steak, of course, isn't the only ingredient that goes well with pepper. Thick white fish such as red snapper may need something to help the cracked pepper stick to it, but that gives you the excuse to add some rich, thyme-flavored aioli. If striped bass is in season, try using that instead.

Serves 4 as an entrée

1 cup Aioli (page 11)
2 teaspoons fresh thyme leaves
3 tablespoons Dijon mustard
Salt, to taste
4 (6-ounce) red snapper fillets
3 tablespoons very coarsely ground black pepper

1. Preheat oven to 250°F.
2. In a wide, shallow bowl, stir together the aioli, thyme, and mustard. Season with salt.
3. If the fillets are thicker than ½ inch, sandwich them one at a time between layers of plastic wrap and gently pound until ¼ to ½ inch thick. If they are thin when you buy them, do not pound them.
4. Place each fillet in the aioli mixture, turn to coat, and transfer to a sheet pan. Repeat with the remaining fillets.
5. Heat a large cast-iron skillet over medium-high heat. Sprinkle cracked pepper evenly over one side of the fillets. When the pan is smoking hot, sear one fillet, pepper-side down, for 3 minutes; turn over the fillet and cook for 2 minutes more, or until a small amount of translucence is visible when you gently cut into the fish. Transfer back to the sheet pan, pepper-side up. Repeat with the remaining fillets.
6. Bake the fillets for 3 minutes to warm through, then serve.

SHRIMP-STUFFED SQUID

ALL IT TAKES is one bite of a rubbery piece of squid to think that you don't like it. But blame the cook, not the food, because when prepared properly, squid is perfectly tender, with a rich flavor all its own. This recipe doesn't give the squid time to get tough, and it gives your guests a tangy shrimp stuffing inside.

Serves 4 as an entrée

½ pound shrimp, peeled and deveined
3 scallions, roughly chopped
4 sprigs fresh cilantro
1 small carrot, peeled and chopped
1 tablespoon peeled and chopped ginger (about 1-inch piece)
2 cloves garlic, peeled
Juice and zest of 1 lime
2 teaspoons red pepper flakes
1 tablespoon fish sauce
1 teaspoon kosher salt
8 large squid bodies (at least 6 inches long), cleaned and tentacles removed
2 tablespoons canola oil
½ cup Vietnamese Cilantro Dipping Sauce (page 16)

1. Preheat oven to 425°F.

2. To guard against bacteria development, freeze or refrigerate food processor bowl and blade until cold. Combine the shrimp, scallions, cilantro, carrot, ginger, garlic, lime juice and zest, red pepper flakes, fish sauce, and salt in the food processor and pulse until the mixture forms a paste. Using a small spoon or your fingers, stuff the squid bodies with shrimp purée (about 2 tablespoons per squid).

3. Heat the oil in a large oven-safe nonstick sauté pan over medium-high heat. Sear the squid for 3 minutes. Turn over the squid, transfer the pan to the oven, and roast for 3 to 5 minutes or until firm.

4. Spoon the dipping sauce onto a serving platter or divide among 4 plates and spread around with the back of a spoon. Using a very sharp knife, slice the squid bodies into ¼-inch rings, being careful not to squeeze out any stuffing, and arrange on top of the sauce.

SIMPLE SPAGHETTI AND CLAMS

ESPECIALLY IN NEW ENGLAND, quahog clams deserve better than to always end up swimming with the potatoes and cream in chowder. We like to pair them with pasta for this classic, homey, satisfying dish. You could use cherrystone or manila clams, too—as long as they're fresh. If you're tempted to use canned clams for this, think again, and visit your fishmonger instead.

Serves 4 as an entrée

1 pound spaghetti
4 tablespoons extra-virgin olive oil, divided
4 shallots, peeled and minced
4 cloves garlic, peeled and minced
½ teaspoon red pepper flakes
½ cup dry white wine
½ cup butter, cut into cubes
1 tablespoon chopped fresh oregano
12 shucked quahog clams with juices, pulsed in food processor
½ cup chopped flat-leaf Italian parsley
½ cup freshly grated Parmesan cheese
Salt and freshly ground black pepper, to taste

1. Cook the spaghetti in a large pot of boiling salted water until al dente. Drain well, and return to the pot. Toss with 2 tablespoons of the oil, cover the pot, and set aside.
2. While the spaghetti is cooking, heat the remaining 2 tablespoons oil in a 2-quart saucepan over medium heat. Add the shallots, garlic, and red pepper flakes; cook, stirring occasionally, until the shallots soften, about 3 minutes. Add the wine and raise heat to high; boil, stirring occasionally, until only about 2 tablespoons of liquid remain, 3 to 5 minutes.
3. Turn heat to low and add the butter, stirring until melted. Add the oregano, clams, and clam juice; bring to simmer, and cook for 2 minutes. Pour the mixture over the spaghetti. Add the parsley and cheese, and toss until well combined. Season with salt and pepper.

TUNA STEAKS are like beef steaks: If the quality of the fish or meat is excellent, they're best eaten rare. In the case of tuna, pay a little more to get sushi-quality (also known as No. 1 tuna), and eat it pretty close to raw. Our take on seared tuna gives a curry punch to its exterior, leaving the interior red and creamy—the perfect foil for a coconut-lime sauce. This dish, with its pink, white, and green colors, looks as beautiful as it tastes. Serve with plain steamed rice and kimchi.

1. Rub the tuna steaks with 2 tablespoons canola oil. Sprinkle the curry evenly over the tuna and refrigerate until needed.

2. Heat the remaining 1 tablespoon canola oil, the sesame oil, red pepper flakes, and ginger in a heavy-bottomed sauté pan on medium-high; cook, stirring frequently, for 1 to 2 minutes, until the ginger begins to brown. Reduce heat to medium, add the coconut milk and brown sugar, and bring to a simmer.

CURRY-SEARED TUNA WITH COCONUT SAUCE

Serves 4 as an entrée

4 (8-ounce) sushi-quality tuna steaks (at least 1 inch thick)
3 tablespoons canola oil, divided
1 tablespoon Tremont 647 Curry (page 8) or commercial curry powder
1 teaspoon sesame oil
½ teaspoon red pepper flakes
1 tablespoon peeled and minced ginger (about 1-inch piece)
1 (14.5-ounce) can unsweetened coconut milk
3 tablespoons brown sugar
3 tablespoons fish sauce
¼ cup freshly squeezed lime juice (about 2 limes)
1 teaspoon cornstarch
2 scallions, cut into ¼-inch rings
Salt and freshly ground black pepper, to taste
¼ cup fresh cilantro leaves
2 limes, cut into quarters

3. In a small bowl, combine the fish sauce, lime juice, and cornstarch, and whisk together with a fork until the cornstarch is fully incorporated. Whisk the mixture into the pan and simmer for 3 minutes. Remove from heat and set aside.

4. Meanwhile, heat another heavy-bottomed sauté pan or cast-iron skillet over medium-high heat. Sear the tuna for 1 to 3 minutes per side, leaving it rare in the center. Remove from pan and cut into 1-inch slices.

5. Stir the scallions into the coconut sauce and season with salt and pepper. Evenly ladle the sauce into 4 shallow bowls, fan the tuna on top, and garnish with cilantro and limes.

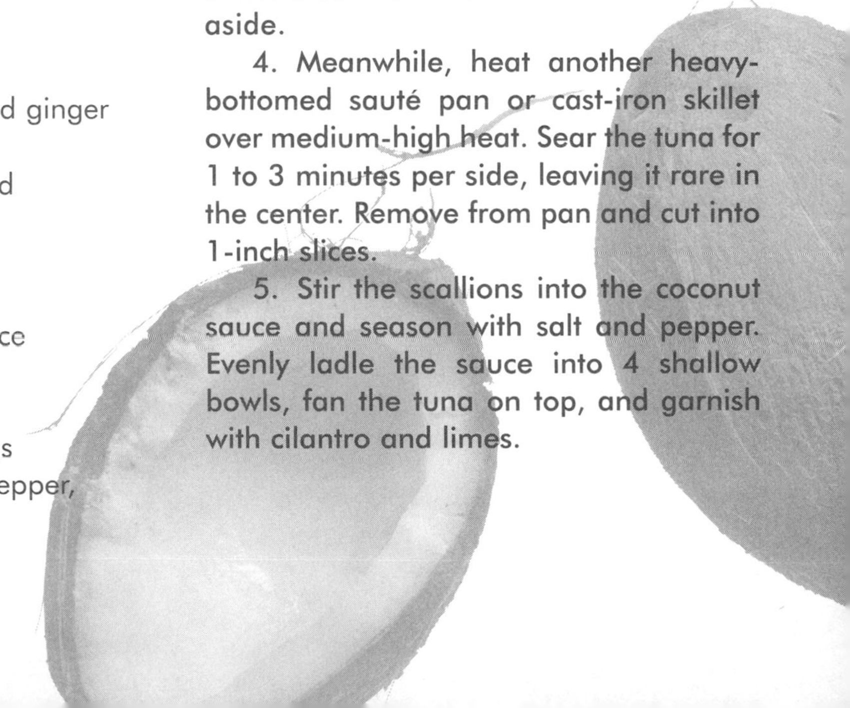

CORIANDER-LIME-GLAZED SWORDFISH KEBABS

SWORDFISH, with its meaty texture, is particularly well suited to grilling; it won't fall apart as easily as thinner, flakier fish, and its flavor is hearty enough to stand up to smoke, fire, and spice. This recipe combines a salty marinade with a sweet-and-sour glaze for a delicious Asian-style take on kebabs. Just make sure your peaches aren't too ripe, or the juices will burn and you might lose the fruit between the grates. Serve with Ginger Fried Rice (page 144).

Serves 4 as an entrée

8 large bamboo skewers, soaked in water for at least 3 hours
1½ pounds swordfish, cut into 1-inch cubes
2 large red onions, peeled, cut into quarters, and pieces separated
2 large red bell peppers, cored, seeded, and cut into large squares
2 barely ripe peaches, pitted and quartered
2 cups Soy Sake Sauce (page 13)
6 tablespoons honey
Juice of 2 limes (about ¼ cup)
2 teaspoons coriander seeds, toasted and very coarsely cracked
1 tablespoon minced fresh cilantro leaves
1 teaspoon kosher salt
2 teaspoons freshly ground black pepper
2 tablespoons canola oil

1. Thread the fish, onions, and red peppers alternately on the skewers, adding a peach wedge in the center of each. Transfer the kebabs to a shallow dish and pour the Soy Sake Sauce over them. Marinate in the refrigerator for 1 to 3 hours.

2. Prepare a hot fire in the grill.

3. Combine the honey, lime juice, coriander, cilantro, salt, and pepper in a small saucepan. Put the pan on the coolest part of the grill or over low heat on the stovetop and cook, stirring occasionally, until the ingredients are incorporated and warm.

4. When the grill is hot (you can keep your hand 5 inches above the grates for only 1 to 2 seconds), remove the skewers from the marinade, brush lightly with oil, and grill on each side for 3 to 4 minutes, watching carefully so they don't burn. When the meat is firm but not flaking apart, move the skewers to the coolest part of the grill and brush with glaze, turning to brush all sides. (If in doubt, use a thin knife to poke into the center of the fish; it should have a tiny bit of translucent flesh in the very center, but should otherwise be opaque.) Serve immediately.

SNAPPER IN CORNHUSKS

CORNHUSKS are not just for tamales; like banana leaves and paper (for what in French kitchens is called *en papillote*), they also make perfect little packages for cooking fish. Unlike paper, though, these take well to the grill. They'll blacken but won't burn, they give the snapper a hint of earthy corn flavor, and they make for a dynamic presentation—all with a minimum of effort. Everything should be this easy.

Serves 4 as an entrée

2 pounds skinless snapper fillet, cut into 4-inch by 1-inch strips
1 package (at least 6 ounces) dried cornhusks, removed and soaked in very hot water at least 1 hour
Salt and freshly ground black pepper, to taste
1 cup Salsa 101 (page 24)
8 (2-foot) lengths kitchen twine
3 limes, cut into 6 wedges each

1. Prepare a hot fire on one side of the grill.
2. Divide the fish into 8 portions. Remove 2 cornhusks from the water, shaking off excess water. Arrange the husks on a work surface with the cut (straight) ends overlapping by 1 to 2 inches. Place 1 portion of fish in the center of the husks, season with salt and pepper, and spoon 2 tablespoons of salsa on top. Fold up the husks around the fish to enclose completely, and tie the package with 1 piece of the kitchen twine. (If the husk tears, wrap another around it before tying.) Repeat with the remaining fish and husks.
3. When the grill is hot (you can hold your hand 5 inches above the hot side for only about 1 to 2 seconds), grill the husks for 1 minute on each side, or until black spots start to appear; move the husks to a cooler part of the grill and cook until the fish is done, 3 to 5 minutes more. Test for doneness by cutting 1 open slightly and checking to make sure the fish is white and flaky.
4. To serve, cut the strings and slit the packages lengthwise. Place 2 packages on each plate, pushing the ends in slightly to expose the fish. Garnish with lime wedges and serve the Salsa 101 on the side.

Carnivores Galore

MEAT AND POULTRY

GO OUT TO EAT WITH A CHEF, AND WE'LL ORDER A **STEAK**. Maybe it's because after a long day at our own restaurants, tasting all sorts of flavors, the comforting mildness of meat hits the spot like nothing else.

When it comes to cooking meat and poultry, match the cut to the cooking style, and you're well on your way to success. Lean stuff, like beef tenderloin and chicken breast, demands speed—sear it, grill it, or roast it under high heat. A lamb shank, pork butt, or short rib, on the other hand, needs a long, slow approach like braising to help break down all that connective tissue and fat. The payoff: a rich, deep taste and near-melting texture.

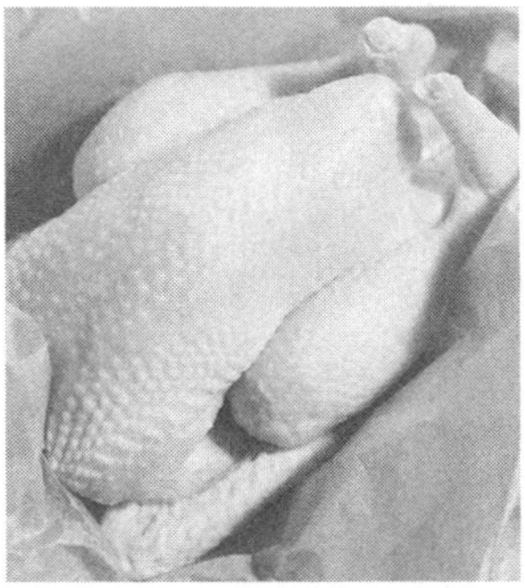

Then there's good old barbecue, which is harder than you might think. The elements have to be just right, from good hard wood to a low, controlled fire and plenty of patience. A few cold beers don't hurt, either.

No matter which technique you choose, as long as you've got the right cut of meat, substitution possibilities are endless. And fear not: If all else fails, you can always just grill up a steak. Just make sure to invite a chef over.

MEAT/POULTR

carnivores galore

PINEAPPLE-GLAZED ROAST PORK SHOULDER

THE BEST BANG for your buck on a pig is the shoulder, either the picnic shoulder or the oddly named Boston butt. Cook it slowly, and it rewards you with falling-apart tenderness, and no fuss. This is a great dinner party dish, not only because the crispy, sweet glaze and rich meat are such crowd pleasers, but because both rub and glaze can be made a day or two ahead. That will make it a favorite of busy hosts, too.

Serves 6 to 8 as an entrée

4 cloves garlic, peeled and minced
½ cup olive oil
2 tablespoons kosher salt
1 tablespoon dried oregano
1 tablespoon chili powder
2 teaspoons cumin seeds, toasted and ground
2 teaspoons coriander seeds, toasted and ground
1 teaspoon cayenne pepper
Juice of 2 limes (about ¼ cup)
5- to 6-pound bone-in pork shoulder (Boston butt or picnic shoulder)
3 cups pineapple juice
¼ packed cup brown sugar
Salt and freshly ground black pepper, to taste

1. Preheat oven to 425°F.
2. In a food processor or blender, combine the garlic, olive oil, salt, oregano, chili powder, cumin, coriander, cayenne, and lime juice; blend well.
3. Make shallow cuts 1 to 2 inches apart over the entire surface of the pork shoulder. Reserving 1 tablespoon of the seasoning mixture, rub the remainder over the pork, working it into the slits. Put the pork on a rack in a roasting pan and roast for 30 minutes.
4. Meanwhile, in a small saucepan, combine the pineapple juice, brown sugar, and reserved 1 tablespoon seasoning mixture over medium-high heat and bring to a boil. Simmer until reduced by half, stirring occasionally to prevent scorching. Season to taste with salt and pepper.
5. When the pork has roasted for 30 minutes, lower heat to 350°F and brush with the pineapple glaze and pan drippings, repeating every 30 minutes until the pork reaches an internal temperature of 145°F, 2 to 2½ hours.
6. Transfer to a cutting board and let rest for 15 minutes before carving. Drizzle the pork slices with some remaining pineapple glaze before serving.

YUCATAN ROASTED PORK

UNWRAP this in front of your guests, and the fragrant steam alone will have them singing your praises. Little do they know, the recipe's a breeze. The marinade, banana leaves, low heat, and long hours do the work for you, leaving the pork fork-tender, spicy, and perfect with Salsa 101 (page 24), Limed Sour Cream (page 22), and tortillas. You can roast this on a grill instead of in the oven, as long as you keep the heat low and consistent.

Serves 4 as an entrée

1½ cups Yucatan Chili Sauce (page 12)
1 cup roughly chopped fresh cilantro
3-pound boneless pork shoulder (Boston butt or picnic shoulder)
Kitchen twine
2–3 large banana leaves, cut into 2-foot-long sections (see "Leave It to Bananas," below)

1. In a large bowl or sealable plastic bag, combine the chili sauce and cilantro, and mix well. Add the pork and coat it generously with the sauce. Cover and refrigerate for at least 24 hours.

2. Preheat oven to 275°F.

3. To wrap the pork, clear a large work surface and have a roll of butcher's twine ready. Spread out the banana leaves so they overlap by about 2 inches. Remove the pork from the marinade, and place it in the center of the leaves. Fold over the leaves, one at a time, to enclose the pork like a package. Use twine to tie it up like a present, so the banana leaves stay tight.

4. Place a small pan of water inside a larger roasting pan, and place a flat roasting rack on top. Arrange the pork package on the rack, and cover loosely with foil. Roast until you can feel the pork falling apart inside its package if you push on it, about 4 to 5 hours. If you're not sure, err on the side of longer cooking; you really can't overcook this dish.

5. Let the roast cool for 10 minutes before transferring to a serving platter. Remove the twine, and serve immediately, opening the banana leaves at the table and allowing guests to serve themselves. Serve hot.

LEAVE IT TO BANANAS

We love banana leaves for steaming meats and seafood, especially since they give a dish that great little opening-a-package effect at the table. But where do you find them? Look in Asian and Latin markets, and head straight for the frozen-food aisle.

Always buy more than you think you need, because once you get them home, you'll discover their main challenge: They can rip easily. Preventing the ripping means preheating, which makes them more pliable. Either remove the leaves from the package and steam, covered, for 1 to 2 minutes, until hot, or—and this is our favorite way—microwave the entire unopened package for 2 minutes on high. It will puff up and self-steam. Then, if you don't use them all, seal in a large plastic freezer bag, and put back in the freezer until next time.

ITALIAN-STYLE MEAT LOAF

IF YOU THINK good Italian food is all pasta, come to Sage in Boston's North End, where I was so wowed by a version of this three-meat loaf that I asked chef Tony Susi to share the recipe. I couldn't resist tinkering, and added the pancetta as an Italian nod to the bacon strips that baste American diner meat loaf; the pancetta adds a unique flavor and an irresistible moistness.

Serves 4 to 6 as an entrée

1 tablespoon canola oil
1 medium-size yellow onion, peeled and minced
4 cloves garlic, peeled and minced
2 portobello mushrooms, stems trimmed
1/4 bunch flat-leaf Italian parsley
10 fresh basil leaves
1/4 cup balsamic vinegar, divided
2 eggs, beaten
3/4 cup bread crumbs
1/2 cup milk
2 teaspoons dried oregano
1 teaspoon dried thyme
3/4 pound ground beef
3/4 pound ground veal
1/2 pound ground pork
2 tablespoons freshly ground black pepper
1 tablespoon kosher salt
3/4 cup ketchup, divided
8 thin slices pancetta (about 1/4 pound)

1. Preheat oven to 350°F.

2. Heat the oil in a small sauté pan over medium heat. Add the onion and garlic; cook, stirring, until the onions are tender, 5 to 7 minutes. Transfer to a large mixing bowl and let cool to room temperature.

3. Crumble the mushrooms into a food processor bowl, and pulse until chopped. (Work in batches if necessary.) Add the parsley, basil, and 2 tablespoons of the balsamic vinegar; process until minced. Add to the onion-garlic mixture, along with the eggs, bread crumbs, milk, oregano, and thyme; mix to combine thoroughly.

4. Add the beef, veal, pork, pepper, salt, and 1/4 cup of the ketchup; mix well. Transfer to a baking sheet and form into a loaf.

5. In a small bowl, combine the remaining 1/2 cup ketchup and remaining 2 tablespoons balsamic vinegar; mix well. Spread evenly over the meat loaf. Arrange the pancetta slices in a layer on top, and bake to an internal temperature of 150°F, about 90 minutes. Allow to rest 10 minutes before slicing.

BILLY'S CRISPY PORK CHOPS WITH MAPLE CHILI GLAZE

CHEF DE CUISINE Billy Barlow is the token Southerner at Rouge, so when we asked him to contribute a recipe to the book, he replied with that sweet charm, "Why, sure." We weren't surprised that he came up with fried pork chops, but the maple glaze was a nice twist. Serve with Chow-Chow (page 74).

Serves 4 as an entrée

4 (1-pound) porterhouse pork chops, about ¾ inch thick
2 cups buttermilk
1½ cups cornmeal
¾ cup all-purpose flour
1 tablespoon paprika
1 teaspoon kosher salt
1 teaspoon freshly ground black pepper
About 3 cups peanut *or* canola oil, for frying
Salt and freshly ground black pepper, to taste
1 tablespoon canola oil
1 teaspoon red pepper flakes
2 cloves garlic, peeled and minced
½ cup maple syrup
Juice of 1 lime (about 2 tablespoons)

1. Soak the chops in the buttermilk in the refrigerator for at least 2 hours.
2. In a medium-size bowl, combine the cornmeal, flour, paprika, salt, and pepper, and mix well.
3. Preheat oven to 350°F.
4. Add the oil to a large, deep frying pan to a depth of about ½ inch. (Do not fill the pan more than halfway.) Turn heat to medium-high. While the oil is heating, remove the chops from the buttermilk. One at a time, dredge the chops in the cornmeal mixture, turning to coat thoroughly. When the oil is sizzling hot, fry pork chops until golden brown, 3 to 5 minutes per side, working in batches if necessary to avoid crowding the pan.
5. Transfer the chops to a rack set on a baking sheet and bake until the chops reach an internal temperature of 150°F, 5 to 7 minutes. Remove from oven and season with salt and pepper.
6. While the chops are baking, make the glaze: In a small saucepan, heat the 1 tablespoon canola oil over medium heat. Add the red pepper flakes and garlic, and cook, stirring, for 1 minute. Remove from heat and add the maple syrup and lime juice; mix well. To serve, spoon the glaze over the chops.

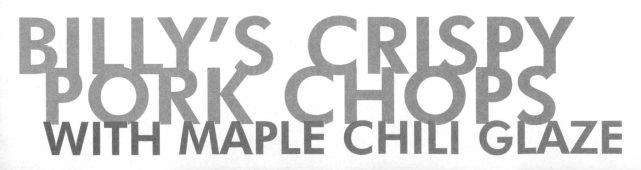

TWELVE-SPICE TURKEY BREAST WITH CUCUMBER-YOGURT SAUCE

JOHN DELPHA, friend and accomplished chef, scribbled this recipe onto a cocktail napkin over drinks one night. The chunky sauce, reminiscent of a Greek tzatziki, cools off the peppery turkey. For a more informal meal, stuff slices of turkey in a toasted pita, spoon in some of the yogurt sauce, and add some texture in the form of chopped red onions.

Serves 6 to 8 as an entrée

For the Twelve-Spice Turkey Breast:

1 (4–6-pound) turkey breast with skin, soaked overnight in Basic Brine (page 9)
1 tablespoon granulated sugar
1 teaspoon kosher salt
2 teaspoons paprika
1 1/2 teaspoons white peppercorns, ground
1 1/2 teaspoons black peppercorns, ground
2 teaspoons garlic powder
2 teaspoons onion powder
2 star anise, ground (about 1 1/2 teaspoons)
1 teaspoon ground cinnamon
1 teaspoon ground cardamom
1 teaspoon coriander, toasted and ground
1/2 teaspoon cumin seeds, toasted and ground
1/2 teaspoon ground cloves

For the Cucumber-Yogurt Sauce (makes about 2 1/2 cups):

2 cups plain yogurt
1 small cucumber, peeled, seeded, and minced (about 1 cup)
Juice of 1 lemon (about 1/4 cup)
1 teaspoon minced fresh mint leaves
1 teaspoon minced fresh oregano
1/2 teaspoon cumin seeds, toasted and ground
Salt and freshly ground black pepper, to taste

1. Preheat oven to 450°F.

2. Remove the turkey from the brine and pat dry. Combine all the remaining turkey breast ingredients, and mix well. Rub the spice mixture under and over the turkey skin, using all of the rub.

3. Roast the turkey until an instant-read thermometer registers an internal temperature of 155°F, 50 to 60 minutes. Transfer the turkey to a cutting board and allow it to rest for 10 minutes.

4. While the turkey rests, combine all the sauce ingredients in a bowl and mix well. Season with salt and pepper.

5. To serve, divide Cucumber-Yogurt Sauce among serving plates. Cut turkey into thick slices, and fan over sauce.

STILL COOKING

If you're using an instant-read thermometer when roasting meat, remember that because the heat penetrates from the outside in, the internal temperature will keep rising by 5° to 10°F within the first few minutes after you remove it from the oven. So if you want your whole chicken to end up at 165°F, pull it out at 160°F; if you want your pork to reach 140°F, pull it out at 135°F. The higher the oven temperature, the greater the rise.

SWEET-AND-SOUR SHORT RIBS

THERE'S REALLY no such thing as overcooked short ribs. Like veal shanks (osso buco) and oxtails, they need time. Done right, they're delectable; undercooked, they turn out chewy and gnarly. These seem barbecued because of the sauce, but they're really braised (slow-cooked in liquid). As with most braises, the cooking liquid is reduced—and becomes the rich, thick, sweet-sour sauce.

Serves 4 as an entrée

1 (28-ounce) can whole peeled tomatoes
1 cup water
1 large white onion, peeled and diced
¼ cup peeled and minced garlic
2 teaspoons prepared yellow mustard
½ cup molasses
¾ cup cider vinegar
½ cup Worcestershire
1 cup of your favorite beer
2 teaspoons red pepper flakes
1 teaspoon paprika
4 pounds bone-in beef short ribs
Kosher salt and freshly ground black pepper, to taste
¼ cup canola oil

1. Preheat oven to 325°F.

2. In a large mixing bowl, make the braising liquid by combining the first 11 ingredients; mix well and set aside. Season the ribs liberally with salt and pepper.

3. In a heavy-bottomed pot or Dutch oven just large enough to hold the ribs in a single layer, heat the oil over medium-high heat. When the oil is hot but not smoking, add the ribs and sear until dark brown, 2 to 4 minutes per side, working in batches if necessary to avoid crowding the pan.

4. Transfer the ribs to the bowl of braising liquid; drain off and discard the fat in the pan.

5. Return the ribs to the pot along with enough braising liquid to come ⅔ up the sides of the meat. Bring the liquid to a boil. Cover the pot tightly with 2 layers of foil, pressing it down the sides of the pot and directly onto the surface of the meat. Cover with a lid, and transfer to the oven. Bake until a skewer inserted into the meat encounters no resistance, about 2 hours.

6. When the ribs are done, transfer to a platter and cover loosely with foil. Place the pot of braising liquid over medium heat and simmer, stirring occasionally, until it has reduced to the consistency of ketchup, about 20 minutes. Season to taste with salt and pepper, pour over the meat, and serve.

Just A Bit

Don't bother with those commercial bacon bits: In texture and flavor, they're nothing like the real thing, which could hardly be easier to make. To get 1 cup of the crispiest possible bacon bits, chop 1 pound of the best-quality bacon you can find, such as applewood smoked. Heat a heavy-duty cast-iron skillet over medium-high heat, and cook until well browned and crisp, about 10 to 15 minutes. Transfer to a plate lined with paper towels for draining and cooling, then store in an airtight container in the refrigerator, for up to 1 week.

Basil-Crusted Pork Tenderloin with Bacon Corn Relish

I WAS SO CLOSE and yet so far to perfecting this recipe, when ROUGE chef Billy Barlow said it all: "Everything's better with bacon." Eureka! The relish, with its sweet corn and salty bacon, perfectly complements the basil pork, making for a summery delight that pairs nicely with Dirty Rice (page 145).

Serves 4 to 6 as an entrée

1 lightly packed cup fresh basil leaves
2 cloves garlic, peeled
2 tablespoons balsamic vinegar
2 tablespoons olive oil
Salt and freshly ground black pepper, to taste
2 (1- to 1½-pound) pork tenderloins
1 cup fresh corn kernels (about 2 large ears)
2 tablespoons fresh-squeezed lemon juice (about ½ lemon)
½ small red onion, peeled and cut into ¼-inch dice
1 tablespoon extra-virgin olive oil
¼ cup pitted and chopped green olives
¼ cup chopped flat-leaf Italian parsley
½ cup bacon bits (see "Just a Bit," above)
2 tablespoons minced chives (optional)

1. Preheat oven to 425°F.

2. In a food processor or blender, combine the basil, garlic, balsamic vinegar, and olive oil; purée, and season with salt and pepper. Rub the mixture into the pork tenderloins, coating them completely.

3. Heat a large, heavy-bottomed ovenproof sauté pan over high heat. Sear the pork until browned on all sides, 2 to 4 minutes. Transfer the pan to the oven and roast the tenderloins to an internal temperature of 135°F, 10 to 15 minutes.

4. Meanwhile, in a medium-size bowl, combine the corn, lemon juice, onion, extra-virgin olive oil, olives, parsley, bacon bits, and chives, and season generously with salt and pepper.

5. When the pork is done, transfer to a cutting board and allow to rest for 5 minutes. Slice crosswise into ¼-inch–thick pieces, and arrange overlapping slices on a platter. Spoon some relish over the pork, and pass the remaining relish on the side.

BIRRIA (MEXICAN MEAT STEW)

THIS DISH sounds a lot better if you don't speak Spanish; it means "deformed" or "grotesque." Don't worry: That's just how it looks, not how it tastes. This spicy multiple-meat stew is rich, hearty, and ideal for wrapping in tortillas. It's also ripe for substitution: In Mexico's roadside taquerias, you'll see organ meats in the mix, but unless your guests are heartier of constitution than most of our friends are, skip that approach. (Veal breast, chicken legs, rabbit, or venison, however, are all fair game; just keep it to 3 pounds of meat total.) Serve with Fiery Three-Onion Salsa (page 25).

Serves 4 to 6 as an entrée

1 small yellow onion, peeled and chopped
4 jalapeño chilies, stemmed and chopped
8 cloves garlic, peeled
1/4 cup white vinegar
2 tablespoons chili powder
2 tablespoons dried oregano
2 teaspoons cumin seeds, toasted and ground
2 teaspoons coriander seeds, toasted and ground
2 teaspoons ground cinnamon
2 teaspoons kosher salt
1 teaspoon ground allspice
1 teaspoon ground cloves
1-pound lamb shank
1-pound pork shoulder
1-pound beef brisket
3/4 cup water
3 tablespoons all-purpose flour
2 large tomatoes, cored and chopped, or 1 (14.5-ounce) can diced tomatoes
Salt and freshly ground black pepper, to taste

1. Preheat oven to 325°F.

2. In the bowl of a food processor, or in a blender, combine the onion, chilies, garlic, vinegar, and seasonings; process to form a paste. Rub the paste liberally on the lamb, pork, and beef.

3. Add 1 inch of water to a heavy pot or Dutch oven, preferably enamel-coated cast iron, with a tight-fitting lid. Add the meat to the pot.

4. In a small bowl, whisk together 3/4 cup water and the flour until smooth. Rub some of the paste along the rim of the pot to form a seal and immediately cover. Set aside the remaining paste.

5. Bake without peeking for 2 1/2 hours, or until the meat is very tender. Remove from oven and uncover. Transfer the meat to a plate. Wait 10 minutes for the juices to settle in the pot, skim the surface with a spoon to remove excess fat, then add the tomatoes to the juices in the pot; bring to a boil over medium-high heat. Stir the remaining flour-water mixture to reblend, and whisk into the boiling sauce. Adjust heat to a simmer, and cook, stirring occasionally, for 5 minutes. Season generously with salt and pepper.

6. When the meat is cool enough to handle, shred it, discarding any bones and large pieces of fat. Transfer to a large serving platter or bowl, and pour the sauce over the meat.

BRAISED LAMB SHANKS WITH EGGPLANT AND CHICKPEAS

LAMB is a seasonally schizophrenic meat: Grilled chops, left rosy inside, evoke spring like nothing else, while few foods make us feel as cozy in winter as braised shanks. This recipe plays up their richness with hearty spices, eggplant, and chickpeas. For extra complexity, we suggest trying the addition of figs, olives, and almond slivers, listed as optional here, but the dish is plenty interesting without them. Serve with rice, couscous, polenta, or Mashed Potatoes with Salt Cod (page 178), along with Green Olive Bread (page 251).

Serves 4 as an entrée

1 large eggplant, peeled and cut into 1-inch cubes
1 teaspoon kosher salt
2 tablespoons canola oil
4 (about 1-pound) lamb shanks, trimmed of excess fat
2 cloves garlic, peeled and minced
1 red bell pepper, seeded and cut into ½-inch dice
1 medium-size red onion, peeled and cut into ½-inch dice
1 tablespoon Ethiopian Spice Mix (page 5)
2 cups tomato juice
2 cups Lamb Stock (page 119), Chicken Stock (page 118), or water
1 (15- to 19-ounce) can high-quality chickpeas (such as Progresso), drained
¼ cup diced figs (optional)
¼ cup diced pitted green olives (optional)
¼ cup almond slivers, toasted (optional)
Juice of 1 lime (about 2 tablespoons)
Salt and freshly ground black pepper, to taste
¼ cup chopped fresh mint leaves
¼ cup chopped fresh parsley leaves

1. Preheat oven to 350°F.

2. Set a colander over a large plate. Toss the eggplant and salt together in the colander, and place another plate directly on the surface of the eggplant. Weight down the plate with a heavy object (such as a jar or milk jug filled with water), and set aside for at least 1 hour. Rinse with cold water and gently squeeze out excess liquid.

3. Heat the oil in a heavy-bottomed sauté pan or cast-iron skillet over high heat. Liberally season the lamb with salt and pepper, and sear on all sides, working in batches if necessary to avoid crowding the pan. Transfer the lamb to a large roasting pan (preferably with a lid), and return skillet to heat.

4. Add the eggplant, garlic, bell pepper, and red onion; cook, stirring frequently, until the vegetables begin to brown, 8 to 10 minutes. Add the Ethiopian Spice Mix, cook for 1 minute, then add the tomato juice and stock or water and bring to a boil, scraping up any browned bits stuck to the bottom of the pan.

5. Spoon the vegetable mixture over the shanks (the liquid should reach about halfway up the sides of the shanks and sides of the pan), cover tightly with lid or foil, and bake for 90 minutes. Carefully remove the roasting pan from the oven. Turn over the shanks and add the chickpeas, along with the figs, green olives, and almonds, if using. Cover and bake for 30 to 45 minutes more, or until the meat easily pulls away from the bone.

6. Transfer the shanks to shallow bowls or plates. Season the braising liquid with lime juice, salt, and pepper, and spoon the vegetables and liquid over the lamb. Garnish with chopped mint and parsley.

A Done Deal

In a busy kitchen cranking out lots of grilled steaks, we don't have time to pull out the meat thermometer at every turn, so I try to teach my cooks how to tell the doneness of a steak without it. The technique involves comparing different parts of the flesh on your palm to the way steaks at different doneness levels feel, but frankly, it's a pretty tough thing to teach. For home cooks, we recommend either slicing into a piece and looking at the redness, or using a good instant-read thermometer. Here's what to look for:

Rare: Done only on outside, bloody and dark red throughout inside (120–125°F)
Medium-rare: Rosy throughout, with a bloody red spot in the center (130–135°F)
Medium: Rosy throughout, with a slightly darker center (140–145°F)
Medium-well: Slightly rosy throughout, including center (150–155°F)
Well-done: Gray throughout (160°F and higher)

BRASSERIE-STYLE STEAK AND MUSSELS

TO BE HONEST, we've never seen this particular combination in Paris, but separately all the pieces are brasserie classics. Here, they fit just fine. The pan-fried steak is seasoned with the briny saltiness of the mussels, a mound of shallots, and beer. Serve with French fries, of course; take out the barbecue spice in our Barbecued French Fries (page 174), and you're all set.

Serves 4 as an entrée

4 (6-ounce) New York strip steaks
Salt and freshly ground black pepper, to taste
2 tablespoons canola oil
4 large or 8 small shallots, peeled and cut into thin slices (about 1 1/2 cups)
2 cloves garlic, peeled and minced
1 teaspoon dried thyme
2 pounds mussels, washed well and debearded (see sidebar on page 48)
1 (12-ounce) bottle any light ale, such as Rolling Rock
1/4 cup cold butter, cut into small cubes
1/2 cup chopped fresh parsley leaves

1. Dry the steaks well, and season liberally with salt and pepper.

2. Heat the oil in a heavy-bottomed sauté pan over high heat. Sear the steaks for 3 to 4 minutes per side or to desired doneness, and remove, leaving the pan on heat.

3. Immediately add the shallots, garlic, and thyme to the pan; cook, stirring constantly and scraping up juices and steak bits stuck to the pan, until the shallots soften, about 1 minute. Add the mussels and beer, and mix well to combine.

4. Lower heat to medium, cover the pan, and cook for 2 minutes, shaking the pan often. Add the butter and continue to cook, covered, until all the mussels are open, 2 to 4 minutes more. (Discard any mussels that do not open.) Toss with parsley, and season with salt and pepper. Spoon the mussels and sauce over the steaks.

GRILLED GIANT PARTY STEAK

SOMETIMES—actually, lots of times, in our book—summer parties just demand a good steak. Few things are as festive as a steak that can serve several people, but it does require some planning. You need to see a good butcher to get a steak this size, and you'll have to be sure to pull it out of the refrigerator a couple of hours before grilling, to get it to room temperature and make for more even cooking. Save this recipe for people who appreciate a medium-rare steak; no offense, but it's too good to waste on that well-done crowd. And in keeping with the party atmosphere, serve with Fontina-Stuffed Crispy Taters (page 172) and Black Pepper Bread (page 249).

Serves 4 to 6 as an entrée

4-pound strip loin or your favorite other top-quality steak, at least 2 inches thick, fat trimmed to 1/8-inch
Salt and freshly ground black pepper, to taste
1 stick butter, cut into cubes and at room temperature
2 cloves garlic, peeled and minced
Zest of 1 lemon, minced
1 teaspoon minced fresh sage leaves
1 teaspoon minced fresh rosemary

1. Prepare a medium-hot fire, preferably with hardwood charcoal, on one side of the grill.
2. Liberally season the steak with salt and pepper, pressing seasoning in, and let sit at room temperature, covered with plastic wrap, for 1 hour while the grill is heating.
3. When the fire is medium-hot (you can hold your hand 5 inches above the grate for only 4 to 5 seconds), grill the steak on each side until the meat begins to char, 2 to 4 minutes per side. Move to unheated side of grill and cook to desired doneness (see "A Done Deal," page 218, for temperature guide), 10 to 15 minutes per side.
4. Meanwhile, in a small bowl, combine the butter, garlic, lemon zest, sage, rosemary, and more salt and pepper to taste, and mix well. Cover with plastic wrap and set aside.
5. When the steak is done, transfer to a large platter. Spread half of the butter mixture on top, loosely cover with aluminum foil, and let rest for 5 to 10 minutes.
6. Slice the steak across the grain into 1/4-inch-thick slices, and fan out on a serving platter. Spread the remaining butter evenly over the slices.

GRILLS, GRILLS, GRILLS

We know it's tempting to use a gas grill—or even an electric one—but if you never use a good-old fire-burning grill, you're missing out on one of the most important benefits of barbecuing and grilling: that smoky taste that you get only when you play with fire.

But even once you commit to a real grill, let go of the charcoal-soaked-in-lighter-fluid approach. Instead, use dry wood or hardwood charcoal, which is free of all those fillers found in most briquettes. As a bonus, it also lights easier and burns hotter.

BUTTERMILK FRIED CHICKEN WITH GREEN ONION GRAVY

MOST down-home Southern fried chicken is bone-in, which is fine, but we like this method because it's quicker and it leaves the chicken so crispy on the outside and so succulent inside. The buttermilk, which we spike with Louisiana hot sauce, helps tenderize the chicken, which we pair with a nice punchy gravy. Serve with Collard Greens with Smoked Turkey Butt (page 153) and your choice of biscuits: Flaky Yankee Biscuits (page 244) or Fluffy Southern Biscuits (page 243).

Serves 4 as an entrée

2 cups buttermilk
1 tablespoon kosher salt
½ cup Louisiana hot sauce
4 (about 6-ounce) boneless, skinless chicken breasts, pounded to ¼-inch thickness (see "Pound for Pound," page 230)
4 (about 4-ounce) boneless/skinless chicken thighs, trimmed well of extra fat and pounded to ¼-inch thickness (see "Pound for Pound," page 230)
1½ cups, plus 3 tablespoons all-purpose flour
1½ cups yellow cornmeal
1½ tablespoons Creole Seasoning (page 4)
Salt and freshly ground black pepper, to taste
3 tablespoons butter
8–10 cups canola *or* peanut oil, for frying
1 tablespoon canola oil
1 link (about 4 ounces) andouille sausage, cut into ¼-inch dice
2 garlic cloves, peeled and minced
2 cups Chicken Stock (page 118)
4 scallions, cut into ¼-inch slices
1–2 teaspoons Tabasco

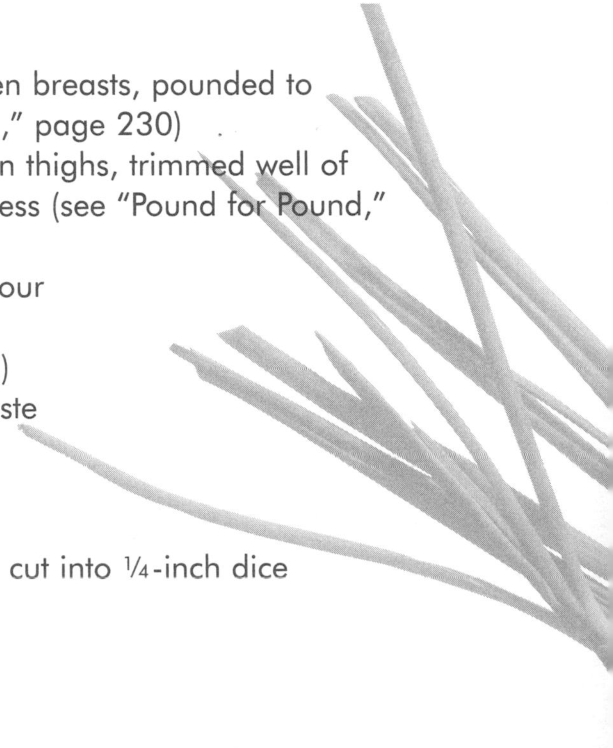

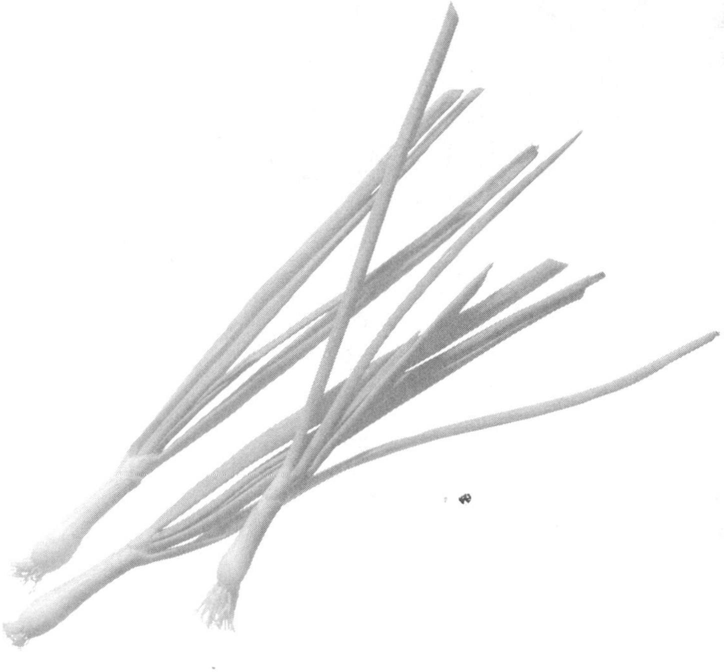

1. Combine the buttermilk, salt, and Louisiana hot sauce in a medium-size bowl and mix well. Add the chicken breasts and thighs, cover, and refrigerate for at least 4 hours and as long as 24 hours.

2. Preheat oven to 200°F.

3. In a medium-size bowl, combine the 1½ cups flour, the cornmeal, Creole Seasoning, and salt to taste. Remove the chicken from the buttermilk marinade, shaking off excess. Dredge in the flour mixture, thoroughly coating, and transfer to a plate.

4. In a small saucepan over medium-low heat, make a roux by heating the butter until melted, then stirring in the 3 tablespoons flour with a wire whisk or fork. Return to low heat and cook for 15 minutes, stirring frequently to avoid burning, until the roux is light golden brown. Remove from heat, transfer to a small bowl, and set aside.

5. Fill the Dutch oven 2 inches deep with canola or peanut oil and place over medium-high heat. When the oil is hot, use tongs to lower the chicken pieces carefully into the oil, working in batches to avoid overcrowding; fry for 4 to 6 minutes or until golden brown. Transfer to a plate lined with paper towels to drain. Season immediately with salt and pepper, then put in a warm oven to keep hot until the rest of the chicken and the gravy is done.

6. To make the gravy, heat the 1 tablespoon canola oil in a medium-size saucepan over medium-high heat. Add the sausage and cook, stirring occasionally, until browned, about 5 to 7 minutes. Add the garlic and cook for 30 seconds. Add the chicken stock, increase heat to high, and bring to a boil.

7. Ladle out some boiling stock and pour it into the bowl of roux, whisking well to combine; repeat with 2 more ladles of stock. Pour the mixture back into the boiling stock, whisking until fully incorporated. Lower heat to medium and simmer for 5 minutes. Add the scallions and season with Tabasco and salt and pepper. Remove the chicken from the oven, pour gravy over the top, and serve immediately.

MY COOKS at TREMONT 647 were exhausted and hungry one night, so I asked one of the day cooks, Jorge Tomayo, to whip up a quick meal. We had some leftover skirt steak strips, and Jorge made quick work of them. He chopped them up and dropped them into the fryer, rendering the beef crunchy and browned, then simply seasoned them with salt, pepper, and lime. Now I make these at home all the time, rolled up in soft tacos with some lettuce, avocado—and, of course, Salsa 101 (page 24) and Limed Sour Cream (page 22).

Serves 4 as an entrée

1 cup canola oil
1 ½ pounds skirt steak, cut into ¼-inch-wide, 4-inch-long strips, making sure to cut against the grain
Salt and freshly ground black pepper, to taste
Juice of 1 lime (about 2 tablespoons)
1 avocado
8 (8-inch) flour tortillas
1 cup Salsa 101 (page 24)
1 cup Limed Sour Cream (page 22)
¼ head of iceberg lettuce, shredded

CRUNCHY SKIRT STEAK TACOS

1. Heat the oil in a large, heavy-bottomed sauté pan or cast-iron skillet over medium-high heat. Season the steak strips with salt and pepper, and add to the pan. Cook, stirring occasionally, for 5 to 10 minutes or until the meat is crispy and browned. Remove from the pan and season with 1 tablespoon of the lime juice and additional salt and pepper to taste.

2. Peel the avocado, cut into 8 wedges, and drizzle with the remaining 1 tablespoon lime juice.

3. Pour off and discard the oil from the pan. Place the tortillas, one at a time, in the pan for 20 to 30 seconds on one side, to heat.

4. To make the tacos, divide the steak into 8 equal portions. Roll each tortilla (oily side up) with the steak, 1 slice avocado, 2 tablespoons each salsa and sour cream, and lettuce, and serve.

APPLE-STUFFED GAME HENS

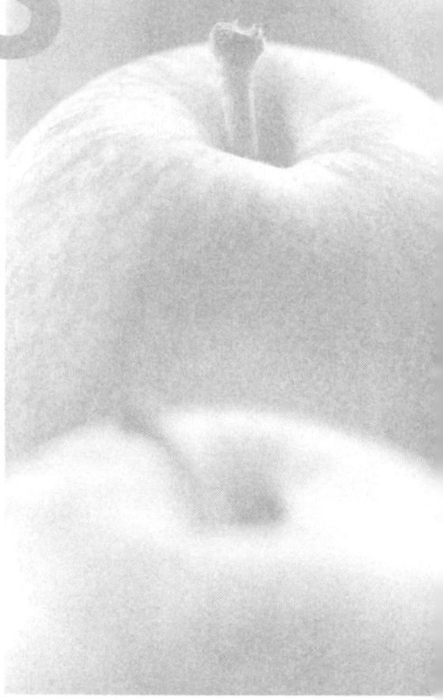

CORNISH HENS, with their tender flesh and easy-to-get-crispy skin, make for an elegant entrée at a sit-down dinner party. For one thing, they're tidy and self-contained; for another, they're just the right amount of food, so your guests will feel satisfied, not as stuffed as the little birds they just ate. That means they can also enjoy such accompaniments as Sweet-and-Sour Cipollini (page 156) and Scalloped Sweet Potatoes with Chipotle (page 176).

Serves 4 as an entrée

6 tablespoons unsalted butter, divided
1 small yellow onion, peeled and cut into ¼-inch dice
2 cloves garlic, peeled and minced
4–5 slices sourdough bread, cut into ½-inch cubes (about 1½ cups)
½ cup dried apples, cut into ½-inch chunks
2 tablespoons milk (optional)
1½ tablespoons minced fresh sage
1 teaspoon kosher salt
1 teaspoon freshly ground black pepper
4 Rock Cornish Game Hens, innards removed
Salt and freshly ground black pepper, to taste
6-inch piece butcher's twine
1 tablespoon minced fresh rosemary
2 tablespoons honey

1. Preheat oven to 350°F.

2. Heat 2 tablespoons of the butter in a medium-size saucepan over medium heat. Add the onion and garlic; cook, stirring occasionally, for 5 to 7 minutes or until the onions are soft. Transfer to a mixing bowl and let cool to room temperature.

3. Add the bread cubes, dried apples, milk (as needed if the mixture seems dry), sage, salt, and pepper, and mix well.

4. Season the hens generously with more salt and pepper inside and out. Stuff with the bread mixture and tie the legs together with a 6-inch piece of butcher's twine. Transfer to a rack placed over a sheet pan, and roast for 30 minutes.

5. Meanwhile, in a small bowl, combine the remaining 4 tablespoons butter, the rosemary, and honey; mix well.

6. Once the hens have roasted for 30 minutes, brush each with about 2 teaspoons rosemary butter and continue roasting and basting every 15 minutes until the hens are done—about 60 to 75 minutes total cooking time. The hens are done when the juices run clear after the thigh is pricked or when the thigh reaches an internal temperature of 160°F.

BARBECUED CHICKEN SANDWICHES

SAVE THIS RECIPE for when you're having a party; it takes awhile, but if you're feeding a barbecue-loving crowd, it's worth it. With these sandwiches, your guests forget the knife and fork and tuck into a soft bun, spicy, tender chicken, and the crunch of some kickin' coleslaw. Such tastes and textures, all in one bite: What could be better?

Serves 8 as an entrée

8 (8-ounce) chicken thighs (or 4 pounds smaller thighs), skin-on and preferably boneless, soaked in Basic Brine (page 9) for at least 2 hours
½ cup Basic Barbecue Rub (page 7)
2 tablespoons distilled white vinegar
2 tablespoons Tabasco
2 teaspoons paprika
2 teaspoons kosher salt
8 hamburger buns
1 recipe UFO Social Club Coleslaw (page 73)

1. Prepare a charcoal or wood fire on one side of the grill, near the opening where the handles are, if you are using this style of grill. (You will need to add charcoal periodically through this hole.) Bring grill to low temperature, about 225°F (you can hold your hand 5 inches above the grate for only 5 to 6 seconds).

2. Remove the chicken from the brine and pat dry with paper towels. Season evenly with the barbecue spice.

3. Lay the thighs skin-side down on the side of the grill *opposite* the fire, and cover the grill, with lid vents open. Cook for 30 minutes. Check the coals, adding more as needed to maintain temperature, and turn the thighs over. Repeat until the chicken is fork-tender, with no sign of redness near the bone, about 1½ to 2 hours.

4. Meanwhile, in a small bowl, combine the vinegar, Tabasco, paprika, and salt; set aside.

5. Transfer the chicken to a plate and let cool slightly. Add more coals, and bring the temperature to medium-high (you can hold your hand 5 inches above the grate for only 2 to 3 seconds).

6. If the chicken was cooked bone-in, remove the bones as soon as the chicken is cool enough to handle: Turn one thigh skin-side down on a cutting board. Use a small, sharp knife to cut neatly along the sides of each bone, without cutting through the skin. Separate the bone from the meat, and reshape the thigh as neatly as possible. Repeat with remaining thighs.

7. Grill the buns cut-side down for about 30 seconds, being careful not to burn them. Transfer to a plate and keep warm. Return the chicken thighs to the grill, skin-side down, to crisp them quickly, 10 to 30 seconds.

8. To serve, put one thigh on each bun heel, sprinkle the vinegar mixture over, and top with the coleslaw and top of bun.

EASY GRILLED PORK CHOPS WITH SWEET PEAS AND CORN

IN SUMMER, and with access to a local farm stand, this is a no-brainer. The vegetables are barely cooked because they're so fresh and in season, the pork is juicy and flavorful from the brine, and they come together like the sun and the earth on a warm day. Don't be afraid to leave the pork a little rosy in the center; if you get it from a reputable source, trichinosis is unlikely. If you don't, cooking it until it reaches 137°F makes sure it's both juicy and safe. Serve with Black Pepper Bread (page 249).

Serves 4 as an entrée

4 center-cut pork chops, 1 inch thick, soaked in Basic Brine for about 3 hours (see page 9)
Salt and freshly ground black pepper, to taste
3 tablespoons canola oil
4 leaves fresh sage, chopped
1 teaspoon cumin seeds, toasted
2 tablespoons butter
1½ cups fresh corn kernels (about 3 large ears)
1½ cups fresh English peas (about 1 pound) *or* 1 pound sugar snap peas, cleaned

1. Prepare a medium-hot fire on one side of the grill.
2. Remove the pork from the brine and pat dry. Season with salt and pepper. Combine the oil, sage, and cumin in a food processor or blender, and blend well. Rub the mixture on the pork.
3. When one side of the grill is medium-hot (you can hold your hand 5 inches above the grate for only 4 to 5 seconds), grill the chops until browned, 2 to 4 minutes per side; move the chops to the cooler side of the grill and cover with an aluminum sheet pan. Continue cooking until the pork reaches an internal temperature of 135°F, 4 to 6 minutes more.
4. While the chops are cooking, heat the butter in a sauté pan on the hot side of the grill. Add the corn and peas; cook, stirring frequently, until the peas are just barely tender, 4 to 6 minutes. Season with salt and pepper, and serve with the chops.

NECTARINE AND LAMB KEBABS

IN THE SUMMERTIME, there are few things we like better than grilled meat and fresh fruit, so why not combine them on a stick? A recipe for something this tasty is rarely so easy: As long as you trim the lamb well and make sure the nectarines are just ripe but not mushy, you're golden. Serve with Tomato-Ginger Chutney (page 29).

Serves 4 as an entrée

2 pounds lamb leg, trimmed and cut into 1-inch cubes
6 nectarines, pitted and quartered
2 red bell peppers, seeded and cut into 1½-inch squares
1 teaspoon kosher salt
1 teaspoon freshly ground black pepper
6 tablespoons olive oil
6 mint leaves
1 tablespoon chopped fresh oregano leaves
3 cloves garlic, peeled
8 (10-inch) wooden skewers, soaked in water for 30 minutes
2 limes, cut in half

1. Prepare a medium-hot fire on one side of the grill.
2. In a large bowl, combine the lamb, nectarines, red peppers, salt, and pepper. Set aside.
3. In a food processor or blender, combine the olive oil, mint, oregano, and garlic; process until the mixture forms a paste. Pour the mixture over the lamb, tossing to coat. Thread the lamb, nectarines, and red peppers alternately on the skewers.
4. When the grill is at medium (you can hold your hand 5 inches above the grate for only 3 to 4 seconds), grill the kebabs, turning occasionally, until lightly charred on all sides and cooked to your liking (cut into one and peek), 6 to 8 minutes for medium-rare. Transfer to a serving platter and squeeze lime juice over the kebabs.

LIGHT MY FIRE

The easiest way to light a fire in a grill or smoker is to use one of those nifty chimney starters, which you can buy in any good hardware store. Or, you can make your own: Remove both the top and bottom from an old coffee can and use an old skeleton key or skewer to poke holes into each side, near the bottom. Then, with either device, fill the bottom with balled-up newspaper and pour the hardwood charcoal over the top. Light the paper through the holes on the side.

After a few minutes, when you cannot hold your hand over the can for more than 10 seconds, the coals should be ready. Use a pair of tongs to remove the can (carefully), and set it aside. Pour more coal over the hot coals and add chunks of wood if you've got them.

Then, get cooking. But don't forget: When the coals are at their hottest, they are also on the decline, meaning that if you're grilling or barbecuing for a while, the best approach is to continually add small bits of coal. Feed the fire, and it will feed you. Beautifully.

ROASTED CHICKEN BREASTS WITH CRANBERRY-ORANGE SAUCE

WE'RE NOT SURE who first paired cranberries and oranges, but we're forever grateful. The combination, of course, is the basis of a holiday classic, that jewel-like cranberry sauce we like to spoon over our roast turkey, even swirl into our mashed potatoes. Here, we treat it more elegantly, adding a hint of mint and using it to glaze simply roasted chicken breasts. This dish is still perfect for a homey holiday meal when you don't want to fuss over a whole stuffed bird.

Serves 4 as an entrée

2 small to medium navel oranges
4 (8-ounce) bone-in, skin-on chicken breasts
Salt and freshly ground black pepper, to taste
2 tablespoons canola oil
2 shallots, peeled and minced
1 cup fresh or frozen cranberries, thawed if frozen
¼ packed cup brown sugar
1 teaspoon cornstarch
½ cup Chicken Stock (page 118) or water
2 tablespoons chopped fresh mint leaves

1. Preheat oven to 425°F.

2. Using a sharp paring knife, cut the entire peel and all of the bitter pith off the oranges. Working over a bowl, hold the peeled fruit in one hand and with the other, cut down both sides of one white membrane all the way to the core to release a segment of orange. Work around the fruit, cutting between the membranes and sections until the orange is segmented, removing seeds if need be. Reserve the sections and any juice squeezed from the membranes in separate bowls.

3. Pat the chicken dry and season generously with salt and pepper. Heat the oil in a heavy-bottomed, ovenproof stainless steel or other nonreactive sauté pan over high heat. Pan-fry the chicken, skin-side down, until the skin is crisp and golden brown, about 4 to 6 minutes. Turn and cook the second side just until opaque, 1 to 2 minutes. Transfer the chicken to a plate and set aside.

4. Discard all but about 1 tablespoon oil from the pan, and return pan to medium-high heat. Add the shallots and cook, stirring, until softened, about 4 minutes. Add the cranberries, brown sugar, and reserved orange juice to the pan and mix well, scraping up browned bits from the bottom of the pan. Whisk the cornstarch into the stock or water to blend, and stir into the cranberry mixture. Bring to boil.

5. Return chicken to the pan skin-side up, along with any juices on the plate, and transfer the pan to the oven. Roast until the juices run clear when one of the breasts is pierced, 15 to 20 minutes. (Test for doneness by poking into a breast to make sure the flesh is opaque and there is no sign of redness near the bone.)

6. Remove the chicken from the pan. Add the mint and orange sections to the pan sauce, and season with salt and pepper. To serve, place the chicken on a platter or individual serving plates and spoon the sauce over the top.

ROAST LEG OF LAMB
WITH MASHED PARSNIPS AND CARROTS

WITH APOLOGIES to our vegetarian friends, our favorite way to prepare root vegetables is to roast them with our favorite meat, whose juices are the best seasoning we could imagine. In this dish, we baste sweet parsnips and carrots in rich lamb flavor, then pull them out and—for even more richness—mash them with butter and cream. The technique is simple, and the result sublime.

Serves 4 to 6 as an entrée

5-pound bone-in lamb leg
2 ½ cups Red Onion Vinaigrette (page 19)
2 pounds parsnips, peeled and cut into large chunks
2 pounds carrots, peeled and cut into large chunks
12 cloves garlic, peeled
1 cup water
2 tablespoons butter
¼ cup heavy cream
Salt and freshly ground black pepper, to taste

1. Preheat oven to 475°F.

2. Cut shallow slits all over the surface of the lamb, and place it in a shallow plastic container or glass baking dish and pour the vinaigrette over the lamb. Let marinate at room temperature, covered, for 2 hours, turning every 30 minutes and redistributing the vinaigrette over the meat.

3. Remove the lamb from the vinaigrette and place in a large roasting pan. Scatter the parsnips, carrots, and garlic around the lamb, and pour the water over the top. Roast until well browned, about 20 minutes. Reduce oven temperature to 325°F and continue to roast until the lamb reaches an internal temperature of 130°F and is tender and rosy inside, 40 to 50 minutes more. Transfer the lamb to a cutting board and let it rest for 10 minutes.

4. Use a slotted spoon to transfer the vegetables to a mixing bowl. Add the butter and cream, and mash. Season with salt and pepper. To carve the lamb, hold it vertically and cut into slices from top to bottom. Serve with mashed parsnips and carrots.

SCHNITZEL AND SPAETZLE

OK, I admit it: I first combined these because I liked saying "schnitzel and spaetzle," much in the same way Joe once stuffed pasta tubes with a white-bean mixture just so he could call it "cannellini cannelloni." Word games aside, the combination is as tasty as you would imagine fried breaded meat and buttered homemade noodles would be.

Serves 4 as an entrée

3 1/4 cups all-purpose flour
3 eggs
1/2 cup milk
2 cups fine bread crumbs
2 teaspoons dried thyme
2 teaspoons kosher salt, divided
1 teaspoon freshly ground black pepper
4 (4-ounce) pieces boneless pork butt or pork chops, trimmed of fat and pounded to 1/4-inch thickness (see "Pound for Pound, page 230)
3/4 cup heavy cream
1/2 cup (1 stick) butter, cut into cubes
Olive oil, for frying (about 1 cup)
1/4 cup chopped flat-leaf Italian parsley
Salt and freshly ground black pepper, to taste

1. Place 1 cup of the flour on a large plate. In a mixing bowl, lightly beat 2 of the eggs and add the milk; whisk to blend. Combine the bread crumbs, thyme, 1 teaspoon of the salt, and the pepper in another mixing bowl.

2. One at a time, dredge the pork cutlets in the flour to coat completely, shaking off excess; then, using tongs, dip in the egg and lift out, allowing excess to drip back into the bowl. Transfer the cutlets to the bread crumbs, and coat completely. Set aside the breaded cutlets.

3. Combine the remaining 2 1/4 cups flour, 1 egg, 1 teaspoon salt, and the heavy cream in the bowl of a food processor; pulse until a dough forms. Remove the dough from the processor and set aside.

4. Preheat the oven to 200°F. Bring 2 quarts water to a boil in a large saucepan. Put the butter in a large bowl beside the stove.

5. In a large, heavy-bottomed sauté pan over medium-high heat, add the oil to a depth of 1/4 inch. When the oil is sizzling hot, add the cutlets, frying in batches if necessary to avoid crowding the pan. Cook until golden brown and crisp, 4 to 6 minutes per side. Transfer the cutlets to a rack set on a baking sheet, and transfer to the oven to keep warm.

6. Add salt to the boiling water. Hold a coarse grater over the pot, and run the dough over it so the spaetzle falls into the boiling water. Cook for 2 to 4 minutes, using a slotted spoon to transfer the spaetzle to the bowl of butter as they float to the surface of the water.

7. To serve, divide the schnitzel among serving plates, and spoon spaetzle over each. Garnish with parsley.

Pound for Pound

When a recipe calls for a pounded meat or poultry cutlet, get out that pounder—the flat side of a meat tenderizer or, better yet, one of those wonderful French pounders that look like a flattened metal spoon. Their heaviness makes quick work of this job. Here's how to do it:

Place a large piece of plastic wrap over your cutting board, folding the ends over the edges of the board, and put the meat in the center. Place another large piece of plastic wrap on top, again covering the entire board. Strike the meat from the center outward, so that you stretch it from the center, working around in a circle and toward the edges until it reaches the desired thinness.

To remove the meat without tearing, peel off the top layer of plastic wrap and discard, then lift the bottom piece, slide your hand underneath, and pick it up. Turn over onto a pan or plate, peel off the plastic wrap, and proceed with the recipe.

SIMPLE ROAST CHICKEN WITH THYME PAN SAUCE

EVERYBODY has a favorite way of roasting a chicken. After talking to friends and coworkers, we settled on this method. Rubbing garlic and seasoning under and over the skin helps add flavor, brining makes it almost foolproof, and the gravy's to die for.

Serves 4 as an entrée

1 whole 3-pound chicken, soaked in Basic Brine if desired for about 3 hours (page 9)
2 cloves garlic, peeled and minced
1 tablespoon olive oil
1 tablespoon kosher salt
1 tablespoon freshly ground black pepper
1 tablespoon butter, softened
2 tablespoons all-purpose flour
1½ cups Chicken Stock (page 118) or water
1 teaspoon minced fresh thyme
Salt and freshly ground black pepper, to taste

1. Preheat oven to 450°F.
2. Rinse the chicken thoroughly inside and out and pat dry.
3. Combine the garlic, olive oil, salt and pepper, and rub over the surface of the chicken and underneath the skin, being careful not to tear the skin.
4. Place the chicken breast-side down on a roasting rack in a pan, and roast for 15 minutes. Using tongs or wadded-up paper towels, turn the chicken breast-side up and reduce oven temperature to 350°F. Baste once with the softened butter, and roast to an internal temperature of 160°F, 35 to 45 minutes more.
5. Pour the juices from the roasting pan into a saucepan over low heat, scraping up browned bits stuck to the pan. Whisk in the flour and cook, stirring, for 5 minutes. Slowly add the stock or water, whisking constantly to keep the mixture smooth, and add the thyme; adjust heat to a simmer and cook until thickened, about 5 minutes. Adjust seasoning with salt and pepper and serve the gravy alongside the chicken.

SPICY DUCK AND PEANUT STIR-FRY

IF YOU DON'T see duck legs in your supermarket, buy two whole ducks, cut off the legs, and freeze the breasts for another use. Or you can braise the breasts along with the legs in this recipe and then use the breasts as a substitute for the turkey in Corn, Turkey, and Tomato Quesadillas (page 40). We love the combination of tender duck, still-crisp vegetables, crunchy peanuts, and Asian spices here, but you could also use leftover chicken meat or even shrimp. Serve with steamed rice.

Serves 4 as an entrée

4 tablespoons canola oil, divided
4 (6- to 8-ounce) duck legs
Salt and freshly ground black pepper, to taste
3 tablespoons chopped fresh ginger (about 3-inch piece), divided
4 cups Chicken Stock (page 118), canned chicken stock (low-sodium), or water
1 tablespoon soy sauce
4 star anise
2 tablespoons sesame oil
2 cloves garlic, peeled and minced
2 serrano or any hot pepper, stems removed and minced
1 small red bell pepper, cored, seeded, and julienned
1 small green bell pepper, cored, seeded, and julienned
1 small red onion, peeled and cut into 1/4-inch dice
1 small carrot, peeled and julienned
1/2 cup Vietnamese Vinaigrette (page 21)
3/4 cup bean sprouts
3/4 cup toasted and coarsely chopped peanuts
3 tablespoons chopped fresh mint leaves
3 tablespoons chopped fresh cilantro leaves
3 tablespoons chopped fresh basil

1. Preheat oven to 325°F.

2. Heat 2 tablespoons of the oil in a Dutch oven over medium-high heat. Liberally season the duck with salt and pepper, and sear for 3 to 5 minutes per side or until golden brown. Work in batches if necessary to avoid overcrowding the pan. Remove the duck and set aside.

3. Pour off and discard all the oil from the pan, and return the duck to the pot. Add 2 tablespoons of the ginger, the stock *or* water, soy sauce, and star anise. Bring to a boil, cover, and transfer to the oven. Braise for 1 to 1½ hours or until the duck is easily pierced with a fork.

4. Transfer the duck to a platter and let cool. (The liquid can be strained, defattened, frozen, and reused as a duck stock, following the instructions in step 5 for meat stock on page 119.) When cool enough to handle, pull the meat off the bones, discard the skin and bones (or save the bones to make even more duck stock), and set aside the meat.

5. Heat the remaining canola oil and the sesame oil in a wok or large sauté pan over medium-high heat. Add the garlic, remaining 1 tablespoon ginger, and the chili pepper; cook, stirring, for 1 minute. Add the red and green peppers, onion, and carrot; cook, stirring occasionally, for 3 minutes. Add the duck meat and cook, stirring, for 1 minute. Quickly add the vinaigrette, stir well, then add the bean sprouts, peanuts, mint, cilantro, and basil; toss to combine, and serve immediately.

BRAISING is a miracle, really. Under that tight foil covering, meat with lots of connective tissue practically steams from the inside out, and the result is delectable. In this recipe, both the bold zinfandel wine (a syrah or shiraz would work nicely, too) and the ancho peppers give a kick to the beef. For a comfort-meal indulgence, serve with Mashed Potatoes with Salt Cod (page 178).

ZINFANDEL-BRAISED BEEF BRISKET

Serves 4 to 6 as an entrée

- 4- to 6-pound beef brisket
- 2 tablespoons canola oil
- Salt and freshly ground black pepper, to taste
- 4 cloves garlic, peeled and minced
- 4 stalks celery, cut into 1-inch pieces
- 2 large carrots, peeled and cut into large chunks
- 1 large yellow onion, peeled and cut into large chunks
- 1 (750-milliliter) bottle red zinfandel wine, the spicier the better
- 1–2 dried ancho chilies, stemmed, seeded, and roughly chopped
- 2 teaspoons chopped fresh thyme leaves
- 1 bay leaf, crumbled
- 3 tablespoons butter
- 3 tablespoons all-purpose flour
- 2 cups cooked navy beans, strained (see Master Bean Recipe, page 123)

1. Preheat oven to 500°F.

2. Pat the brisket dry, and arrange fat-side up in a large, heavy, deep roasting pan, preferably one with a lid. Rub the brisket with the oil, and season liberally with salt and pepper. Roast, uncovered, until well browned, 20 to 30 minutes. Remove pan from oven, and reduce oven temperature to 350°F.

3. Using large forks or turkey lifters, transfer the brisket to a large platter. Place the roasting pan on a stovetop over 2 burners, and turn heat to medium-high. Add the garlic to the drippings in the pan and cook for about 30 seconds, using a spoon or spatula to scrape up any juices and bits stuck to the bottom of the pan. Add the celery, carrots, and onion; cook, stirring, until the onions soften, about 5 minutes.

GET TO THE POINT!

Beef brisket consists of two parts: the flat and the point, separated by a thick layer of fat. In supermarkets, you are more likely to find the flat, which is leaner, but our favorite is the point. There's no real difference in cooking method or time between the two, but the point is fattier and more flavorful. In barbecue competitions, we call the point "cotton candy" because of all that sweet juiciness.

4. Add 1 cup of the wine to the pan, along with the chilies, thyme, and bay leaf, scraping the bottom of the pan well. Remove pan from heat. Carefully arrange the brisket on top of the vegetables, and pour the remaining wine around the meat. Add additional water as necessary so that the liquid reaches $2/3$ up the sides of the meat. Tightly cover with foil, pressing the foil down the sides of the pan and pressing directly on top of the meat; then cover with a lid. Braise in the oven for 90 minutes. (If the pan does not have a lid, use 3 layers of heavy-duty foil.)

5. While the meat is braising, melt the butter in a medium-size saucepan over medium heat. Whisk in the flour until thoroughly blended; cook, stirring constantly, until the roux is lightly browned and has a nutty aroma, 3 to 5 minutes. Remove from heat and set aside.

6. Remove the brisket from the oven and uncover carefully, being careful not to burn yourself on the steam. Carefully turn over the brisket, and scatter beans around the meat. Cover tightly again, and braise until the meat offers no resistance to a large fork and pulls apart easily, about 1 hour more. Transfer the brisket to a large cutting board and tent loosely with foil. Use a large slotted spoon to transfer the vegetables from the roasting pan to a serving platter.

7. Strain the pan juices into a tall, cylindrical container or gravy separator, and let stand until the fat rises to the surface; spoon off the fat. Return the pan with the roux to medium heat, and when it is hot, add the braising liquid, 1 cup at a time, whisking vigorously with each addition. Bring the sauce to a boil, stirring frequently to prevent burning, and simmer for 5 minutes. Season with salt and pepper.

8. To serve, slice the meat and arrange around the vegetables on a serving platter, drizzling the zinfandel sauce on top. Serve the remaining sauce on the side.

VENISON is a beautiful meat, but so lean that we won't cook it beyond medium, and prefer it rare to medium-rare, because without any marbling, it can dry out in a flash. We like to pair it with this tart-sweet sauce, which depends on the short availability of gorgeous fresh red currants. If you can't find them, don't substitute dried currants—they're actually tiny raisins, not currants at all; instead, find some dried cherries and add 2 tablespoons of red wine vinegar along with the molasses to balance out the sweetness.

SEARED VENISON LOIN WITH RED CURRANT–MOLASSES SAUCE

Serves 4 as an entrée

2 tablespoons olive oil
4 (8-ounce) pieces of venison loin, about 1 inch thick
Salt and freshly ground black pepper, to taste
2 shallots, peeled and minced
½ cup dry red wine
½ cup dark molasses
2 tablespoons red wine vinegar (optional; if using dried cherries instead of red currants)
1 teaspoon fresh sage, minced
2 tablespoons butter, cut into cubes
1½ cups fresh red currants or ½ cup dried cherries

1. Preheat oven to 425°F.

2. Heat the oil in a heavy-bottomed ovenproof sauté pan over high heat. Season the venison with salt and pepper, and sear on one side for 2 to 4 minutes or until golden brown.

3. Turn over the venison and transfer the pan to the oven. Roast for 5 to 10 minutes or until the internal temperature reaches 125°F. Remove from oven, transfer venison to a plate, and let rest.

4. Meanwhile, pour out and discard the oil from the pan and return to medium heat. Add the shallots and cook, stirring, for 3 minutes. Add the wine and cook, stirring to scrape up the browned bits at the bottom of the pan, until the wine is reduced by about half. Add the molasses, vinegar (if using dried cherries), sage, and the juices that have accumulated on the plate where the venison is resting; stir well to combine. Remove from heat and quickly stir in the butter until melted, and add the currants or dried cherries.

5. To serve, slice the meat into ¼-inch slices, fan out the slices on each serving plate, and drizzle sauce over and around the meat.

On the Rise

BAKED GOODS

HERE'S ONE AREA WHERE JOE AND I DIFFER CONSIDERABLY. He's a **BAKER AT HEART,** loving the precision and the chemistry, while I can't follow recipes, even my own. I like to zip around and throw in this and that. Years ago, for example, when I tried to improvise while coming up with a recipe for naan—that wonderful soft Indian bread—the result was hard as a cracker. Thankfully, it was a great cracker, and the renamed Sesame Flatbread has remained a signature component of Tremont 647's bread basket ever since.

Usually things don't go so well during baking experiments. Changing the type of flour—even measuring it differently—can drastically change the result, unpredictably, and usually for the worse.

That said, this chapter is for people who love eating baked goods but aren't bakers. If you veer from these ratios, we can't be held responsible for the results. If your "mistake" results in something even better, though, you owe us.

BAKED GOO

on the rise

SESAME FLATBREAD

THIS RECIPE, which we call the non-naan, was one of the best mistakes I ever made. It's a fantastic flatbread, thin and crackerlike. Set it out on an appetizer table along with North African Hummus (page 130) and Gloria's Crab Dip (page 45), and watch the fingers fly.

Makes 10 large crackers

½ cup plus 2 tablespoons warm water, about 110°F
½ teaspoon active dry yeast
¼ cup plain yogurt
2 ¾ cups bread flour, divided
3 tablespoons canola oil, divided
1 tablespoon white sesame seeds, toasted
1 tablespoon black sesame seeds
½ teaspoon Tremont 647 Curry (page 8) or store-bought curry powder
½ teaspoon salt
½ cup cornmeal
2 tablespoons extra-virgin olive oil
2 tablespoons butter
1 teaspoon fresh rosemary leaves
1 clove garlic, peeled and minced
Salt and freshly ground black pepper, to taste

1. In a small bowl, combine the water and yeast, and let sit until the yeast bubbles, about 5 minutes. Add the yogurt and mix well. Add ½ cup of the bread flour, mix well, and set aside for 15 minutes.

2. Using a mixer with a dough hook, or in a large bowl by hand, combine the yeast mixture with 2 tablespoons of the canola oil, the white and black sesame seeds, curry, and salt; mix until smooth. Measure out 1¾ cup of the bread flour, and gradually add it, ½ cup at a time, mixing until the dough pulls away from the side of the bowl. (You may not need all the flour.) Increase speed to medium and mix until the dough is smooth and elastic, about 5 minutes, or remove to counter and knead by hand for 8 to 10 minutes.

3. Put the remaining 1 tablespoon canola oil in a large mixing bowl and add the dough, turning to coat. Cover tightly with plastic wrap and let rise in a warm place until doubled, 1 to 2 hours. Punch down the dough and divide into 10 equal-sized balls. Cover each ball with plastic wrap and let rest in a warm place for another 30 minutes, or store in the refrigerator, covered, until the next day.

4. Preheat oven to 450°F with pizza stone or large, heavyweight baking sheet in it.

5. Combine the remaining ½ cup flour with the cornmeal. Sprinkle a work surface and rolling pin generously with the cornmeal mixture, and roll each piece of dough into a very thin, rough circle at least 8 inches in diameter.

6. In a small saucepan, combine the olive oil, butter, rosemary, and garlic. Place the pan over low heat and bring to a simmer; cook gently for 5 minutes. (If the garlic starts to burn, immediately remove pan from heat.)

7. Dust the pizza stone or baking sheet with more cornmeal. Place as many pieces of dough on the pizza stone or baking sheet as possible without overlapping. Bake until golden and dry, 4 to 5 minutes, then flip and continue baking for 3 to 5 minutes more, until the second side is golden. Remove from oven, brush with the butter mixture, and season with salt and pepper. Let cool to room temperature, then break into pieces and serve.

CLASSICALLY, popovers were served with prime rib, and the fat from the meat was used to grease the popover tins. When I was a kid, though, my mom would serve her crunchy, gooey popovers with tuna fish salad. I'd eat four or five of them at a pop. At **TREMONT 647** and **ROUGE** we use cast-iron muffin pans, and we heavily grease them with duck fat, but shortening works just as well. Serve these with Buttermilk Fried Chicken with Green Onion Gravy (page 220) or any good barbecue dish.

Shortening, for greasing
1¾ cups all-purpose flour
½ cup pecans, toasted and chopped into pebble-sized pieces
1 tablespoon cumin, toasted and ground
½ tablespoon salt
4 eggs
2 cups milk
1 cup melted butter

Makes 10 to 12 large or 18 small popovers

1. Preheat oven to 450°F. Liberally grease 12 standard or jumbo muffin cups or 18 popover cups, preferably nonstick.

2. In a medium-size bowl, combine the flour, pecans, cumin, and salt. Mix well and set aside.

3. In a separate bowl, lightly whisk the eggs and stir in the milk and butter. Add the liquid ingredients to the dry ingredients all at once, and stir until fully incorporated. (Small lumps are okay.) Divide the batter among the cups of the prepared pan, filling each halfway.

4. Bake for 20 minutes. Reduce the heat to 350°F, and bake until the popovers are dark golden brown, about 20 to 40 minutes more. Serve immediately.

PECAN CUMIN POPOVERS

STACY'S SPICY CORN BREAD

THIS RECIPE, developed by Stacy Breen while she was a pastry chef on Block Island, is probably my favorite corn bread of all time. It's perfect for a summer cookout, and makes punchy croutons for Achiote Caesar Salad (page 66).

Serves 8

Canola *or* corn oil, for greasing
3 ½ cups all-purpose flour
2 cups cornmeal
2 ½ tablespoons baking powder
1 tablespoon salt
¼ cup cumin seeds, toasted and ground
½ tablespoon ground cinnamon
1 teaspoon cayenne
½ cup chopped chives
1 stick butter, softened
1 cup granulated sugar
2 eggs
2 cups buttermilk
2 cups fresh corn kernels (about 4 large ears corn)

1. Preheat oven to 400°F. Grease a 10-inch cast-iron skillet with canola *or* corn oil.
2. In a large bowl, combine the flour, cornmeal, baking powder, salt, cumin, cinnamon, cayenne, and chives; mix well.
3. In another large mixing bowl, cream the butter and sugar until light and fluffy. Add the eggs, one at a time, blending well after each. Stir in the buttermilk. Fold in the dry ingredients in 3 batches, and then fold in the corn.
4. Pour the batter into the prepared pan and bake until it begins to brown and a skewer inserted near the center comes out clean, 30 to 40 minutes. Let cool in the pan for 10 minutes, then turn out; serve hot.

647 PIZZA

PIZZA toppings are limited only by your imagination, and it's fun to experiment, but you've got to start with a good crust. We lighten ours by adding apple juice, which helps give a boost to the yeast. It gets nice and crispy in the restaurant's brick oven, but at home try using a pizza stone or a preheated cast-iron skillet. We like to go easy on the toppings, starting with a thin spread of the chunky sauce: A crust this good deserves to be showcased.

Serves 2 to 3 as an entrée (makes two 10-inch pizzas)

3/4 cup hot tap water
1/2 cup apple juice
1 teaspoon active dry yeast
1 garlic clove, peeled and minced
2 teaspoons extra-virgin olive oil
1 1/2 teaspoons granulated sugar
1 teaspoon minced fresh rosemary
1 teaspoon honey
3 cups all-purpose flour
1 1/2 teaspoons kosher salt
1 teaspoon ground black pepper
1 tablespoon olive oil
1/2 cup fine cornmeal
Toppings of your choice (see "Top This Pizza," page 241)

1. Combine the water and apple juice in a glass measuring cup; it should be warm to the touch, about 110°F. (If not, microwave for 20 to 30 seconds to warm it.) Add the yeast and let sit until the yeast bubbles, about 5 minutes. Add the garlic, extra-virgin olive oil, sugar, rosemary, and honey; mix well with a fork.

2. In the bowl of a mixer fitted with a dough hook (or in a large bowl, using your hands), combine 2 1/2 cups of the flour, salt, and pepper. Add the yeast mixture, and blend on medium speed until the flour is thoroughly moistened and the dough starts to pull away from the sides of the bowl, 3 to 5 minutes. Increase speed to medium-high and beat until elastic and smooth, 7 to 10 minutes (or turn out onto a floured surface and knead vigorously by hand for 12 to 15 minutes).

3. Put the olive oil in a large, clean bowl. Shape the dough into a ball and add to the oiled bowl, turning to coat. Cover with a damp cloth and let rest in a warm place until doubled in size, 1 to 2 hours. Punch down the dough and divide in half. (The dough may be covered tightly and refrigerated for up to 2 days.)

4. Preheat oven to 500°F. Roll each piece of dough into a ball, place on a floured surface, and cover with a damp cloth. Let rise again until almost doubled, 30 to 45 minutes.

5. Mix together the remaining 1/2 cup flour and the cornmeal. Sprinkle the work surface, dough, and rolling pin with the flour mixture and roll out each ball or stretch by hand to a thickness of 1/4 inch. Top with sauce (see following) and toppings, and place on a pizza stone, large preheated cast-iron skillet, or preheated baking sheet that has been dusted lightly with some of the flour mixture. Bake until the edges of the dough brown, 8 to 10 minutes.

TOP THIS PIZZA

Our favorite pizza toppings:

1. Sliced local tomatoes, a drizzle of extra-virgin olive oil, and grated fontina cheese
2. BLT: Bacon slices and extra-virgin olive oil, topped with fresh tomatoes and lettuce after cooking
3. Fresh basil leaves and hot Italian sausage
4. Mashed Potatoes with Salt Cod (page 178), thinly sliced scallops, and prosciutto bits
5. Pepperoni and Great Hill or other blue cheese
6. Quattro formaggio: Fontina, Great Hill or other blue cheese, Parmigiano-Reggiano, and fresh mozzarella

ANDY'S PIZZA SAUCE

Makes about 3 cups

2 tablespoons olive oil
1 small yellow onion, peeled and thinly sliced
3 cloves garlic, peeled and minced
1 small red bell pepper, seeded and julienned
1 cup dry red wine
2 teaspoons dried oregano
1 (14.5-ounce) can of chopped tomatoes
8 leaves fresh basil, julienned
Salt and freshly ground black pepper, to taste

1. Heat the oil in a heavy-bottomed, 2-quart saucepan over medium-high heat. Add the onions and cook, stirring occasionally until translucent, about 5 minutes. Add the garlic and red pepper; lower heat to medium-low and cook slowly, stirring occasionally, until the vegetables are very soft and caramelized, 15 to 20 minutes.

2. Add the wine and oregano; increase heat to medium-high and cook, stirring frequently, until the wine has reduced by half. Add the tomatoes and lower heat to a gentle simmer. Cook, stirring occasionally, until the sauce is thick, about 30 minutes.

3. Remove from heat, stir in the basil, and season with salt and pepper. Let cool slightly before spreading on pizza dough.

CHEDDAR-BASIL CORN MUFFINS

THESE FLAVORFUL little muffins combine sharp Cheddar with sweet basil and a kick of Tabasco, rendering them as hard to resist as fresh tortilla chips. At the restaurant, we bake them throughout the night so they're never more than 30 minutes old when served. That's when they're at their lightest—and most addictive.

Makes about 2 dozen muffins

2 tablespoons unsalted butter, softened
2 cups all-purpose flour
½ cup fine cornmeal
½ cup granulated sugar
2 teaspoons kosher salt
2 tablespoons baking powder
1 teaspoon baking soda
2 tablespoons dried basil
4 eggs
1 cup whole milk
½ cup half-and-half
½ cup olive oil
¾ cup unsalted butter, melted
2 teaspoons Tabasco sauce
½ teaspoon freshly ground black pepper
6 ounces sharp Cheddar cheese, cubed and pulsed in a food processor until finely chopped (about 1½ cups)

1. Preheat oven to 325°F. Grease muffin tins with the softened butter.

2. In a large bowl, sift together the flour, cornmeal, sugar, salt, baking powder, and baking soda; stir in the basil.

3. In a second large bowl, beat the eggs. Add the milk, half-and-half, olive oil, butter, Tabasco, and black pepper. Add the wet mixture to the dry mixture in 3 additions, mixing just to blend after each. Stir in 1 cup of the Cheddar cheese.

4. Spoon the batter into the muffin tins, not filling each cup more than two-thirds full. Sprinkle the remaining cheese on top of the muffins, and bake until golden brown and a toothpick inserted in the center of a muffin comes out clean, 25 to 30 minutes.

FLUFFY SOUTHERN BISCUITS

JOE'S SISTER TERI, the picture of Southern grace and an amazing cook, has been making these for decades. These have crispy edges from the high heat of the oven and the skillet, but inside they're lush and tender, thanks to the use of that lower-protein White Lily flour that Southern cooks swear by. When guests in Teri's Florida kitchen eat them hot out of the oven, smeared with her good-as-gold fig preserves (and more butter), they think they've died and gone to Savannah, if not heaven.

Makes 6 very large biscuits

6 tablespoons butter
2 cups White Lily flour *or* 1½ cups all-purpose flour plus ½ cup cake flour
1 tablespoon granulated sugar
2 teaspoons baking powder
1 teaspoon baking soda
1 teaspoon kosher salt
¼ cup cold shortening, cubed
1 cup cold buttermilk

1. Preheat oven to 500°F.

2. Melt the butter in a 10-inch cast-iron (or heavy, nonstick) skillet. Keep skillet hot on the stove until ready to bake the biscuits.

3. Sift the flour, and measure 1¾ cups into a large mixing bowl. Add the sugar, baking powder, baking soda, and salt, and mix well. Add the shortening and toss to coat. Cut the shortening into flour using a fork or your fingers until the size of large peas.

4. Make a well in the center of the flour mixture and pour in the buttermilk. Stir with light, quick strokes just until the dough is combined, but do not overwork. Dough will be very wet.

5. With a large spoon, drop the dough into the hot skillet, forming 6 mounds spaced evenly apart. Immediately turn each biscuit over to coat with butter, and place the pan in the center of the oven. Reduce oven temperature to 475°F.

6. Bake until golden brown on top and puffed, 12 to 14 minutes. Serve immediately with more butter.

WE'RE GIVING you two biscuit recipes because, frankly, we couldn't choose between them. Joe's sister Teri's biscuits are fluffy and cakelike, while these are flaky and have more structure. Besides geography—the Northern approach versus the Southern—it's a matter of taste, and of use. The Fluffy Southern Biscuits are best enjoyed all alone with preserves, while these might be better as part of a hearty dinner, such as Buttermilk Fried Chicken with Green Onion Gravy (page 220). Like the Fluffy Southern Biscuits, they are best when hot out of the oven.

Makes 12 large biscuits

2 ½ cups all-purpose flour, plus extra for cutting
2 teaspoons baking powder
2 teaspoons kosher salt
¼ teaspoon baking soda
¼ cup cold vegetable shortening, diced, plus extra for greasing
½ cup (1 stick) cold unsalted butter, diced
1 ½ cups cold buttermilk

1. Preheat oven to 425°F.

2. In a large mixing bowl, sift together the flour, baking powder, salt, and baking soda. Add the shortening and butter, and toss to coat. Squeeze bits of shortening and butter through your fingers (or use two knives or a pastry blender to cut into the flour) until they are the size of large peas.

3. Make a well in the center of the flour and pour in the buttermilk. Stir with light, quick strokes just until the dough is combined, but do not overwork. The dough will be very sticky.

4. Sprinkle your hands and a work surface liberally with flour, and transfer the dough to the floured surface. Quickly pat the dough to an even 1-inch thickness. Dip a sharp, 2-inch biscuit or cookie cutter into the flour, then cut out the biscuits, reflouring as needed. If necessary, very gently gather any large scraps together, without squeezing the dough, and cut more biscuits. Transfer to a well-greased 9" × 13" baking pan.

5. Bake the biscuits until light golden brown, 15 to 20 minutes. Serve hot.

FLAKY YANKEE BISCUITS

ALMOND-PEACH COFFEE CAKE

BRUNCH is one of our favorite meals, and at Tremont 647 we've been doing it for years in our pajamas, which our customers just love. A good brunch needs a signature breakfast pastry, and at a restaurant it's helpful to have ones that we can adapt seasonally. We've made this delicious coffee cake with apples in the fall, rhubarb in the spring, and peaches in the summer, and so can you. However you make it, though, know that it seems to taste best when you're still in your jammies.

Serves 12

For the cake batter:

3/4 cup (1 1/2 sticks) unsalted butter, softened
1 cup granulated sugar
3 eggs
2/3 cup sour cream
1 tablespoon vanilla extract
2 cups all-purpose flour
1 teaspoon baking powder
1 teaspoon kosher salt
1/2 teaspoon baking soda

For the streusel:

1 cup sliced almonds, toasted
1/3 packed cup brown sugar
2 tablespoons granulated sugar
2 teaspoons ground cinnamon
2 barely ripe peaches, pitted and sliced 1/4 inch thick
1 tablespoon cornstarch
1/4 cup (1/2 stick) unsalted butter, softened, plus extra for greasing
1/4 cup all-purpose flour
2 tablespoons quick-cooking oats

1. Preheat oven to 350°F.

2. For the cake: In a large mixing bowl with an electric mixer, cream together the butter and sugar until light and fluffy, 2 to 3 minutes. Add the eggs one at a time, beating well and scraping down the sides of the bowl after each addition. Add the sour cream and vanilla; blend until well combined.

3. In a separate bowl, sift together the flour, baking powder, salt, and baking soda. Turn mixer speed to low, and add the dry mixture to the wet mixture in 3 additions, scraping down the sides of the bowl each time. When all the flour has been added, turn the mixer to high and beat for 1 minute to thoroughly combine.

4. For the streusel: In a medium-size bowl, combine the almonds, both sugars, and cinnamon; mix well and set aside. In another bowl, toss together the peaches and cornstarch, and set aside.

5. Lightly grease a 10-inch springform pan with butter. Spread about half of the batter in the pan, smoothing with a spatula. Sprinkle half of the sugar-almond mixture on top, and arrange the peach slices over the streusel. Spoon the remaining batter evenly over the peaches, scraping the bowl well. Smooth the surface with a spatula so the peaches are covered.

6. Add the remaining streusel mixture to the mixing bowl (no need to wash). Add the butter, flour, and oats; blend on medium speed until crumbly but not creamy. Scatter the topping evenly over the batter.

7. Bake until a toothpick or skewer inserted in the center comes out clean, 50 to 60 minutes. Let cool for at least 20 minutes before releasing the sides of the pan. Serve warm or at room temperature.

BANANA-ALMOND BREAD

WHEN LIFE gives you overripe bananas, make banana bread. But what if you don't have a spare hour, and the bananas look a day away from rotten? Simple: Just peel them, stick them in a plastic bag, and freeze for later. That way you can make the bread on your own time, not the banana's. When you do get around to it, you'll be glad you did. In this version, ground almonds give the crust extra texture, while sour cream and lemon add tang to a beautifully light interior.

Serves 6 to 8

Shortening, for greasing
1 cup toasted and finely ground almonds
2 cups all-purpose flour
1 1/2 teaspoons baking powder
1/2 teaspoon baking soda
1 teaspoon kosher salt
1/2 cup (1 stick) butter, softened
3/4 cup granulated sugar
3 overripe bananas
1 egg
Zest of 1 lemon
1 teaspoon vanilla extract
1/3 cup sour cream

1. Preheat oven to 350°F. Grease a 9" × 5" × 3" loaf pan well with the shortening.

2. Pour the ground almonds into the pan, turning the pan to coat the insides completely with almonds. Pour excess onto a plate and reserve.

3. In a mixing bowl, sift together the flour, baking powder, baking soda, and salt; set aside.

4. In the large bowl of an electric mixer, cream together the butter and sugar until fluffy, about 3 minutes, scraping down the sides of the bowl. Crumble the bananas into the mixer bowl, and continue beating until fully incorporated. Add the egg, beating to blend. Add the lemon zest, vanilla, and sour cream, and beat on medium speed until well blended. Add the dry ingredients and mix on low until well blended.

5. Transfer the batter to the prepared pan, and sprinkle the remaining ground almonds on top. Bake until golden brown and a toothpick inserted in the center comes out clean, 45 to 55 minutes. Let cool for 10 minutes in the pan; finish cooling on a wire rack.

A CLEAN SWEEP

Back when every kitchen had an old-fashioned straw broom, cooks would pull out a piece of straw and use it as a cake tester, sticking it into the center of a cake and pulling it out; if any batter stuck to the straw, the cake wasn't done. Nowadays, it's probably easier to use a toothpick or a skewer, but the reasoning is still the same; just because the cake has browned nicely on top, doesn't mean the inside is ready.

GINGER-LIME MUFFINS

HAVING a brunch party, or hosting afternoon tea? With their crunchy, sweet-and-sour top and moist interior, these would get scarfed right up. Just be careful not to overbake, and serve them within a few hours of cooling.

Makes 12 muffins

Shortening, for greasing
Grated zest of 2 limes, plus 1 teaspoon more
1/2 cup turbinado sugar (such as Sugar in the Raw)
2-inch piece fresh ginger, peeled
1 3/4 cups all-purpose flour
1 tablespoon ground ginger
2 teaspoons baking powder
1 teaspoon baking soda
1 teaspoon kosher salt
4 tablespoons unsalted butter, softened
3/4 packed cup dark brown sugar
2 eggs
3/4 cup buttermilk
1/4 cup, plus 2 tablespoons finely chopped crystallized ginger
1/2 cup golden raisins (optional)

1. Preheat oven to 375°F. Grease a 12-cup muffin tin with the shortening.

2. In a food processor, combine the lime zest from the 2 limes and the turbinado sugar. With the machine running, add the fresh ginger and process until smooth; set aside.

3. In a mixing bowl, sift together the flour, ground ginger, baking powder, baking soda, and salt; set aside.

4. In the large bowl of an electric mixer, cream together the butter, brown sugar, and the 1 teaspoon lime zest until fluffy, about 3 minutes, scraping down the sides of the bowl. Add the eggs one at a time, scraping down the sides of the bowl after each addition and mixing until fully incorporated, 1 to 2 minutes. Add the flour mixture in 3 additions, alternating it with the buttermilk. Mix thoroughly and scrape down the sides of the bowl between additions. Fold in the 1/4 cup crystallized ginger and the raisins, if using.

5. Divide the batter between the cups of the prepared muffin tin, filling each 3/4 full. Scatter a scant teaspoon of the turbinado sugar mixture over each muffin, and sprinkle with the remaining 2 tablespoons crystallized ginger. Bake until puffed and golden brown, and a toothpick inserted in the center comes out clean, about 20 minutes. Do not overbake. Let cool in the pan for 5 minutes, then transfer to a wire rack.

JUST SCRAPING BY

There are risks in the move to electric mixing: It's pretty easy to miss unmixed pockets in your batter, especially on the sides and bottom of your bowl. That's why our recipes remind you to scrape down the sides whenever using an electric stand or hand mixer. If you didn't, a pouch of salt or sugar or spice could easily end up in your final product, creating an unwelcome surprise to the unlucky diner who takes a wrong bite.

SPICED PUMPKIN BREAD WITH MAPLE-CAYENNE BUTTER

JUST BECAUSE you're not a kid anymore doesn't mean you don't want something hot and delicious to snack on when you get home after a hard day's work. Those urges seem to be even stronger in the fall, when we crave a cup of tea and the tastes of pumpkin, cinnamon, nutmeg, and maple. To take the chill off even further, this recipe spikes the butter with the burn of cayenne pepper, just to remind you that even if your comfort-food urges make you feel like a child, your palate is all grown up.

Serves 12

Shortening, for greasing
3 cups all-purpose flour
2 teaspoons ground cinnamon
1 teaspoon baking powder
1 teaspoon baking soda
1 teaspoon kosher salt
1/2 teaspoon ground nutmeg
3/4 cup unsalted butter, softened
2 cups granulated sugar
1 teaspoon vanilla extract
3 eggs
1 small zucchini, shredded (about 1 cup)
1 cup canned or fresh pumpkin purée
1 tablespoon peeled and minced fresh ginger (about 1-inch piece)
1/3 cup buttermilk
1/2 cup lightly toasted and coarsely ground pecans

For the maple-cayenne butter:
1/2 cup unsalted butter, softened
2 tablespoons maple syrup
1 teaspoon cayenne pepper
Salt, to taste

1. Preheat oven to 350°F. Grease two 9" × 5" × 3" loaf pans or a 12-cup muffin tin with the shortening.

2. In a mixing bowl, sift together flour, cinnamon, baking powder, baking soda, and salt; set aside.

3. In the large bowl of an electric mixer, cream together the butter and sugar until fluffy, about 3 minutes, scraping down the sides of the bowl. Add the vanilla, then add the eggs one at a time, scraping the sides of the bowl after each addition and mixing until fully incorporated, 1 to 2 minutes. Add the zucchini, pumpkin, and ginger, and mix on low just until combined. Add the flour mixture in 3 additions, alternating with the buttermilk. Mix thoroughly and scrape down the sides of the bowl between additions. Blend for 30 seconds more on medium, and divide the batter evenly between the prepared pans or tins (if using muffin tins, fill each cup about two-thirds full). Sprinkle the pecans on top.

4. Bake until golden brown and a toothpick inserted in the center comes out clean: 45 to 55 minutes for loaves, 25 to 35 minutes for muffins.

5. While the bread is baking, make the maple-cayenne butter by stirring together all the ingredients in a small mixing bowl.

6. Serve the warm bread or muffins with the maple-cayenne butter.

Spice Is Nice

Too many cooks are afraid to experiment with bread and other baked goods. True, baking is more precise than other cooking, but you can easily play around with flavors by adding or subtracting spices, particularly with yeast breads, without worrying about changing the texture. Simply add the spices to the flour before mixing with your other ingredients, and make sure to keep the total amount under 1 tablespoon for each loaf of bread. Some of our favorite additions: dried thyme, toasted ground cumin, cayenne pepper, chili powder, dried rosemary, whole fennel seeds, and whole caraway seeds.

BLACK PEPPER BREAD

WHEN I WAS CHEF at East Coast Grill, we needed a bread whose flavor was big enough to pair with the smoky steaks, so I came up with this. When we reworked it for this book, we cut back on the pepper—not every home cook is as fearless as those jalapeño-popping East Coast Grill diehards, after all—but it still stands up to just about any grilled meat. Serve with Grilled Giant Party Steak (page 219) or Easy Grilled Pork Chops with Sweet Peas and Corn (page 225).

Makes 1 loaf

3/4 cup very hot tap water
1/4 cup tomato juice
2 teaspoons dry active yeast
1 egg, beaten
3 3/4 cups all-purpose flour
1 tablespoon cracked black pepper
2 teaspoons finely ground black pepper
2 teaspoons cumin seeds, toasted and ground
2 teaspoons kosher salt
4 tablespoons butter, melted
2 tablespoons canola oil
Shortening, for greasing
1 tablespoon butter, chilled

1. In the large bowl of a mixer fitted with the paddle attachment, combine the water and tomato juice. (The mixture should be warm to the touch, about 110°F.) Add the yeast and let sit until bubbly, about 5 minutes. Add the egg, beating just to blend with the yeast. Add the flour, cracked and ground pepper, cumin, salt, and melted butter; beat until evenly moistened.

2. Switch to a dough hook attachment and beat on medium speed until the dough is elastic, 4 to 6 minutes. (Or knead by hand on a lightly floured surface for 8 to 10 minutes.)

3. Put the oil in a large bowl. Transfer the dough to the bowl, turning to coat with the oil. Cover with a damp towel and let rise in a warm place until doubled, 1 to 2 hours.

4. Preheat oven to 350°F. Grease a 9" × 5" × 3" loaf pan with the shortening.

5. Punch down the dough, roll it into a ball, and shape into a cylinder about 9 inches long. Transfer to the prepared pan and let rest for 30 minutes.

6. Make a 1/2-inch-deep lengthwise slash down the center of the loaf. Put the chilled butter in the center of the slash, and bake until golden brown, about 45 minutes. Remove from the pan and let cool for at least 30 minutes before slicing.

BUTTER BREAD

THIS RICH BREAD, somewhat like a quick brioche, gets its flavor from butter and buttermilk. It has become our staple bread at Rouge, where we toast it and serve it with the Barbecued Shrimp with Hominy appetizer (page 33), and for French toast. Of course, it also makes a superb sandwich bread.

Makes 2 medium loaves

2 teaspoons active dry yeast
2 tablespoons warm water, about 110°F
4 tablespoons granulated sugar, divided
1/3 cup butter
2 cups buttermilk
5 1/4 cups all-purpose flour
1 tablespoon kosher salt
1 tablespoon canola oil
Shortening, for greasing
2 tablespoons chilled butter

1. In the large bowl of an electric mixer, combine the yeast, water, and 1 tablespoon of the sugar. Let sit until the yeast bubbles, about 5 minutes.

2. Meanwhile, in a small saucepan over low heat, melt the 1/3 cup butter along with the remaining sugar, stirring occasionally to dissolve the sugar. Remove from heat.

3. Add the buttermilk and butter-sugar mixture to the yeast, and mix on low speed until thoroughly combined. Add the flour and salt; mix on low speed until fully incorporated. Switch to a dough hook, and beat until the mixture forms a ball and pulls away from the sides of the bowl. Increase speed to medium and beat for 5 minutes, or transfer to a lightly floured work surface and knead by hand until the dough is elastic, 8 to 10 minutes.

4. Put the canola oil in a large bowl. Transfer the dough to the bowl and turn to coat with oil. Cover with a damp cloth and let rise in a warm place until doubled in size, 1 to 2 hours.

5. Grease two 9" × 5" × 3" loaf pans with the shortening. Punch down the dough and divide in half; roll each half into a cylinder about 8 1/2 inches long. Transfer to the prepared pans and let rest for 30 minutes.

6. Preheat oven to 350°F.

7. Make a 1/2-inch-deep lengthwise slash down the center of each loaf, and tuck 1 tablespoon of the cold butter in each slash. Bake until golden brown, about 30 minutes. Remove from pan and let cool on a wire rack for at least 30 minutes before slicing.

GREEN OLIVE BREAD

THIS BREAD is meant to pair with any rich slow-roasted or braised meat dish whose juices are so tasty they demand sopping. The briny olives (substitute your favorite) make it a perfect match for the Braised Lamb Shanks with Eggplant and Chickpeas (page 217). If both bread and lamb are left over, you've got all the makings of an excellent sandwich the next day.

Makes 1 loaf

½ cup whole milk
½ cup very hot tap water
2 teaspoons active dry yeast
1 cup large pitted green olives, smashed
¼ cup whole-wheat flour
¼ cup extra-virgin olive oil
1 teaspoon whole caraway seeds
½ teaspoon kosher salt
2 ¾ cups all-purpose flour
1 tablespoon canola oil
Shortening, for greasing
1 egg
¼ cup cold water

1. Combine the milk and hot water in a glass measuring cup; it should be warm to the touch, about 110°F. (If not, microwave for 20 to 30 seconds to warm it.) Add the yeast and let sit for a few minutes, until the yeast bubbles.

2. Put the yeast mixture in the bowl of an electric mixer fitted with a dough hook. Add the olives, whole-wheat flour, olive oil, caraway seeds, and salt. Mix until blended, about 2 minutes, then add the all-purpose flour and mix until the dough pulls from the sides of the bowl and forms a ball around the hook, 3 to 4 minutes. Increase speed to medium-high and beat until the dough becomes elastic and smooth and loses most of its stickiness, 10 to 15 minutes.

3. Pour the canola oil in a large bowl. Transfer the dough to the bowl and turn to coat with oil. Cover with a damp cloth and let rise in a warm place until doubled in size, 1 to 2 hours.

4. Preheat oven to 400°F. Grease a 9" × 5" × 3" loaf pan with the shortening.

5. Punch down the dough and roll into a ball, then shape into a cylinder about 8½ inches long. (The dough will be soft.) Transfer to a loaf pan. In a small bowl, combine the egg and water and beat to blend; brush the loaf with the egg mixture, cover with plastic wrap, and let rest for another 30 to 40 minutes in a warm place.

6. Remove the plastic wrap, brush again with the egg mixture, and bake until dark golden brown, 45 to 55 minutes, or until the interior reaches 190°F on an instant-read thermometer. Let cool on a wire rack for 30 minutes before serving.

FEED THAT YEAST

Why do you often see sugar as an ingredient in an otherwise-savory yeast bread? It helps feed and activate the yeast. When using yeast, it's important to "proof" it, or to combine it with water and a little sugar (or something that has sugar in it, such as fruit juice or milk) and wait until it bubbles. That's how you know your yeast is alive, kicking, and ready to do what you put it in the dough to do: rise, rise, rise.

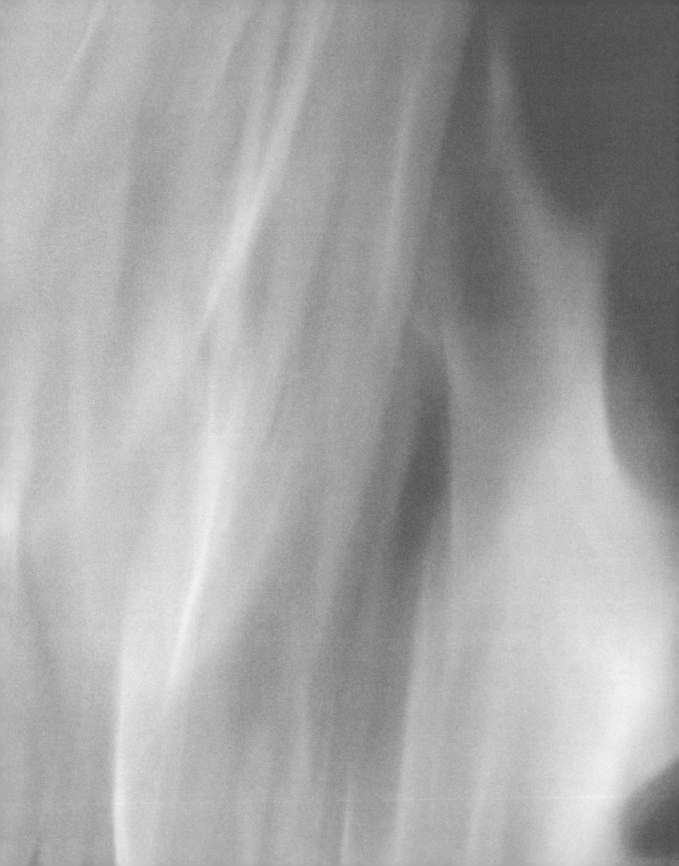

Sweet Nothings

DESSERTS

IF APPETIZERS ARE THE WARM-UP BAND, **DESSERTS** ARE THE FINAL ENCORE. The meal could've been the best ever, but a disappointing dessert is as hard to take as the ringing of annoying music in your ears.

We're not scientists, but, frankly, that's part of being an expert pastry chef. These recipes, then, after much trial and even more error, have emerged as goof-proof; if I can make them, anyone can.

If you're skittish, go with simplicity, and make sure you have top-of-the-line ingredients. Just-picked wild strawberries, dipped in imported dark chocolate and topped with farm-fresh cream, can rival any dessert. That'll leave your diners with a last taste they'll be glad to remember.

WATCH YOUR TEMPER

When we need to add delicate items such as eggs, sour cream, or even roux to a hot custard, soup, or sauce, we don't want them to scramble, curdle, or become lumpy in reaction to the sudden heat, so we temper them. Tempering—hot to cold, cold to hot—is a way to buffer the heat transfer, to gently heat up the cold ingredients before adding them back to the hot ones, so the transition isn't so bumpy.

Here's how to do it: Put your cold ingredients in a small stainless steel bowl. Slowly ladle in some of the hot liquid, whisking the entire time, until you feel the bowl warm up, then slowly whisk that liquid back into the custard, soup, or sauce.

BANANA CREAM PIE

EVERYBODY loves banana cream pie; all you have to do is check Tremont 647's trash barrels and try to count all those banana peels at the end of a busy night. Different pastry chefs have made their mark on other parts of the restaurant's dessert menu, but this is one pie that won't change, and for good reason: The combination of bananas, vanilla pastry cream, whipped cream, and flaky crust just plain works, while the peanut-chocolate topping gives it an extra flair.

Makes one 10-inch pie

1 recipe All-Purpose Pie Dough (page 256)
3/4 cup plus 2 tablespoons granulated sugar
1 tablespoon cornstarch
1 tablespoon all-purpose flour
2 1/2 cups heavy cream, divided
2 cups whole milk
1 vanilla bean, split
4 egg yolks, whisked to blend
3 tablespoons cold unsalted butter, diced
2 just-ripe bananas
1 1/2-ounce chocolate candy bar, chilled and finely chopped
1/4 cup toasted and finely chopped peanuts

1. Roll out the dough into a 12-inch circle, and fit into a 10-inch deep-dish pie plate. Blind-bake according to the instructions for All-Purpose Pie Dough, page 256.

2. In a heavy-bottomed stainless steel or other nonreactive saucepan, whisk together the 3/4 cup sugar, the cornstarch, and flour. Add 1/2 cup of the heavy cream and all the milk, whisking until smooth. Scrape the seeds from the vanilla bean into the pan. Bring to a boil over medium-high heat, stirring and scraping the bottom of the pan constantly to prevent scorching. When the mixture boils, adjust heat to simmer and cook for 5 minutes, stirring and scraping the bottom of the pan frequently. Remove the custard from heat.

3. Slowly add 1/2 cup of the hot custard to the egg yolks, whisking constantly to warm the eggs without scrambling them. Whisk the warmed yolk mixture back into the custard, and return the pan to medium heat. Cook, stirring constantly, just until bubbles begin to break on the surface. Remove from heat and stir in the butter until melted. Pour into a shallow bowl or pan. Cover with plastic wrap, pressing the wrap directly onto the surface of the custard, and cut several slits with a knife. Refrigerate for several hours, until cold.

4. To assemble the pie, slice the bananas and arrange in the bottom of the baked pie shell. Whip the remaining 2 cups heavy cream with the 2 tablespoons sugar until stiff peaks form. Using a rubber spatula, gently fold 3/4 cup of the whipped cream into the chilled custard, and spread evenly over the bananas. Pile on the whipped cream, spreading it out evenly. For best flavor, chill the finished pie for several hours, then toss together the chocolate and peanuts, and sprinkle on top.

ALL-PURPOSE PIE DOUGH

YOU'VE probably heard it before, but it bears repeating. These are the keys to a flaky, tender pie crust: Keep the butter in big pieces for flakiness, and for tenderness, don't handle the dough too much with your hands, don't add too much liquid, and keep everything really cold. Those last three tips keep the dough from developing too much gluten, which is what gives baked goods their structure—and, if overdeveloped, their toughness, which is the last thing you want in a good pie crust.

Makes 1 single-crust pie

1¼ cups all-purpose flour, plus extra for dusting
½ teaspoon kosher salt
6 tablespoons chilled butter, cut into 6 pieces
2 tablespoons chilled shortening, cut into 2 pieces
About ¼ cup ice water

1. In a food processor, combine the flour and salt. Pulse a few times to blend. Scatter the butter and shortening over the flour, and pulse just until the butter chunks are the size of grapes. Transfer the mixture into a large bowl.

2. A little at a time, begin adding the water, tossing with a fork to blend. Add just enough water to evenly moisten the flour (depending on many factors—including the humidity—you may need only 3 tablespoons, or as much as ½ cup water). To test, pinch the dough; it should hold together easily but not feel wet or sticky.

3. Lightly gather the dough into a ball and flatten it into a disk. Wrap in plastic wrap and refrigerate until cold and firm, at least 30 minutes.

4. Lightly dust a work surface and rolling pin with flour. Unwrap the dough and roll out to a circle roughly 2 inches larger than the pie or tart pan and about ⅛ inch thick. Lift the dough occasionally as you roll, to be sure it is not sticking to the work surface. If the dough starts to stick, sprinkle lightly with more flour.

5. Gently fold the dough in half and transfer to the pan; unfold and tamp gently into the corners. Trim off excess pastry (or fold inward and press against the sides for a smooth, raised edge).

6. To bake the empty shell (a.k.a., "blind-bake"), prick the bottom and sides of the crust all over with a fork, and cover with plastic wrap. Freeze the crust until cold and firm.

7. Preheat oven to 400°F. Remove the plastic wrap and line the crust with foil. Pour a layer of dried beans or pennies into the crust. Put the pie pan on a baking sheet and bake for 10 minutes. Remove from oven, remove foil and weights, and bake for another 5 to 10 minutes or until golden brown. Transfer to a wire rack to cool.

SAVORY HERBED PIE DOUGH

THIS SIMPLE variation on the All-Purpose Pie Dough (page 256) is meant for anytime you want to fill this crust with something savory, such as the Caramelized Onion and Green Apple Tart (page 50).

Follow the directions for All-Purpose Pie Dough (page 256), adding the thyme and pepper with the flour and salt in the food processor at the beginning of the recipe.

Makes 1 single-crust pie

1 ¼ cups all-purpose flour
½ teaspoon kosher salt
1 tablespoon fresh thyme leaves
2 teaspoons freshly ground black pepper
6 tablespoons chilled butter, cut into 6 pieces
2 tablespoons chilled shortening, cut into 2 pieces
About ¼ cup ice water

STRAWBERRY-CITRUS CURD TART WITH CORNMEAL-THYME CRUST

WE LOVE CURDS—not the kind that Miss Muffet ate with her whey, but fruit juice custards that walk the line between tart and sweet and make a wonderfully refreshing base for a fruit tart. In this version, three citrus fruits replace the standard lemon in the curd, and cornmeal gives extra texture to the crust, which is perfumed with the ever-so-subtle flavor of thyme. As for the berries, feel free to branch out. If fresh, local, and in season, blackberries, raspberries, or blueberries—or a combination—would work well, too.

Serves 6 to 8 (makes one 12-inch tart)

For the tart shell:

3/4 cup all-purpose flour, plus extra for dusting
1/2 cup yellow cornmeal
2 tablespoons granulated sugar
1 tablespoon fresh thyme leaves
1/2 teaspoon kosher salt
1/2 cup cold unsalted butter, diced
About 1/4 cup very cold water

For the citrus curd:

6 egg yolks, beaten to combine
1 cup granulated sugar
6 tablespoons butter, diced
Juice and finely grated zest of 1 lemon
Juice and finely grated zest of 1 lime
2 tablespoons fresh orange juice
1 teaspoon finely grated orange zest
Pinch kosher salt
1 pint strawberries, stems removed and thinly sliced
4 tablespoons seedless fruit preserves
2 sprigs fresh mint leaves, for garnish

1. To make the tart shell, combine the flour, cornmeal, sugar, thyme, and salt in a food processor; blend for 10 seconds. Add the butter and pulse until the pieces are the size of large peas. Transfer the mixture to a large bowl.

2. Add the water a little at a time, tossing with a fork to blend. Add just enough water to evenly moisten the flour; the dough should hold together easily when pinched but not feel wet or sticky.

3. Lightly gather the dough into a ball and flatten into a disk. Wrap in plastic wrap and refrigerate until cold and firm, at least 1 hour.

4. To make the curd, combine the egg yolks, sugar, butter, citrus juices and zest, and salt in a stainless steel or Pyrex bowl set over, not in, simmering water. Cook, stirring frequently, until the butter melts; then stir constantly, scraping the bottom of the bowl until the curd becomes very thick and the spoon leaves a path in the bottom of the pan, about 20 minutes. Be careful not to let the mixture boil or it will curdle. Immediately remove from heat and pour through a fine-mesh strainer into a stainless steel bowl. Cover with plastic wrap, pressing the wrap directly onto the curd, and pierce in several places with a knife. Refrigerate for at least 2 hours.

5. Meanwhile, lightly dust a work surface with flour and roll out the dough into a 14-inch circle. Carefully transfer the dough to a 12-inch tart pan with a removable bottom, gently fitting the dough into the corners and up the sides, trimming to fit. Pierce the surface of the dough with a fork, and freeze for 30 minutes. Preheat oven to 400°F while the dough is chilling.

6. Bake the crust until golden brown, 8 to 10 minutes. Let cool completely, and spread the citrus curd evenly inside. Layer fresh strawberries by starting from the outside and arranging in overlapping concentric circles until the shell is filled.

7. Spoon the preserves into a small microwave-safe bowl and microwave for 20 to 30 seconds or until melted. Brush the glaze on top of the strawberries, garnish with fresh mint, and serve.

PAN PREP

Grease and flour the pan: You read it in many recipes, including ours. But why? It gives cake batter something to grab onto, helping it rise properly, but most importantly, it helps you get the cake out of the pan, creating a nonstick barrier.

You can use butter, vegetable oil spray, or oil, but our favorite is shortening, which seems to grab just the right amount of flour. Use a paper towel dipped in shortening, and smear it generously around the pan. Then, scoop about ½ cup of all-purpose flour into the pan and, working over a receptacle, tilt the pan in all directions until the flour completely coats the bottom and sides; then turn it over and give a couple of taps to get rid of any excess flour.

One more thing: Do all this before you make your cake batter, so that when it's ready, it can go right in the pan, and right into the oven.

SUBLIME WALNUT CAKE

THIS CAKE is the height of subtlety, with a beautiful texture and delicate flavor—whispering, not screaming, of walnuts. Tomiko Khalid-Khan, one of our servers at Rouge, brought us this recipe from her mom. Well, after trying it, then trying to improve on it, and then realizing that we didn't need to change a thing, all we have to say is this: Mother knows best.

Serves about 16 (makes 1 cake)

Shortening, for greasing
1 cup (2 sticks) unsalted butter, slightly softened
6 large eggs
2 cups granulated sugar
1½ teaspoons vanilla extract
1 teaspoon Myers's or other dark rum
1½ cups all-purpose flour, plus extra for flouring pan
½ teaspoon baking powder
1 cup ground walnuts, divided
1 tablespoon fresh lemon juice

1. Preheat oven to 325°F.
2. Grease and flour a 10- or 12-cup bundt pan.
3. In the large bowl of an electric mixer, cream the butter until light. Add the eggs, 1 at a time, alternating with ⅓ cup of the sugar each time. Mix well and scrape down the sides of the bowl between additions. Add the vanilla and rum; blend well.
4. Sift together the flour and baking powder; blend into the batter in 3 additions, mixing for 30 seconds on low speed after each addition. Increase speed to high and beat for 1 minute. Fold in ¾ cup of the walnuts and the lemon juice.
5. Pour the batter into the prepared pan and sprinkle with the remaining ¼ cup walnuts. Bake until a toothpick or skewer inserted into the center comes out clean, about 1 hour. Let cool in the pan for 15 minutes, and turn out onto a cooling rack.

VODKA GIMLET GRANITA WITH CITRUS SHORTBREAD

PASTRY CHEF Michelle Vernier, originally from Detroit, has been a great addition to TREMONT 647, and she perfectly captured our sense of fun and funkiness with this granita recipe. Where sorbets and ice creams are smooth, granitas are coarse and even crunchy, with the consistency of thick slush. That makes them somewhat whimsical to eat, and wonderfully easy to make (no ice cream maker required). Michelle's version pairs the flavors of the classic cocktail with a rich shortbread, letting the tartness in each bridge the gap between them.

Serves 6

For the granita:

½ cup fresh lime juice (about 4 large limes)
Zest of 2 large limes
1¼ cups water
¾ cup granulated sugar
2 tablespoons vodka

For the citrus shortbread:

¾ cup unsalted butter, slightly softened but cold
½ cup granulated sugar
1 teaspoon vanilla extract
2 cups all-purpose flour, plus extra for flouring
½ teaspoon kosher salt
1 teaspoon lime zest
1 teaspoon lemon zest
1 teaspoon orange zest

1. Combine all the granita ingredients in a glass or stainless steel mixing bowl. Stir until the sugar is completely dissolved, about 2 minutes. Pour the mixture into a nonstick loaf pan (or other nonreactive metal pan), and freeze, stirring about every 30 minutes until frozen but still slightly mushy, about 2 to 3 hours. While the granita is freezing, make the shortbread.

2. In the bowl of a mixer fitted with the paddle attachment, cream together the butter and sugar until smooth. Add the remaining ingredients and mix just until fully blended.

3. Turn out the dough onto a lightly floured work surface. Gently roll or pat the dough to an even ½-inch thickness. Work quickly so the dough does not get too soft. Wrap the dough lightly with plastic wrap and place on a plate. Chill until cold and firm, about 30 minutes.

4. Preheat oven to 350°F.

5. Unwrap the dough and cut out rounds with a 1-inch cookie cutter. Arrange the cookies at least 1 inch apart on a baking sheet lined with parchment paper or foil. Using the tines of a fork, press decorative marks on top of the cookies, and put the pan in the oven while the dough is still cold. Bake until the bottoms of the cookies are golden, about 15 minutes. Let cool for 5 minutes before transferring the cookies to a wire rack to cool.

6. When the shortbread is cool and the granita is ready, spoon the granita into serving dishes and push 2 pieces shortbread into each serving.

THIS is baking for nonbakers: nearly foolproof, and easy to manipulate. Bread pudding is akin to a baked French toast, meaning the custard and bread combine to create something better than either one alone. You can play with the bread, using sourdough or even corn bread instead of the classic brioche. You could also add nuts, or substitute chocolate or other fruits—just stay away from high-water ones like bananas and strawberries, or you'll thin out the custard.

Serves 6 to 8

8 cups sourdough bread, cut into 1½-inch cubes
8 eggs
3 cups milk
1 cup heavy cream
1 cup granulated sugar
1 tablespoon vanilla extract
1 teaspoon salt
½ tablespoon ground cinnamon
1 teaspoon ground nutmeg
1 teaspoon ground ginger
2 cups blueberries

1. Preheat the oven to 425°F.
2. Place the bread cubes on a baking sheet and toast until golden brown. Set aside and let cool to room temperature. Reduce oven temperature to 350°F.
3. While the bread is toasting, whisk the eggs thoroughly in a large bowl. Add the milk, cream, all but 2 tablespoons of the sugar, the vanilla, salt, cinnamon, nutmeg, and ginger; mix well.
4. Transfer the croutons to a 9" × 13" baking dish, scatter the blueberries on top, and slowly pour the custard over them. Sprinkle the reserved sugar over the pudding and bake until the custard is just set but still wobbles slightly, about 1 hour. Serve immediately with Quick Caramel Sauce (following), or chill and serve cold.

QUICK CARAMEL SAUCE

Makes 1½ cups

½ cup (1 stick) butter
1 cup brown sugar
½ cup bourbon
½ cup water

In a small, heavy-bottomed saucepan over high heat, combine all the ingredients and bring to a boil. Boil until the mixture is smooth and syrupy, stirring occasionally, about 4 minutes. Serve immediately. (If you don't serve immediately, the sauce will separate but will still taste great.)

BLUEBERRY BREAD PUDDING

JAMAICAN RUM-BAKED BANANAS

HERE'S a tropical answer to Bananas Foster. The spices, especially the unexpected bite of curry, give this sauce a rich burnt-mustard color and will surprise the palates of even your most sophisticated tasters. Serve with Rich Vanilla Ice Cream (page 273).

Serves 4 to 6

4 bananas, barely ripe and still firm
½ cup brown sugar
½ cup toasted and lightly chopped peanuts
1 tablespoon cornstarch
2 teaspoons ground cinnamon
1 teaspoon grated nutmeg
1 teaspoon curry powder
1 teaspoon ground allspice
¼ cup butter, melted or at room temperature
1 cup dark Jamaican rum
2 teaspoons vanilla extract
1 recipe Rich Vanilla Ice Cream (page 273)

1. Preheat the oven to 425°F.
2. Peel the bananas, leaving them whole, and arrange in a 9" × 9" baking dish.
3. Combine the brown sugar, peanuts, cornstarch, and spices in a medium-size bowl and mix well. Blend in the butter, then add the rum and vanilla, and stir until incorporated.
4. Pour the rum mixture evenly over the bananas; bake, basting once, until the bananas are heated through and the sauce is thick and bubbly, about 15 to 20 minutes.
5. Divide the bananas between serving dishes. Top each with a scoop of ice cream, and ladle the sauce on top. Serve immediately.

LEMON-LIME BARS

WE CAN NEVER settle for a mere lemon when there are limes around, too. The combination is something more interesting than either fruit alone, especially when some ground ginger plays a part, too. Serve these as part of a dessert buffet or platter, alongside fresh fruit and some dark chocolate, or pack them into gift tins lined with bright paper at holiday time. Just be careful: Serve once, and you'll be expected to bake them regularly.

Makes 24 bars

2 ¼ cups all-purpose flour
½ cup confectioners' sugar, plus extra for dusting
¼ teaspoon kosher salt
1 cup (2 sticks) unsalted butter, softened
4 large eggs
2 cups granulated sugar
2 teaspoons finely grated lime zest
2 teaspoons finely grated lemon zest
2 tablespoons fresh lemon juice (about ½ large lemon)
2 tablespoons fresh lime juice (about 1 large lime)
2 teaspoons ground ginger

1. Preheat oven to 350°F.
2. In the large bowl of an electric mixer, sift together 2 cups of the flour, the confectioners' sugar, and salt. Add the butter, and mix on low speed until thoroughly combined but not creamy. Press evenly into the bottom of an ungreased 9" × 13" baking pan.
3. Bake until pale golden, about 25 minutes. Let cool to room temperature.
4. While the crust is cooling, beat the eggs in another large mixing bowl. Add the granulated sugar, lemon and lime zest, lemon and lime juice, ground ginger, and remaining ¼ cup flour; whisk until thoroughly combined. Pour over the cooled crust.
5. Reduce oven temperature to 325°F, and bake until firm, 35 to 40 minutes. Remove from the oven and run a knife around the edge of the pan to loosen. Allow to cool completely, and dust with confectioners' sugar. Cut into bars, and serve.

MANGO MARGARITA TRES LECHES CAKE

WHILE its exact origins are a mystery, pastel de tres leches, or "cake with three milks," is popular throughout Central America, where cooks soak their cake in a combination of evaporated, sweetened condensed, and regular milk, add some flavorings, and either leave the top plain or top with a soft meringue or whipped cream. Being such margarita fans, we spike ours with tequila, add some mangoes to the batter, and throw in some Triple Sec. The result is a decadently moist confection, and a soothing end to a spicy Latin meal.

Serves 12 (makes 1 cake)

For the cake:

1 1/2 cups all-purpose flour
1 1/2 teaspoons baking powder
1 1/2 teaspoons kosher salt
1 cup granulated sugar
1/2 cup unsalted butter, softened
5 large eggs
1 teaspoon Triple Sec
2 ripe mangoes, peeled and cut into 1/4-inch dice

For the tres leches mixture:

1 cup whole milk
3/4 cup sweetened condensed milk
3/4 cup evaporated milk
1/4 cup Sauza Gold or other high-quality tequila
1 tablespoon Triple Sec or other orange liqueur

For the topping:

1 1/2 cups heavy cream
2 teaspoons Triple Sec
2 teaspoons confectioners' sugar
1 ripe mango, peeled and cut into 1/4-inch dice
1/2 cup toasted coconut, minced
Grated zest of 1 lime

1. Preheat oven to 350°F. Grease and flour a 9" × 13" baking pan.

2. To make the cake, sift together the flour, baking powder, and salt in a medium-size bowl; set aside. In the large bowl of an electric mixer, cream together the sugar and butter until light and fluffy. Add the eggs, 1 at a time, beating well after each. Scrape down the sides of the bowl and add the Triple Sec.

3. Add the flour in 3 additions, mixing well and scraping down the sides of the bowl after each addition. With a rubber spatula, gently fold in the mangoes. Spread the batter in the prepared pan, and bake until the cake just begins to pull away from the sides of the pan and the toothpick or skewer inserted in the center comes out clean, about 30 minutes. Let the cake cool in the pan.

4. While the cake is cooling, make the tres leches: In a mixing bowl, combine all the tres leches ingredients, and whisk to blend.

5. When the cake is completely cool, poke holes all over the surface with a toothpick. Pour the tres leches mixture evenly over the cake. Cover with plastic wrap and refrigerate for at least 4 hours, preferably overnight.

6. In a chilled bowl, whip the heavy cream with the Triple Sec and confectioners' sugar to stiff peaks. To serve, arrange squares of cake on individual plates. Top each with 1 to 2 tablespoons diced mango, a dollop of whipped cream, and garnish with toasted coconut and lime zest.

APPLE EMPANADAS

IF YOU'RE UP early enough on Saturday to watch CBS's *The Early Show,* you've probably seen the great segment called Chef on a Shoestring, in which they challenge a guest chef to cook a three-course meal for four for under $30. I've been featured on the segment twice, and once I made a Latin-inspired meal that ended with these easy and delicious little fried apple pies. Serve with Rich Vanilla Ice Cream (page 273), after a meal of Yucatan Roasted Pork (page 210) and Crispy Plantain Cakes (page 166).

Makes 8 empanadas

2 tablespoons butter
1 pound Granny Smith or Golden Delicious apples (2 large or 3 small apples), peeled, cored, and cut into ½-inch dice
1 tablespoon granulated sugar
½ teaspoon ground cinnamon
Pinch freshly grated nutmeg
8 (6-inch) flour tortillas
1 egg, beaten
2 cups canola oil, for frying
Confectioners' sugar, for dusting

1. In a medium-size sauté pan, melt the butter over medium heat. Add the apples and sprinkle with the sugar, cinnamon, and nutmeg; stir to combine. Cook, stirring occasionally, until the apples are soft but still hold their shape, about 10 minutes.

2. If the tortillas are brittle, soften by placing on a plate under a damp paper towel and microwaving on high for 30 seconds.

3. Lay a single tortilla on a work surface and brush the edges with some of the beaten egg. Spoon 2 to 3 tablespoons of apples in the center of the tortilla and fold over, flattening the apples slightly and pressing the tortilla firmly around the apples to seal. Repeat with the remaining tortillas.

4. Heat the canola oil in a cast-iron or other heavy-bottomed sauté pan over medium-high heat until shimmering hot (a bit of tortilla will sizzle immediately on the surface). Fry the empanadas, working in batches if necessary to avoid crowding the pan, until crispy and golden brown, 3 to 4 minutes per side. Transfer to a plate lined with paper towels to drain. Let cool for at least 5 minutes, and sift confectioners' sugar heavily over the tops.

MINI GRAPEFRUIT TRIFLES

EVEN BEFORE Michelangelo said, "Trifles make perfection, and perfection is no trifle," poor perfectionists have been worrying about the smallest thing. When it comes to desserts, trifles are not something to fuss or worry over in the least. Cake too dry, or doesn't rise? Cut it up into cubes, arrange with pastry cream and fruit in a trifle bowl (glass, to show the layers), and accept your accolades. Our version is a bit more constructed, but you can still make all but the whipped cream the day before, which should help you perfectionists stop all that worrying.

Makes 8 individual trifles

For the grapefruit curd:

6 egg yolks, slightly beaten
1 cup granulated sugar
6 tablespoons butter, diced
1/2 cup freshly squeezed red grapefruit juice
1 tablespoon grapefruit zest, minced
Pinch salt

For the spiced yellow cake:

2 cups cake flour
2 teaspoons baking powder
1 teaspoon ground cinnamon
1/4 teaspoon ground nutmeg

For the spiced yellow cake (continued):

1/8 teaspoon ground allspice
1/2 teaspoon kosher salt
8 tablespoons (1 stick) butter, softened
1 cup granulated sugar, plus extra to taste
3 egg yolks
1 teaspoon vanilla extract
3/4 cup milk
1/4 cup peach *or* other fruit liqueur
3 large red grapefruits
1 cup heavy cream
1 tablespoon confectioners' sugar
8 perfect fresh mint leaves

1. To make the grapefruit curd, combine all the ingredients in a stainless steel or other nonreactive saucepan over medium heat. Cook for about 10 minutes or until the butter melts and the curd thickens enough to coat the back of a spoon, stirring constantly with a wooden spoon and making sure to scrape the bottom of the pan. Immediately remove from heat and pour through a fine-mesh strainer into a stainless steel bowl. Cover with plastic wrap, pressing the wrap directly onto the curd, and pierce in several places with a knife. Refrigerate for at least 2 hours.

2. To make the spiced yellow cake, preheat oven to 350°F. Grease and flour an 8-inch round cake pan. Sift together the flour, cinnamon, nutmeg, allspice, and salt in a mixing bowl and set aside.

3. Using a mixer fitted with the paddle attachment, or an electric hand mixer, cream together the butter and the 1 cup granulated sugar for 2 to 3 minutes on medium speed. Scrape down the sides of the bowl, then add the egg yolks one at a time, beating for 30 seconds after each addition and scraping the sides of the bowl. Add the vanilla extract. In alternating batches, add ⅓ of the flour mixture and ¼ cup of the milk at a time, mixing for a minute or so after each addition.

4. Pour the batter into the cake pan and bake for 40 to 50 minutes or until a toothpick or skewer inserted in the center comes out clean. Remove, let cool in the pan for 10 minutes, then turn out of the pan onto a wire rack and let cool to room temperature.

5. With a serrated knife, score around cake's horizontal equator, then cut in half horizontally. Using biscuit cutters or a water glass, cut 8 circles out of each half, and brush each circle liberally with the fruit liqueur.

6. Using a sharp paring knife, cut off the entire peel and all of the bitter pith from the grapefruit. Working over a bowl, hold the peeled fruit in one hand and with the other, cut down both sides of one white membrane all the way to the core to release a segment of grapefruit. Work around the fruit, cutting between the membranes and sections until the entire grapefruit is segmented, removing seeds if need be; repeat with remaining fruit. Reserve juice for another use. Toss the grapefruit segments with granulated sugar to taste.

7. Beat the cream and confectioners' sugar in a small mixing bowl until stiff peaks form.

8. Assemble the trifles on individual serving plates or in small glass fruit bowls: For each serving, layer 1 circle of cake, then 1 tablespoon of the whipped cream, 1 tablespoon of the curd, another circle of cake, 1 tablespoon of curd, 4 grapefruit sections, and a dollop of whipped cream, in that order. Garnish each serving with a mint leaf, and serve.

I HAD SO MANY blackberries at home when growing up in Seattle, I'd play hide-and-seek among the bushes, and get scratched every time. Once the blackberries were ready to pick, they were so plump and sweet I would forget my scars. With fruit that good, you don't need to fuss, so my mother would merely combine seasoned sour cream with the berries under a brown sugar topping and pop it under the broiler. You can follow her lead, but only when the blackberries are perfect. Otherwise, substitute wild Maine blueberries and crème fraîche.

HOT BLACKBERRIES AND CREAM

Serves 4

1 cup sour cream, at room temperature
Finely grated zest of 1 lime
1 tablespoon granulated sugar
½ teaspoon ground cinnamon
1 pint fresh blackberries, washed and well drained
½ cup brown sugar

1. Move broiler rack to lowest possible position, at least 6 inches from the top element, and turn on oven broiler.
2. In a mixing bowl, combine the sour cream, lime zest, sugar, and cinnamon. Gently fold in the blackberries, and transfer to small gratin dish. Sprinkle brown sugar on top. Broil until the brown sugar melts and darkens, 1 to 3 minutes, rotating the dish halfway through so it browns evenly but does not burn. Serve hot.

SPICED MOLASSES COOKIES

I DEVELOPED these chewy cookies at Rouge to serve as a little last thank you delivered with the check. I wanted something with a mild sweet-savory combination, which is what the cumin and pepper provide. If you're not handing out checks after your own dinner party, you might serve these with Dark and Stormy Ice Cream (page 275).

Makes about 3 dozen cookies

2 1/4 cups all-purpose flour
2 teaspoons baking soda
1/2 teaspoon kosher salt
2 teaspoons ground ginger
1 teaspoon ground cinnamon
2 teaspoons finely ground black pepper
1 teaspoon cumin, toasted and ground
3/4 cup unsalted butter, softened
1 packed cup brown sugar
1 large egg
1/4 cup molasses
1/2 cup coarse sugar, for dusting
1/2 cup minced crystallized ginger (optional)

1. Sift together the flour, baking soda, salt, ginger, cinnamon, black pepper, and cumin; set aside.

2. In the large bowl of an electric mixer, cream together the butter and brown sugar on medium-high speed until fluffy, about 1 minute. Add the egg and molasses, and mix until combined. Add the flour mixture in 3 additions, mixing just until combined before adding more. Chill the dough for at least 1 hour.

3. Preheat oven to 375°F.

4. Place the dusting sugar in a shallow bowl. Roll the dough into 1-inch balls and roll in the sugar to coat. Place 2 inches apart on an ungreased baking sheet, and flatten slightly. For extra spiciness, press a pinch of minced crystallized ginger onto the tops of the cookies. Bake just until evenly colored on top, 8 to 10 minutes. Let cool on the pan for 2 minutes, then transfer to a cooling rack, or eat warm.

THE ULTIMATE CHOCOLATE CHIP COOKIE

WE'D PUT this against anybody's chocolate chip cookie. The ground oats give a wonderfully chewy texture, especially if you cook the cookies as little as we do. Pull them out as soon as the edges are browned and the center starts to color, and they'll continue to firm up, resulting in a crunchy-gooey combination that drives any cookie lover wild. Serve hot with a tall glass of milk, or with Rich Vanilla Ice Cream (page 273).

Makes 2 dozen large cookies

1¼ cups all-purpose flour
1 cup quick-cooking oats, ground to powder in a food processor
1 (1.55-ounce) plain chocolate candy bar, chilled and ground to powder in a food processor
1 teaspoon baking soda
1 teaspoon kosher salt
1 cup (2 sticks) unsalted butter, softened
½ cup granulated sugar
½ packed cup brown sugar
1 large egg
½ teaspoon vanilla extract
¾ cup bittersweet or semisweet chocolate chips
½ cup toasted and chopped almonds or pecans

1. Preheat oven to 350°F.
2. In a large mixing bowl, stir together the flour, oat powder, ground candy bar, baking soda, and salt.
3. In the large bowl of an electric mixer, cream together the butter, granulated sugar, and brown sugar until well blended and fluffy. Add the egg and vanilla, and mix until combined. Add the flour mixture in 3 additions, mixing until incorporated and scraping down the sides of the bowl after each addition. Fold in the chocolate chips and nuts.
4. Use a large spoon to drop 2-inch mounds of dough about 3 inches apart on an ungreased baking sheet. Bake until the edges of the cookies are golden brown and the centers start to color, 10 to 12 minutes. Remove from the oven and let cool on the baking sheet for 2 minutes, then transfer to a cooling rack.

WARM INDIVIDUAL PEACH COBBLERS

TREMONT 647 pastry chef Michelle Vernier's interpretation of peach cobbler is a wildly popular summer dessert at TREMONT 647. For the home cook, it's no more difficult than any cobbler; rather than putting the filling in one baking dish and topping with biscuit dough, you merely use separate ramekins and separate biscuits. And they can all be prepared a day ahead and refrigerated until ready to bake. While you're at it, be sure to make a few extra for all those guests who will demand seconds.

Makes 8 mini-cobblers

8 peaches, halved and pitted
1 cup granulated sugar
1 cup water
1 cinnamon stick

For the biscuits:

2 cups all-purpose flour
1 tablespoon granulated sugar
1 tablespoon baking powder
1 teaspoon kosher salt
5 tablespoons cold butter, diced
3/4 cup milk
3 tablespoons coarse sugar, for sprinkling

1. Cut the peach halves into ½-inch-thick slices; cut the slices in half, crosswise. Put the peaches in a 3-quart saucepan, along with the sugar, water, and cinnamon stick. Cook over medium heat until the peaches are tender, 15 to 30 minutes (depending on the ripeness of the peaches).

2. Arrange eight 1-cup ramekins on a rimmed baking sheet. Divide the peaches and cooking liquid among the ramekins. Set aside.

3. Preheat oven to 400°F.

4. To make the biscuit dough, stir together the flour, granulated sugar, baking powder, and salt in a large mixing bowl. Add the butter, and toss to coat. Squeeze bits of butter through your fingers (or use two knives or a pastry blender to cut into the flour) until they are the size of small peas.

5. Make a well in the center of the flour mixture and add the milk. Stir with light, quick strokes just until the dough is combined, but do not overwork. Pat out to 1-inch thickness and cut out 8 rounds with a sharp, 2½-inch biscuit cutter or a water glass. Place a single biscuit on top of each ramekin, and sprinkle with the coarse sugar. Bake until the biscuits are golden brown and the peaches are bubbling, about 20 minutes. Serve warm, with a scoop of Rich Vanilla Ice Cream (page 273).

SWIRLED CHOCOLATE CHEESECAKE

MY BIRTHDAY cheesecake when I was a kid is not too sweet but has a strong cream cheese flavor. In case you wonder why good cheesecake recipes always call for letting the cake cool in the oven, that's so the center sets slowly and doesn't crack. Serve this on its own, or with fresh strawberries.

Serves about 16 (makes one 9-inch cheesecake)

For the crust:

1 cup all-purpose flour
3 tablespoons granulated sugar
½ teaspoon kosher salt
6 tablespoons very cold unsalted butter, diced
1 ounce bittersweet chocolate, melted and cooled

For the cheesecake batter:

3 (8-ounce packages) cream cheese, softened
1 cup granulated sugar
¼ cup all-purpose flour
2 teaspoons vanilla extract
6 large eggs
1 cup sour cream
5 ounces bittersweet chocolate, melted and cooled

1. Preheat oven to 400°F.

2. Make the crust: In a large mixing bowl, combine the flour, sugar, and salt. With two knives or a pastry blender, cut the butter into the flour mixture until it resembles small peas. Stir in the chocolate until evenly blended; the mixture will be crumbly but hold together when pressed.

3. Press the dough into the bottom and ½ inch up the sides of a 9-inch springform pan. Prick the crust all over with a fork, and bake just until the edges begin to pull away from the sides of the pan, 10 to 12 minutes. Set aside to cool. Maintain oven temperature.

4. In the large bowl of an electric mixer, beat together the cream cheese and sugar until smooth, about 3 minutes, scraping down the sides of the bowl. Add the flour and vanilla; blend well. Add the eggs, one at a time, beating until smooth and scraping down the sides and bottom of the bowl after each. Stir in the sour cream, mixing just until smooth.

5. Measure 1¾ cups of the batter into a separate bowl; add the chocolate, stirring to blend.

6. Pour half of the plain batter over the crust, smoothing evenly. Reserving half of the chocolate batter, drop large spoonfuls of chocolate over the plain batter. Pour the remaining plain batter evenly over the chocolate, and drop large spoonfuls of the remaining chocolate over it. Use a thin knife or spatula to draw lines through the batter in alternating directions to create a marbleized pattern. (Avoid scraping the crust with the knife.)

7. Reduce oven temperature to 300°F, and bake the cheesecake until the edges look set and the middle still jiggles, about 1 hour. Turn off the oven, open door slightly, and let the cheesecake cool slowly inside the oven for 1 hour, or until the center sets. Finish cooling in a draft-free area for 2 to 3 hours. Cover and chill for at least 8 hours before serving.

RICH VANILLA ICE CREAM

THIS IS a truly French-style ice cream, which means it's basically a frozen rich custard, a fabulous dessert in its own right and the base for our other ice cream recipes. The easiest way to manipulate this is to macerate 2 cups of your favorite fresh fruit in sugar to taste, crush it, and throw it in at the end according to your ice cream maker's instructions. But on its own, it's nothing to scoff at: You could hardly have a more satisfying, richer dessert than this ice cream paired with the Ultimate Chocolate Chip Cookie (page 270).

Makes about 1 quart

1½ cups half-and-half
1½ cups heavy cream
1 vanilla bean, split, *or* 2 teaspoons vanilla extract
6 large egg yolks
1 cup granulated sugar
½ teaspoon salt

1. In a heavy-bottomed saucepan over medium heat, combine the half-and-half, heavy cream, and the vanilla bean; if using vanilla extract, it will be added later, in step 5. Heat until just below a boil, or until you see small bubbles form around the edges of the pan. Remove from heat and set aside.

2. In the bowl of an electric mixer fitted with the paddle attachment, or using a hand mixer, beat together the egg yolks and sugar until thick and light, 2 to 3 minutes on medium speed. (Or beat by hand with a whisk.)

3. With the mixer on medium speed, gradually add about half of the hot cream, beating until smooth. Pour the contents of the mixer bowl back into the remaining cream in the saucepan, and mix well.

4. Place the pan over medium-low heat and cook, stirring constantly, until the mixture thickens enough to coat the back of a spoon and registers just barely 180°F on an instant-read thermometer, about 15 minutes. Watch carefully, stirring constantly and scraping the bottom of the pan. Do not allow the mixture to boil or go over 180°F, or it will curdle.

5. Remove pan from heat and fish out the vanilla bean, if using. Strain custard through a fine-mesh strainer into a bowl. Scrape the vanilla seeds into the cream; or, if using extract, stir it in at this point. Stir in the salt. Refrigerate for 12 to 24 hours, and churn in an ice cream maker, following the manufacturer's instructions.

ICE CREAMS

What other dessert inspires childhood rhymes that we remember until we die? When was the last time you hear somebody chanting, "I scream, you scream, we all scream for cake?" Such is the power of ice cream that the prospect of unlimited access made a childhood tonsillectomy almost seem appealing. Whatever your age, if you're like the average American, you eat 23 quarts of ice cream a year, or about 1 cup every 4 days. Seems kind of low to us, but then again, we live in New England, where the average consumption is 49 quarts a year, or 3 cups a week. That's more like it.

RASPBERRY LIME RICKEY ICE CREAM

AT JUST ABOUT the same time I was ordering a raspberry lime rickey as a kid at a seaside New Hampshire resort, Joe was getting the same from his favorite West Texas drive-in. This ice cream is an ode to one of our favorite childhood flavor combinations. The only thing missing is the soda, but there's an easy way to remedy that: Make a float by scooping the ice cream into a tall glass half full of lemon-lime soda. Serve with both spoon and straw.

Makes about 1½ quarts

½ pint fresh raspberries
Juice and zest of 1 lime
Pinch salt
1 recipe Rich Vanilla Ice Cream custard (page 273), chilled overnight but not frozen

1. In a food processor or blender, purée the raspberries, lime juice, lime zest, and salt. (If raspberry seeds bother you, strain the purée through a fine-mesh sieve.) Stir into the ice cream custard, and chill until very cold (38° to 40°F).
2. Freeze the ice cream according to the manufacturer's instructions, and pack into freezer containers. Chill until firm, about 6 hours.

GET CRANKING

Ice cream makers have come a long way since the hand-cranked, rock-salt versions of our childhoods, but that doesn't make them foolproof. The most popular, cheapest models require that you prefreeze the canister. If your freezer doesn't get cold enough, or you don't leave the canister in it long enough, or you don't prechill the batter properly, you can end up with ice cream soup. Make sure to read the manufacturer's instructions carefully several days before making ice cream, just to be safe.

Our other complaint with most ice cream makers these days is the limited capacity; they usually make only 1 quart, which is enough for four folks who don't eat a lot of ice cream but never seems to feed more than two or three of our friends. If you plan to make much ice cream, buy an extra canister and store both in the back of your freezer. That way, if you run across a recipe that makes more than 1 quart (as some of ours do), or want to double a recipe, you can make one batch right after the other.

Better yet, consider going retro. Some of those old-fashioned pine bucket and rock salt makers, such as the great one made for 150 years by White Mountain, come with electric motors and make up to 6 quarts. They're a bit messy, and they cost more, but there's no prefreezing required, the texture of the resulting ice cream is perfect, and you'll have enough for a party.

DARK AND STORMY ICE CREAM

INSPIRED by one of our favorite drinks, this ice cream has some kick—not just from the rum, but from the ginger. That little burn in the back of your throat is quickly offset by the cold soothing cream, though, so not to worry.

Makes about 1½ quarts

1 (12-ounce) bottle AJ Stephans *or* other dry, spicy ginger beer
2 teaspoons peeled and minced fresh ginger (about ½-inch piece)
1½ cups heavy cream
1¼ cups half-and-half
1 vanilla bean, split, *or* 2 teaspoons vanilla extract
6 large egg yolks
½ cup granulated sugar
½ teaspoon ground ginger
½ teaspoon salt
¼ cup Gosling's *or* other dark rum
Zest of 1 lime, minced
Juice of 1 lime (about 2 tablespoons)

1. In a small saucepan over medium-high heat, combine the ginger beer and fresh ginger, and bring to a boil. Reduce to about ¼ cup, about 10 minutes. Strain out the fresh ginger and set aside the reduced beer.

2. Meanwhile, in a heavy-bottomed saucepan over medium heat, combine the cream, half-and-half, and vanilla bean; if using vanilla extract, it will be added later, in step 5. Heat until just below boiling, or until you see small bubbles form around the edges of the pan. Remove from heat and add the reduced ginger beer.

3. In the bowl of an electric mixer fitted with the paddle attachment, or in a large bowl with an electric hand mixer, beat the egg yolks, sugar, and ground ginger together until thick and light, 2 to 3 minutes on medium speed. (Or beat by hand with a whisk.)

4. With the mixer on medium speed, gradually add about half of the hot cream, beating until smooth. Pour the contents of the mixer bowl back into the remaining cream in the saucepan, and mix well.

5. Place the saucepan over medium-low heat and cook, stirring constantly, until the mixture thickens enough to coat the back of a spoon and registers just barely 180°F on an instant-read thermometer, about 15 minutes. Watch carefully, stirring constantly and scraping the bottom of the pan. Do not allow the mixture to boil or go above 180°F, or it will curdle. Remove from heat. Strain through a fine-mesh strainer into a bowl. Scrape flecks of vanilla from the bean into the cream; if using vanilla extract, stir it in at this point. Stir in the salt. Refrigerate for 12 to 24 hours.

6. Heat the rum over medium heat in a small saucepan and ignite (see "All Aflame," page 276). Cook until the flames die out and the rum is reduced to about 1 tablespoon. Add the lime zest and juice, and chill.

7. Stir the batter well, and freeze in an ice cream maker, following the manufacturer's instructions. Add the rum-lime mixture in the last 5 minutes of processing. Pack into freezer containers and chill until firm.

All Aflame

We often want the flavor of liquor when cooking but don't necessarily want the alcohol, especially when its presence would prevent freezing. The solution: We flame the liquor to burn off the alcohol. It's not difficult, but please, be careful.

Here's how to do it: Pour the liquor into a sauté pan, then put over medium heat. If you have a gas flame, tilt the pan slightly until the flame curls over the top and ignites the liquor, or use a long matchstick. Swirl the pan for a few minutes until the flame dies out, and you're ready to proceed.

Warning: Never, ever pour liquor from the bottle into a flaming pan, or the flame can ignite the stream and travel back up into the bottle, causing it to explode.

DUSTY TENNESSEE ROAD ICE CREAM

THIS GOOF on Rocky Road is really nothing like it. It begins with a sort of Bananas Foster, with bourbon standing in for the rum, and adds pecans for texture. Just don't skip the flaming step; if you don't burn off the alcohol, you may have trouble freezing the ice cream. This also makes more ice cream than most ice cream makers, so if you have an extra frozen canister at the ready, you may want to make multiple batches.

Makes almost 2 quarts

1 tablespoon butter
2 ripe bananas, peeled and roughly chopped
1/4 cup bourbon
1 recipe Rich Vanilla Ice Cream custard (page 273), chilled overnight but not frozen
1/4 cup toasted and chopped pecans

1. In a small sauté pan, melt the butter over medium-high heat. Add the bananas and cook, stirring, for 2 minutes. Add the bourbon, light with a match to flame, and let burn out (see "All Aflame," above); reduce for 3 minutes or until slightly thickened. Spread on a plate and freeze until very cold; transfer to the refrigerator.

2. Freeze the ice cream according to the manufacturer's instructions, adding the banana-bourbon mixture and the pecans during the last 5 minutes of churning. Pack into freezer containers, and chill until firm.

STRAWBERRY CHEESECAKE ICE CREAM

MY STEPSON SAGE claims not to like cheesecake, but I don't believe him, because when he thought the following was merely strawberry ice cream, he gobbled it up with a smile. Smart kid: This ice cream gets a nice tang from the cream cheese, lifting it way beyond the ordinary. Serve with a tall glass of milk.

Makes about 1 quart

3/4 cup half-and-half
1/2 cup heavy cream
1/2 vanilla bean, split, *or* 1 teaspoon vanilla extract
3 large egg yolks
1/2 cup, plus 1 tablespoon granulated sugar
1/4 cup (2 ounces) cream cheese, room temperature
1/2 teaspoon salt
1 cup fresh strawberries, stems removed

1. In a heavy-bottomed saucepan over medium heat, combine the half-and-half, heavy cream, and vanilla bean; if using vanilla extract, it will be added later, in step 5. Heat until just below a boil, or until you see small bubbles form around the edges of the pan. Remove from heat and set aside.

2. In the bowl of an electric mixer fitted with the paddle attachment, or using an electric hand mixer, beat the egg yolks and 1/2 cup sugar together until thick and light, 2 to 3 minutes on medium speed. (Or beat by hand with a whisk.)

3. Add the softened cream cheese, beating just until smooth. With the mixer on medium speed, gradually add about half of the hot cream, beating until smooth. Pour the contents of the mixer bowl back into the remaining cream in the saucepan, and mix well.

4. Place the pan over medium-low heat and cook, stirring constantly, until the mixture thickens enough to coat the back of a spoon and registers just barely 180°F on an instant-read thermometer, about 15 minutes. Watch carefully, stirring constantly and scraping the bottom of the pan. Do not allow the mixture to boil or go over 180°F, or it will curdle.

5. Remove pan from heat and fish out the vanilla bean, if using. Strain through a fine-mesh strainer into a bowl. Scrape the vanilla seeds into the cream; if using vanilla extract, stir it in at this point. Stir in the salt. Refrigerate for 12 to 24 hours.

6. While the custard is chilling, toss the strawberries and the remaining 1 tablespoon sugar in a mixing bowl and mash. Refrigerate until ready to churn the ice cream.

7. Churn the ice cream according to the manufacturer's instructions, adding the macerated strawberries during the last 5 minutes of processing. Pack into freezer containers, and freeze until firm.

MINT MOCHA ICE CREAM

THIS ISN'T YOUR TYPICAL COFFEE ICE CREAM RECIPE. The coffee flavor is limited to chocolate-covered beans, but that means that you might not want to eat this right before bedtime, unless you're an addict like Joe or you wimp out and use decaffeinated. Nonetheless, you'll enjoy the crunchy chunkiness, lightened up with a little splash of mint. (Note: You may not be able to find mint chocolate chips except during the holiday season, but you'll be fine without them.)

Makes about 1½ quarts

1 recipe Rich Vanilla Ice Cream custard (page 273), prepared but not chilled
2 teaspoons mint extract
½ cup mint chocolate chips, *or* semisweet chips if you cannot find mint
½ cup chocolate-covered coffee *or* chocolate-covered espresso beans

1. Stir the mint extract into the ice cream custard, and refrigerate for 12 to 24 hours.
2. Freeze the ice cream according to the manufacturer's instructions, adding the chocolate chips and coffee beans during the last 5 minutes of churning. Pack into freezer containers, and freeze until firm.

With a Twist

COCKTAILS

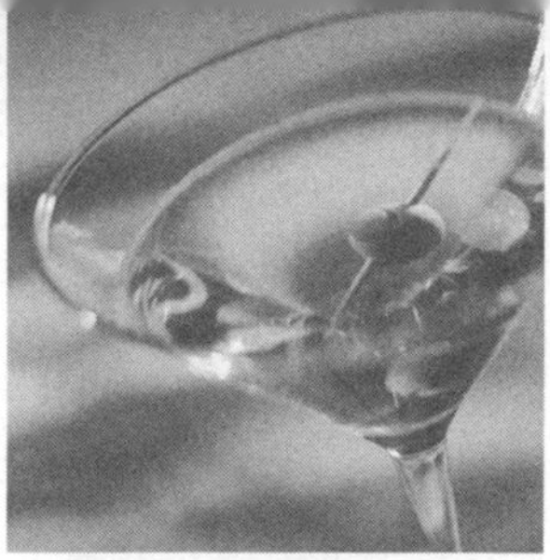

cocktails with a twist

TRENDS COME AND GO, BUT **GOOD COCKTAILS**—like classic cars and the little black dress—never go out of style. They can take you back in time, or to the other side of the world. Besides, their names are often little stories in themselves. In Havana, as the bartender served the U.S. soldiers their rum-Coke concoctions, he toasted (you guessed it), "Por Cuba Libre!"

Even the name "cocktail" has many a story of its supposed origin. Was it from the Western horse traders who fed their horses liquor, which made them cock their tails? Was it from "Octelle," a Southern belle who supposedly served drinks to army officers? Or was it from a young Irish lass who decorated the drinks of her customers with feathers from rooster (cock) tails?

All ideas for you to mull as you stir, mix, shake, and muddle your way through this chapter. Whatever story you believe, and whatever new ones you make for yourself, note that there are indeed some rules to this business of cocktail making. The most important: Use excellent liquors, the freshest ingredients (especially fruits and juices), the coldest ice (hard, not weeping), and prechilled glasses.

Oh, yes, and by all means, drink responsibly. One thing that has never been in style, and never will be, is the sloppy drunk.

Ice, Ice, Baby

People often freeze their vodka so that it's supercold when going into martinis, and that's important, but for other drinks, ice is an integral part. In a Mojito or Caipirinha, as the ice melts, the drink changes, and you keep stirring, sipping from the bottom, and enjoying the development of the drink. Cocktail shakers, those wonderful aluminum cylinders, use ice to get a drink almost as cold as if the liquor had been frozen: Joy Richard, one of the Tremont 647 bartenders, advises shaking until the shaker is so cold your tongue could stick to it.

MY WIFE GRETCHEN and I did extensive research on this drink in 1998 when we went to Vieja ("Old") Havana, where the Mojitos are 2 bucks each. The name translates into "little sauce," and we indeed got a little sauced (but not sloppy) drinking them.

Serves 1

½ loosely packed cup fresh mint sprigs
2 tablespoons fresh-squeezed lime juice
2 tablespoons granulated sugar
2 ounces Bacardi Silver Rum
2 ounces club soda
1 lime wedge, for garnish

Using a wooden muddler or a small wooden spoon, muddle (mash together) the mint, lime juice, and sugar in a highball glass for 1 to 2 minutes, until well bruised. Fill the glass with ice. Add the rum. Top with soda, garnish with lime, and serve. (Option: For a Mojito Especial, add ½ ounce Myers's Original Dark Rum.)

VARIATION: MOJITOS FOR A CROWD

Serves 10

3 loosely packed cups fresh mint leaves
1¼ cups fresh-squeezed lime juice
1½ cups simple syrup (see "Simply Simple Syrup," page 291)
2½ cups Bacardi Silver Rum
2½ cups soda water
2 limes, cut into 5 slices each
½ cup granulated sugar

1. Pulse together the mint, lime juice, and simple syrup in a food processor.
2. Fill a punch bowl or pitcher with ice. Pour the rum over, then the mint-lime mixture, and then the soda.
3. Toss the lime slices in the sugar. Ladle Mojito into each glass, and put a lime slice directly on top (not on the rim).

MOJITO

CAIPIRINHA

OF THE MANY BEAUTIFUL THINGS to come out of Brazil, this drink, made with sugar cane liqueur, is one of the most intoxicating. But to love it, you have to get to know it slowly; a Caipirinha is not something you can just pick up and take home. (It's not that kind of drink.)

Serves 1

½ lime, cut into wedges
2 tablespoons granulated sugar
2 ½ ounces (5 tablespoons) Cachaça 51 (Brazilian sugar cane liqueur)
1 lime wedge

Using a wooden muddler or a small wooden spoon, mash together (muddle) the lime and sugar in a rocks glass for 1 to 2 minutes or until it is the consistency of a gooey paste. Fill the glass with ice. Add the Cachaca, garnish with a lime wedge, and serve.

PETER'S JULEP

PETER WHITE, one of the partners at Rouge, is an award-winning bartender, and all it takes is a few minutes at his bar to see why: He has an amiable way with customers, and can make a mean drink. This is one of his concoctions: It's not a classic mint julep by any stretch, but more like a cross between a julep and a Mojito, making it an ideal brunch drink.

Serves 1

½ loosely packed cup fresh mint sprigs
2 tablespoons freshly squeezed lime juice
2 tablespoons granulated sugar
2 ounces Jim Beam Bourbon
1 ounce Cointreau Orange Liqueur
Large splash ginger ale

Using a wooden muddler or a small wooden spoon, mash together (muddle) the mint, lime juice, and sugar in a highball glass for 1 or 2 minutes, until well bruised. Fill the glass with ice. Add the Jim Beam and Cointreau. Top with ginger ale and serve.

THIS IS OUR SUMMERTIME DRINK of choice: High-quality tequila, fresh sour mix, and good company. What could be better? Well, some chips would be nice. Waiter!

Serves 1

2 ounces Sauza Gold Tequila
½ ounce Grand Marnier Orange Liqueur
½ cup sour mix (see "Sour Power," page 286)
Salt for rimming glass (optional)
1 lime slice, for garnish

Fill a cocktail shaker with ice. Add the tequila, Grand Marnier, and sour mix; shake vigorously. Pour into a margarita or old-fashioned glass, rimmed with salt if desired, and garnish with lime.

GRAND MARGARITA ("BEST OF BOSTON" WINNER)

GETTING EDGY

Margaritas are traditionally served in salt-rimmed glasses, but there's no reason to limit yourself to salt, or to margaritas, for that matter. Specialty stores sell special flavored salts (usually lime flavored) particularly for margaritas, but for those who like their margaritas on the sweeter side, feel free to rim with sugar instead. Our Tremont Tang is rimmed with straight Tang powder, giving it an unbeatable flavor boost.

Here's how to do it: Place a mound of salt, sugar, or Tang on a small, flat dish. Rub the flesh side of lime or lemon wedge around the rim of a glass, then turn the glass over onto the dish, twisting to pick up the salt, sugar, or Tang. Gently tap to remove excess, and you're ready to pour in the drink. If you're making more than one drink at a time, rim all the glasses at once and have them at the ready.

HORNY MARGARITA

Fill an old-fashioned glass with ice. Dump the ice into a cocktail shaker. Add the tequila and Cointreau, and shake vigorously. Rim the old-fashioned with salt if desired, pour in the sour mix and cold liquor, and garnish with lime.

WE'RE FANS of Sauza Tequila and particularly Sauza Hornitos, which in Mexico is what they call *resposado,* meaning it's rested, or aged. That makes it slightly more expensive than your run-of-the-mill tequila, but its musky flavor makes it worth every penny.

Serves 1

2 ounces Sauza Hornitos Tequila
½ ounce Cointreau Orange Liqueur
½ cup sour mix (see "Sour Power," page 286)
Salt for rimming glass (optional)
1 lime wedge, for garnish

WATERMELON MARGARITA

THIS USED TO BE a limited-to-summer drink at Tremont 647, but when we tried to take it off the menu, customers would beg us to leave it. Well, since you can find good watermelons pretty much year-round, we gave in.

Serves 1

10 (1-inch) cubes fresh seedless watermelon
Pinch kosher salt
Salt for rimming glass
1 ounce sour mix (see "Sour Power," page 286)
1½ ounces Sauza Gold Tequila
1 ounce Grand Marnier Orange Liqueur

Fill an old-fashioned or rocks glass with ice. Using a wooden muddler or a small wooden spoon, mash together (muddle) the watermelon and salt in a cocktail shaker. Add the ice from the old-fashioned glass, then rim the glass with salt. Add the tequila and Grand Marnier. Shake vigorously, then pour back into the salt-rimmed glass.

VARIATION: WATERMELON MARGARITAS FOR A CROWD

Serves 10

5 pounds fresh seedless watermelon cubes
2 teaspoons kosher salt
1½ cups sour mix (see "Sour Power," page 286)
2 cups Sauza Gold Tequila
1¼ cups Grand Marnier Orange Liqueur
3 limes, cut into wedges

Purée the watermelon and salt in a food processor. Put in a punchbowl or pitcher. Fill with ice. Pour in the sour mix, tequila, and Grand Marnier; stir well. Serve in salt-rimmed glasses, and garnish with limes.

ROUGE SOUR APPLE MARTINI

DID WE MISS the law that said every hip bar had to serve a sour apple martini? Not that we object: When done right, it will make you pucker and smile at the same time. And if nothing else, that's pretty entertaining to watch.

Serves 1

1½ ounces vodka
1½ ounces Berentzen *or* other high-quality apple schnapps
¼ cup sour mix (see "Sour Power," below)
1 slice Granny Smith apple

Fill a cocktail shaker with ice. Add the vodka, apple schnapps, and sour mix; shake vigorously, and strain into a martini glass. Garnish with the green apple slice.

SOUR POWER

For on-the-rocks margaritas, this freshly made sour mix is far superior to any commercially available instant margarita base, which we find way too syrupy sweet for good margaritas. Start any cocktail party by having plenty of this on hand, and you'll save plenty of time bartending.

Here's how to make 1 cup: Combine the juice of 4 limes and the juice of 1 large lemon with ½ cup simple syrup (see "Simply Simple Syrup," page 291), and stir to combine. Store in an airtight container in the refrigerator for up to 1 day, or freeze for up to 1 week.

Measure BY Measure

Our restaurants' liquor bottles have nozzles on them called speed pours, so that bartenders can count to three when pouring, and know that it results in 1 1/2 ounces of liquor. For home bartenders, you need either a little liquid measuring cup, which looks like a clear shot glass with markings on it, or, better yet, a standard jigger. Our favorite is the hourglass-shaped kind, which measures 1 ounce on one side and 1 1/2 on the other. Just in case you need it, here are some other equivalents for your drink-making pleasure: 1 ounce is 2 tablespoons, 1 1/2 ounces is 3 tablespoons, and 2 ounces is 4 tablespoons, or 1/4 cup.

ORANGE CRUSH

WHY BOTH ORANGE VODKAS? Of course, you could make it with just one of them, and the drink would be fine, but the two are actually significantly different in taste. When combined, they give this drink, named after the soda, a delightfully complex flavor.

Serves 1

1 ounce Stoli Ohranj Vodka
1 ounce Grey Goose L'Orange Vodka
1/2 ounce Cointreau Orange Liqueur
Small splash orange juice
Small splash sour mix (see "Sour Power," page 286)
Splash orange soda

Fill a cocktail shaker with ice. Add the vodkas, Cointreau, orange juice, and sour mix; shake vigorously. Pour into an old-fashioned glass. Finish with a splash of orange soda.

MOONSHINE MASH

GIVEN ROUGE'S SOUTHERN SLANT, we mulled the possibility of setting up a still out back, but then thought better of it—and the legal problems that illegal production of alcohol might just bring. Instead, we found the closest commercially available thing to moonshine, an aged-less-than-30-days corn whiskey made by a company called Shine on Georgia Moon. It's not the most sophisticated liquor in the world, which is exactly what we were going for.

Serves 1

2 (¼-inch-thick) orange slices
2 lemons, cut into eighths
2 limes, cut into sixths
2 tablespoons granulated sugar
2 ounces Shine on Georgia Moon or other corn whiskey
½ ounce Cointreau Orange Liqueur
Splash of lemon-lime soda
1 orange slice

Using a wooden muddler or a small wooden spoon, muddle together (mash) the orange, lemon, lime, and sugar in an old-fashioned glass for 1 to 2 minutes, or until very juicy. Add the whiskey and Cointreau, top with soda, and garnish with the orange slice.

FRENCH KISS

THIS LITTLE MARTINI comes off as sweet and crisp, but it'll sneak up on you, tickle your nose with champagne bubbles (like it's kissing you back), then, just when you're not paying attention, wind up for the punch.

Serves 1

1 ounce vodka
½ ounce Cointreau Orange Liqueur
Splash cranberry juice
Splash champagne
1 maraschino cherry

Fill a cocktail shaker with ice. Add the vodka, Cointreau, and cranberry juice; shake vigorously, and strain into a martini glass. Top with a splash of champagne, and garnish with the cherry, and serve.

Infused with Flavor

Infusing alcohol with the flavor of fruit gives our bartenders a chance to develop new drinks without being limited to commercial products. We sometimes infuse gin, rum, and even tequila, but most of our focus is on vodka because its lack of flavor makes it particularly receptive to additions.

Here's how to do it: Pour out 1 cup of vodka from a 1-liter bottle, and add 1 cup of fruit (blackberries, raspberries, dried papaya, blueberries, pineapples, and mangoes are some of our favorites), to the bottle. Recap the bottle, and let it sit undisturbed at room temperature for at least 1 week and up to 1 month. There's no need to strain; just pour the vodka from the top, letting the fruit remain on the bottom. Actually, now that we think of it, if some of the fruit escapes the bottle, consider it a bonus.

THIS DRINK is the adult version of the good-old raspberry lime rickey, but with a kick from the vodka. Plan ahead; infuse some vodka with fresh raspberries, and then enjoy this drink's zip—and its beautiful reddish pink color.

Serves 1

2½ ounces raspberry-infused vodka (see "Infused with Flavor," above)
1 ounce fresh lime juice
1 ounce simple syrup (see "Simply Simple Syrup," page 291)
1 lime wedge

Fill a cocktail shaker with ice. Add the vodka, lime juice, and simple syrup; shake vigorously, and strain into a martini glass. Garnish with the lime wedge.

RASPBERRY GIMLET

TREMONT TANG

AFTER EXPERIMENTING with dried papaya (found in natural food stores and Middle Eastern markets) that we used to make a vodka infusion, we tested various additions for a drink at **TREMONT 647**. When we reached the taste we wanted, someone said, "This tastes like Tang!" We rushed out to buy some, used it to sugar the rim of the glass, and just like that, a signature drink was born.

Serves 1

2½ ounces papaya-infused vodka (see "Infused with Flavor," page 289)
Splash pineapple juice
Splash lemon-lime soda
Tang for rimming the glass

Fill a cocktail shaker with ice. Add the vodka and pineapple juice, and shake vigorously. Pour a splash of lemon-lime soda in a cocktail glass rimmed with Tang, then add the mix from the cocktail shaker.

JOY'S PINEAPPLE MARTINI

JOY RICHARD, besides all her work doing public relations, communication, and general problem-solving around Tremont 647, is also a hell of a bartender. Her creation reminds us of a coconut Life Savers candy, part of its Tropical Fruits collection. Next up: sour cherry?

Serves 1

1½ ounces House-infused pineapple vodka
1½ ounces Stoli Vanil Vodka
½ ounce simple syrup (page 291)
Splash pineapple juice
1 wedge pineapple

Fill a cocktail shaker with ice. Add the vodkas, simple syrup, and pineapple juice. Strain into a cocktail glass and garnish with the pineapple wedge.

THIS DRINK, which depends on good pear nectar and pear liqueur, is perfect for a nice hot day, when you're sitting by the beach. No, it's perfect for a cold day, when you're sitting by the fire. How 'bout a gray day, when you're sitting in a dark apartment wishing you had a fire or were at the beach? Face it: This sweet drink hits the spot anytime.

Serves 1

2 ounces Bacardi Coco Rum *or* Malibu Rum
1 ounce Belle de Brillet *or* other pear liqueur
1 ounce Goya pear nectar
1 lime wedge
1 maraschino cherry

Fill a cocktail shaker with ice. Add the rum, Belle de Brillet, and pear nectar, and shake vigorously. Strain into a martini glass and garnish with the lime wedge and cherry.

TROPICAL PARADISE

SIMPLY SIMPLE SYRUP

Why make a sugar syrup rather than just add sugar? Simple: If the sugar's already dissolved in the water, it'll easily dissolve in your drink. Sometimes you want that, and sometimes, with drinks like Mojitos and Caipirinhas that require muddling, the layer of sugar in the bottom is part of the appeal.

Here's how to make 1½ cups: Combine 1 cup sugar and 1 cup water in a small saucepan over medium-high heat and bring to a boil, stirring occasionally until the sugar dissolves. Remove from heat, let cool, and transfer to an airtight bottle to store in the refrigerator, for up to 1 month.

CHOCOLATE TEMPTATION

ONCE you make one of these all-alcohol drinks, you'll get more requests, thanks to how cool-looking it is: a clear martini on top, with the dark chocolate liqueur hanging out on the bottom. If there were ever a cocktail to have after dinner, this is it: Skip dessert.

Serves 1

1 ounce Stoli Ohranj Vodka
1 ounce Stoli Vanil Vodka
1 ounce white crème de cacao
1 ounce Godiva Chocolate Liqueur

Fill a cocktail shaker with ice. Add the vodkas and crème de cacao, and shake vigorously. Strain into a martini glass. Slowly pour the Godiva liqueur down the side of the glass, so it sinks to the bottom.

ENTER THE DRAGON

FRIEND AND CHEF KEN ORINGER, who owns the fabulous Clio restaurant, gave us a recipe for a drink that's very much like his food: cutting edge and exotic, using only the best of the perfect ingredients for a truly unique taste. This drink calls for black mint and calamansi (also known as musk) lime juice, both of which you can find in Asian supermarkets, but if you can't, peppermint and a combination of lemon and orange juices will suffice. The taste in any case is sweet and sour, with a little burn from the cayenne.

Serves 1

1 ounce simple syrup (see "Simply Simple Syrup," page 291)
½ cup fresh black mint *or* peppermint sprigs
1½ ounces Stoli Ohranj Vodka
¾ ounce Cointreau Orange Liqueur
1 ounce calamansi lime juice (*or* 2 tablespoons fresh lemon juice plus ½ teaspoon fresh orange juice)
Small pinch cayenne pepper

Using a wooden muddler or a small wooden spoon, muddle (mash) together the syrup and mint in a cocktail shaker. Fill with ice, then add the vodka, Cointreau, lime juice, and cayenne. Shake vigorously and strain into a martini glass.

ESPRESSO MARTINI

THIS IS the speedball of drinks, the yin and yang. Alcohol is a depressant, we've all been told, so why not give it some juice with espresso? As a bonus, the coffee gives it a smoky richness. Make it with decaf if you're a wimp.

Serves 1

1 ounce Stoli Vanil Vodka
1 ounce white crème de cacao
½ ounce Kahlua Liqueur
½ ounce Baileys Irish Cream
1 shot (1 ounce) espresso
3 espresso beans (optional)

Fill a cocktail shaker with ice. Add the vodka, crème de cacao, Kahlua, Baileys, and espresso. Shake vigorously and strain into a martini glass. Garnish with 3 espresso beans.

THE DARK AND STORMY

YOU, of course, are familiar with the classic Cuba Libre, the rum-Coke combination. Well, meet its pirate cousin, who makes old C. L. look like an English schoolmarm. The keys to a good Dark and Stormy are a smoky, spicy rum like Gosling's, and a spicy, not-too-sweet ginger beer like AJ Stephans, made in Massachusetts.

Serves 1

1 (12-ounce) bottle AJ Stephans or other dry, spicy ginger beer
2 ½ ounces Gosling's Black Seal Rum (Bermuda)
Lemon wedge, for garnish

Fill a zombie glass (straight-sided tumbler, 12 ounces or more) halfway with ice. Add the ginger beer until the glass is ¾ full. Slowly pour the rum down the side of the glass so that it floats at the surface of the cocktail. Garnish with the lemon wedge.

A

B

C

D

E

F

G

H

I

J

K

L

M

S

T

U, V

W

Y, Z

About the Authors

andy husbands

Chef Andy Husbands is owner of **TREMONT 647**, **SISTER SOREL**, and **ROUGE**, all in Boston's South End neighborhood, and **KESTRAL** in Providence, Rhode Island.

Born and raised in Seattle, Husbands graduated in 1992 from Johnson and Wales University in Providence, then worked as a sous-chef and later executive chef at the renowned East Coast Grill in Cambridge, under James Beard Award–winner Chris Schlesinger.

In 1996, he and friend Chris Hart opened Tremont 647, serving boldly flavored American cuisine with inventive global influences. In 2000, he opened Sister Sorel (named after his older sister) in the adjoining space, offering a café-style menu. In 2002, he and wife Gretchen teamed up with Peter White to create Rouge, combining his trademark cuisine with award-winning barbecue. In 2003, Andy, Gretchen, Peter, and Jason Santos opened Kestral, an American bistro in Providence.

In 2004, Andy joined with Tessa Edick and Paolo Volpati-Kedra of Sauces 'n Love, Inc. (*www.saucesnlove.com*) to create their version of "Fearless Sauces" (for purchasing information, visit *www.andyhusbands.com*).

His UFO Social Club competitive barbecue team won the Vermont state barbecue championship in 2002 and the New Hampshire state championship in 2003, and has competed nationally.

Andy is on the advisory board of the Massachusetts chapter of Operation Frontline, a program run by Share Our Strength (*www.strength.org*), one of the country's leading hunger relief organizations, that uses chefs to teach cooking and nutrition to low-income families. He is also on the board of directors of United South End Settlements, a community social service agency.

Andy Husbands (left) and Joe Yonan (right).

joe yonan

Joe Yonan writes about travel, food, and other topics
BOSTON GLOBE, where he is the travel editor.

He grew up in West Texas, graduated with a journalism c
from the University of Texas at Austin, and moved in 1989 to
Boston area, where he was a news editor and reporter for the L
Transcript in Dedham and the *News-Tribune* in Waltham. Before j
ing the *Globe* staff in 1996, he was editor in chief at weekly new
papers in Peterborough, New Hampshire, and the South End neigh
borhood of Boston, where he met Andy Husbands.

After deciding that he wanted to combine his two great loves (food and journalism) into one career, he attended the Cambridge School of Culinary Arts, graduating with top honors in January 2000.

He was the driving force behind the *Globe's* popular "Sauce" column, covering new restaurants in Boston, and now writes about kitchen tools in the monthly "Inspect Your Gadgets" column for the Life at Home section. His stories also regularly appear in the Food, Living/Arts, and Travel sections. Under his leadership, the Travel section won a Gold award from the Society of American Travel Writers, designating it the nation's best travel section with more than 500,000 circulation. One of his articles, "Out on the High Seas," was named among the year's top 100 travel stories in "Best American Travel Writing 2003."

Joe also makes regular appearances talking about food and travel on *The Globe at Home* show on New England Cable News, and has hosted online chats about restaurants, cooking, and travel on Boston.com.

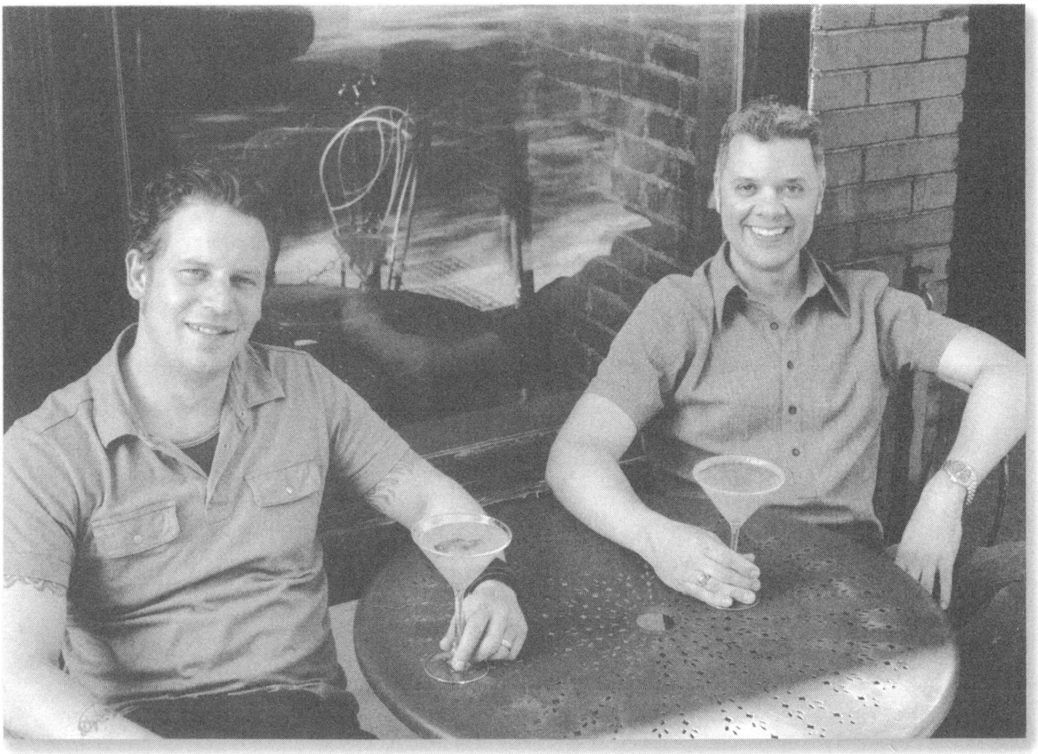

About the Restaurants

TREMONT 647, ROUGE, KESTRAL

TREMONT 647

With an open kitchen, lively bar scene, and wood-fired grill, Tremont 647 has been getting attention for its bold brand of adventurous American cuisine since it opened in the heart of Boston's South End in 1996. Such signature dishes as Tibetan Momos, Atlantic Cod in Banana Leaves, and Banana Cream Pie anchor a menu that changes according to two-month seasons, with a focus on locally available ingredients. The seventy-seat spot, named best neighborhood restaurant in the South End by *Boston Magazine*, offers four- and seven-course chef's tastings, an award-winning wine list, a selection of cocktails based on house-infused liquors, a private dining room at the next-door Sister Sorel café, and a wildly popular Pajama Brunch on Sundays.

TREMONT 647, 647 TREMONT ST., BOSTON, 617-266-4600
www.tremont647.com

ROUGE

Rouge, also in Boston's South End, combines Andy Husbands's trademark adventurous American cuisine with award-winning barbecue. Like Tremont 647, the eighty-seat Rouge is home to a hopping bar scene, in a blood-red room where bourbon-based cocktails and other drinks keep everybody happy. On the other side, in an airy, parlorlike setting with stunning hand-stenciled walls, dishes such as Knife and Fork Fried Chicken, New Orleans Barbecued Shrimp, and assorted applewood-smoked barbecue plates remind Yankees of the glories of Southern flavors.

ROUGE, 480 COLUMBUS AVE., BOSTON, 617-867-0600
www.rougeboston.com

KESTRAL

Kestral, the latest of Andy Husbands's restaurants, opened in December 2003, bringing the tastes of Tremont 647 and Rouge to Providence, Rhode Island, an hour south of Boston.

KESTRAL, 123 EMPIRE ST., PROVIDENCE, R.I., 401-490-2042
www.kestralbistro.com